THE CUBAN KITCHEN

THE CUBAN KITCHEN

Raquel Rabade Roque

ALFRED A. KNOPF
NEW YORK
2011

THIS IS A BORZOI BOOK
PUBLISHED BY ALFRED A. KNOPF

Knopf, Borzoi Books, and the colophon are registered trademarks of
Random House, Inc.

Library of Congress Cataloging-in-Publication Data
Roque, Raquel Rabade.
[Cocina cubana. English]
The Cuban kitchen / Raquel Rabade Roque.
p. cm.
ISBN 978-0-375-71196-1
1. Cooking, Cuban. 2. Cookbooks. I. Title.
TX716.C8R3313 2011
641.597291—dc22
2011006633

Cover photographs by Sabra Krock
with food styling by Mariana Velasquez
Cover design by Carol Devine Carson

Manufactured in the United States of America
First Edition

For my family and friends with love and gratitude.

Thank you for sharing your Cuban recipes and memories.

CONTENTS

INTRODUCTION:

Cuban cooking

lore, history, and anecdotes

THE COOKING OF CUBA is as rich as its landscape and as diverse as its people. It is a fusion and a work in progress. It combines the simplicity of peasant food, which has little regard for measurements, with elegant European cooking traditions. As the Caribbean's largest and most beautiful island, from its early days Cuba boasted an ocean full of fish and a land filled with fruits and vegetables. You will find recipes that come directly from Spanish, French, African, Caribbean, and Chinese origins. You will be surprised by recipes that are just uniquely Cuban. Cuban cooking was at its height in the 1950s. Havana had so many restaurants. One could find Spanish taverns, American diners, Italian eateries, and Jewish delis alongside Chinese kitchens. The streets were jammed with food vendors selling peanuts and *pirulíes* (Cuban candy on a stick) and lined with classy French gourmet restaurants. Cuban cooking was and is glamorous and exciting. Today Cuban cooking is alive in Miami and wherever the roots from Cuba still grow strong. It is a defining cuisine that keeps new generations of Cubans proud of their heritage. It is what we share and what we like to share with others, and that is why I wrote this book.

Through the years, I have realized how much I love being Cuban, even though my own family in Cuba was always very "modern" and *americana*. My parents spoke English, even in Cuba. My dad was a World War II veteran and had studied in Richmond, Virginia. My mom worked outside the home. She was a teacher in a very cool school in Cuba called the Havana Business Academy, which was owned by Canadians. She used to drive her all-American '57

Chevy all around the streets of Habana Vieja, Vedado, and Fontanar. We used to celebrate Halloween when no one else did, and we used to watch Jerry Lewis flicks and love them as much as the Mexican comic actor Cantinflas's films. Our neighbors were *americanos,* and our family always spoke of Miami as if it were an extension of a magical Cuban territory. But now I know how Cuban I have always felt and will always feel. It is the way we eat, dress, dance, and sing. And I do know that, as Cubans, we have always loved to share what it means to feel Cuban. I know of no better way to share that experience, that feeling, than through food. Cooking Cuban is feeling Cuban. This book has all the recipes that shaped me through childhood and adulthood, and that have given my children and, I hope, someday their children a heritage and a way of life. This book is for chefs and novice cooks, for Cubans and non-Cubans, for those who lived on the island and those who have never set foot there. This book is meant to preserve for future generations the rich culinary tradition of a people, and to reflect the best of my two worlds: the Cuba of the 1950s, when I was a child, and our Hispanic presence in today's America. The essence of all this is captured in *The Cuban Kitchen.*

Ever since the days of Ricky Ricardo, the idea of being Cuban has always been fun. So many jokes, so many caricatures, and so much nostalgia ready to tug at us at any moment. We play dominoes, smoke cigars, talk politics, drink Cuban coffee, wear *guayaberas,* and have splendid parties. We are proud that we grew up in a Cuban household:

Where coffee, milk, and sugar were part of a balanced breakfast.

Where all it took was just that *one* look.

Where we loved white rice and fried eggs.

Where lentil soup was considered *comida de presos* (prison food).

Where Spanish was my primary language and the only language I was allowed to speak at home.

Where music and TV were never played on Good Friday, because it was a *pecado capital*—cardinal sin!

Where we ate *bacalao* (dried codfish) on Good Friday because all other fish were too expensive, and if it was good enough for our ancestors in Spain, it was good enough for us!

Where we ate *lechón* (suckling pig) at Nochebuena (the traditional Christmas Eve party), New Year's Eve, birthday parties, and every other social function.

Where *malanga* (a root vegetable) and *manzanilla* (chamomile tea) were the remedies to end all remedies. And they still are!

Where we cured everything with Vicks VapoRub. Okay, I admit I really think it is the cure for everything.

Where I was not allowed to sleep over at anybody's house, but my friends could all come over to our house, and that was completely logical to my parents, to me, and even to my friends.

Where *la carne* (meat) came only from *la carnicería* (meat market) and from your own personal *carnicero* (butcher), who was also your unofficial Cuban shrink, and the meat and potatoes were literally *carne con papas.* And the dish was served over rice.

Where oxtail stew had the colorful name of *rabo encendido,* or "fiery tail."

I grew up in a household where the *frijoles* exploded in the pressure cooker just about every day.

I grew up in a proud Cuban household, survived, and thrived!

THE CUBAN KITCHEN

STOCKING A CUBAN KITCHEN:
Equipment and ingredients

YOU CAN CERTAINLY GO ALL OUT and splurge on your Cuban kitchen, but the basics of a well-stocked kitchen are simple. Don't be tempted by all the gadgets, and remember that ingredients are more important in creating great recipes. Here is a list of must-haves for Cuban (or any other serious) cooking.

POTS AND PANS
A large pot for soup or stew stocks
Roasting pan and rack
Saucepans (at least two different sizes)
Skillets (one nonstick and one cast-iron)

BAKING EQUIPMENT
Cookie sheet
Glass baking dish
Loaf pan
Pie plate
Wire rack

UTENSILS
Colanders
Pastry bag
Rolling pin

Spatulas
Spoons (slotted and long-handled)
Tongs

KITCHEN APPLIANCES
Blender
Electric mixer
Food processor

For the experienced or just plain curious Cuban cook, these are great to add slowly as you acquire more skill:

La Caja China (The Chinese Box—the Cuban roasting box)
Candy thermometer
Churro maker (*churrera*)
Corn-and-meat grinder
Cuban coffeemaker
Electric *palomilla* grill—for off-the-grill flavor
Flan mold
Flying saucer (*platillo volador*) sandwich press
Garlic mortar
Ice-cream maker
Paella pan (straight-sided skillet)
Plantain slicer
Pressure cooker (both traditional and microwave)
Rice cooker
Sandwich press (press grill)
Tostón maker (*tostonera*)

You can find much of this equipment in general superstores, national chains, bodegas, or supermarkets. More specialized items are available online at sites such as www.cubanfoodmarket.com (see Resources, page 417).

BUILDING THE CUBAN PANTRY

These are the herbs, spices, and other flavors to emphasize in your kitchen for Cuban and many other Latin cuisines.

> Bay leaves
> Bijol annatto powder (yellow food coloring)
> Bitter or sour orange juice (see page 120)
> Black pepper
> Cinnamon
> Cumin
> Dry white wine
> Garlic
> Lemons and limes
> Onions
> Oregano
> Paprika (hot)
> Parsley
> Salt
> Star anise
> Tomato sauce
> Vanilla extract

In addition, this is what the Cuban cook buys regularly at the grocery store or bodega; many of these items are available online as well (see Resources, page 417).

> Coco López cream of coconut
> Condensed milk (sweetened)
> Chorizo
> Cuban bread
> Cuban crackers
> Cuban cracker meal
> Evaporated milk
> Frozen tropical-fruit pulp
> Green bell pepper

Guava paste
Ironbeer (soft drink)
Jupiña (soft drink)
Malta beverage (in a six-pack)
Malanga, ñame, cassava, and plantain
Mango and tamarind nectar
Masa harina
Materva (soft drink)
Olive oil
Queso blanco (white cheese)
Rice
Roasted red peppers
Salt cod *(bacalao)*
Sangria (bottled)
Sidra (Spanish cider)
Spanish green olives
Sugarcane juice
Vegetable oil

CLASSIC CUBAN COCKTAILS:
More than
sugar and rum
cócteles clásicos cubanos

THE CREATION of these classic romantic Cuban cocktails dates back to the 1920s, when barmen from all over the world joined the native Cuban bartenders to serve tourists from all over the world. A unique style of cocktail making was soon born, in which tropical fruits were mixed with the smoothest of rums, and numerous celebrities became regulars at the island's famous bars. Over the years, you could often see Ava Gardner, Errol Flynn, Mary Pickford, Nat King Cole, and Greta Garbo having a drink and dancing to the rhythms of the island in their *guayaberas* and smoking Cuban cigars. El Floridita and La Bodeguita del Medio were hangouts for the legendary honorary Cuban Ernest Hemingway in the 1940s and 1950s. Federico García Lorca, the Spanish poet, was also a regular at most of the bars in Havana in the 1930s. What a mecca, and what a legend! Mix one of these drinks, close your eyes, and dream. . . .

STOCKING YOUR CUBAN BAR

These items are essential to create your ultimate Cuban cocktail party. The basics are the same for all good drinks.

Glassware
Drinks always taste better when served in a beautiful glass. When shopping for glassware for your bar, bear in mind that the trend over the years has been to

serve drinks in larger glasses. Not only do they look better, but they can accommodate many different types of drinks, and the home bartender will need to buy less. Some glasses to consider:

SHOT GLASSES—always present in any bar, the original bar measure

PONY GLASSES—stemmed glasses for liqueurs and brandies

COCKTAIL GLASSES—varying in size from 3 to 6 ounces; the most popular glasses. Beloved for their distinctive Y shape.

HIGHBALL GLASSES—straight-sided glasses holding 8–10 ounces

OLD-FASHIONED GLASSES—just the right size for anything on the rocks

CHAMPAGNE GLASSES—for all bubbly drinks

Garnishes and Condiments

Angostura bitters, black pepper, cocktail olives (no pimiento), cocktail onions (pickled), limes, lemons, oranges, grenadine, horseradish, maraschino cherries, Rose's lime juice, salt, coarse salt, sugar, Tabasco sauce, Worcestershire sauce, orange bitters

Mixers

Water, club soda, cola, diet cola, lemon-lime soda, milk, orange juice, tomato juice, tonic water, ginger ale, cranberry juice, pineapple juice, beer

CUBANS AND RUM

Rum and rum drinks are very much part of the Cuban heritage. Don't forget that rum is a product of sugarcane, which for centuries was the major industry in the Cuban economy. After all, Santiago de Cuba, on the southeastern tip of the island nation, was the birth site of the original Bacardi distillery. The highly respected and dominant firm of Bacardi and Company Ltd. began its corporate life in 1862 in a plant that consisted of a tin-roofed shed housing a few essential barrels and fermenting tanks, and also a colony of fruit bats, which eventually became the icon of this famous brand. At the height of rum mania in the 1950s, Havana was full of "rum-tasting" distillery tours. Bacardi had launched its famous Hatuey beer brand and had already erected in the capital city an Art Deco masterpiece, the Havana Bacardi Building. Other brands of Cuban rum are Casa Moreno, Havana Club, and Ron Matusalem.

CUBA LIBRE *Cuba libre*

Viva Cuba! (Long live free Cuba!) was the war cry of the Mambises, the combatants of the Independence Army, who fought to free Cuba from the Spanish colonists. The Cuba libre was one of the first cocktails to be mixed by Cuban bartenders, and throughout the years this drink has also been ironically called La Mentirita, or the Little Lie. You see, the people of Cuba have seldom experienced true liberty. Despite the political context, or perhaps because of it, this drink has gained worldwide fans.

1 DRINK

> **Ice (either crushed or cubes)**
> **5 ounces cola**
> **2 ounces white rum**
> **1 teaspoon lemon juice**
> **Lime slice for garnish**

Place the ice in a chilled glass; pour in the cola, rum, and lemon juice. Mix well, and garnish with the lime slice.

DAIQUIRI *daiquiri*

This cocktail was created at the Daiquiri mines, located in the easternmost region of Cuba, by an engineer who needed relief from the intense humid heat of the area. In the 1920s, the drink was improved and made famous by the bartender at El Floridita bar, known as Constante. This is what Hemingway drank at El Floridita, and what he so vividly describes in his book *Islands in the Stream*. The classic daiquiri uses lime juice, but a daiquiri can also be made with strawberry, pineapple, or other fruit juice. It can be frappé, which is mixed in the blender for a frozen-drink appeal, or *natural*, which is just mixed and served.

1 DRINK

Juice of ½ lime
1 teaspoon sugar
1 cup crushed ice
2 ounces white rum
Lime slice for garnish

In a blender or food processor, blend all the ingredients until frosty. Pour into a chilled cocktail or champagne glass, and garnish with the lime slice.

NOTE You can use your favorite fruit, but always make sure it is fresh and in season for the best flavor. You can also use a combination and call it a tutti-frutti daiquiri. Check out the effect on your guests when you serve multicolored daiquiris at your next get-together. This is a perfect drink for summer weddings, birthdays, and barbecues.

ORANGE DAIQUIRI *daiquiri de naranja*

1 DRINK

½ ounce lime juice
½ ounce fresh orange juice
1 teaspoon sugar
2 drops curaçao
1 cup crushed ice
2 ounces rum

In a blender or food processor, blend all the ingredients for about 20 seconds. Pour into a chilled cocktail or champagne glass.

CHERRY DAIQUIRI *daiquiri de cerezas*

The vibrant color always makes this a huge hit.

1 DRINK

½ ounce lime juice
1 teaspoon cherry liqueur
1 teaspoon grenadine
1 cup crushed ice
1½ ounces white rum
Lime slice for garnish

In a blender or food processor, blend all the ingredients for about 20 seconds, and pour into a chilled cocktail or champagne glass. Garnish with the lime slice.

CHAPARRA PUNCH *Chaparra*

This old Cuban punch is perfect for a weekend of festivities and celebration, since you can refrigerate it for a couple of days and it actually tastes better the second time around. The name is derived from the famous Chaparra sugar mills in Cuba. Serve it in a punch bowl or pitcher. Pour the punch, listen to Arturo Sandoval music, and be transported to Havana in the 1940s.

8 DRINKS

> **Peel of 1 lime**
> **1 bottle white rum**
> **½ bottle sweet vermouth**

Place the lime peel in a jar, and add the rest of the ingredients. Refrigerate for at least 24 hours for better taste. Serve chilled. Refrigerate the rest for future use.

SPECIAL HINT If you would like to make individual Chaparra drinks, stir in a mixing glass 1 ounce white rum and 1 ounce sweet vermouth with ice, and strain. Add a lime twist and serve. But remember that refrigeration serves to blend the two liquors to perfection.

HAVANA SPECIAL *Habana especial*

This true Creole recipe uses tropical pineapple to create the perfect drink. I remember that my father would order this in the restaurant La Roca, which is where our family went for special occasions. It all felt so sophisticated.

1 DRINK

> **2 ounces white rum**
> **2 ounces fresh pineapple juice**
> **1 teaspoon Maraschino liqueur**
> **1 cup crushed ice**
> **1 slice pineapple for garnish**

Pour all the ingredients into a cocktail shaker, and shake vigorously to mix thoroughly. Serve in a tall glass or an old-fashioned glass, and garnish with the pineapple slice.

HEMINGWAY SPECIAL *especial de Hemingway*

A drink named in honor of Ernest Hemingway, who loved our island for its ocean, its folklore, and its nightlife—but mostly for its people. He used to spend many afternoons in the Floridita bar, which is as famous for its drinks as for its drinkers. My mom swears that I sat next to Ernest Hemingway at the circus in 1959, and that he told her, "*Qué linda la niña!*"—"Your girl is so cute!" That is a Cuban mom's tall tale! But I do repeat the story to anyone who will listen. (And I add that it partly inspired my choosing bookselling for a profession.) Back to the cocktail: It has no sugar, and that is how the famous writer liked it. To be enjoyed on hot summer afternoons while reading *The Old Man and the Sea* or *Death in the Afternoon,* or perhaps Oscar Hijuelos's *The Mambo Kings Play Songs of Love,* a modern erotic classic.

1 DRINK

> Juice of ½ lime
> 1 teaspoon Maraschino liqueur
> 2 teaspoons grapefruit juice
> 2 ounces white rum
> ½ cup crushed ice

In a blender or food processor, mix all the ingredients, and pour into a chilled cocktail glass.

ISLE OF PINES *Isla de Pinos*

The Isle of Pines in Cuba (now called Isla de la Juventud) is said to have inspired Robert Louis Stevenson to write his novel *Treasure Island.* It is a lush, beautiful place, and this drink is lush and beautiful as well.

1 DRINK

> 2 ounces grapefruit juice
> 2 ounces white rum
> ½ teaspoon sugar
> ½ cup crushed ice

In a cocktail shaker, mix all the ingredients and shake vigorously for 10 seconds. Pour into a chilled cocktail glass.

THE MOJITO *el mojito*

What can we say about the trendiest drink, the mojito? Just imagine the rounds of mojitos served at La Bodeguita del Medio, the Cuban temple of food and drink and the museum of the decadent era in the 1950s in Havana, where movie stars, intellectuals, and mobsters were equally treated to old-fashioned Cuban hospitality, and where every word seemed just a little shady and every action just a little on the edge. We know that Sir Francis Drake invented the mojito and that Hemingway drank his daiquiris at El Floridita but always, always drank his mojitos at La Bodeguita del Medio. In Cuban street slang, *mojo* is "soul" and *ito* is "little," so try these mojitos for just "a little soul."

1 DRINK

> **3 spearmint leaves, plus 1 for garnish**
> **Juice of ½ lime**
> **½ teaspoon sugar**
> **2 drops Angostura bitters**
> **2 ounces white rum**
> **½ cup crushed ice**
> **Splash of sparkling mineral water**

In a food processor or with a mortar, crush the three mint leaves. Mix the juice, sugar, crushed mint leaves, and the rest of the ingredients except the mineral water in a cocktail shaker. Shake to blend, then add the mineral water. Stir well to make the mineral water bubbly. Serve in a tall or highball glass. Garnish with the mint leaf.

SANTIAGO *Santiago*

Santiago de Cuba is one of the most beautiful provinces of Cuba, and this drink will transport you there.

1 DRINK

¼ ounce lime juice
½ teaspoon sugar
1 ounce white rum
½ cup crushed ice

In a cocktail shaker, shake all the ingredients vigorously for 10 seconds. Pour into a chilled cocktail glass.

YUMURÍ PUNCH *Yumurí*

The Yumurí Valley has been the inspiration of authors, singers, and the country folk of Cuba. This drink brings Cuban Americans back to our roots.

6 DRINKS

Juice of 6 oranges
Juice of 2 lemons
6 teaspoons sugar
4 ounces white rum
3 drops Angostura bitters
2 cups crushed ice
6 pineapple, orange, or lime slices for garnish

In a small pitcher, thoroughly mix together all the ingredients except the garnish. Refrigerate for a couple of hours. Serve in a tall or highball glass with a slice of your preferred fruit as garnish.

CUBANITA *cubanita*

This drink is sweet and very suitable for a lazy afternoon.

1 DRINK

> 2 ounces rum elixir (see Resources, page 417)
> 1 ounce heavy cream

Pour the rum elixir into a cognac or pony glass and top it with the heavy cream. Stir, mix well, and serve.

MULATA *mulata*

Mulatas are some of the prettiest Cuban women, with African Caribbean features and complexions the color of *café con leche* (see page 406). Cuban *mulatas* have long been the muses for painters, writers, and other artists.

1 DRINK

> ½ ounce lime juice
> ¼ ounce coffee liqueur
> 2 ounces white rum
> ½ cup crushed ice

In a cocktail shaker, mix all the ingredients and shake vigorously until blended. Serve cold in a chilled cocktail glass.

CUBAN SPECIAL *cubano especial*
1 DRINK

> 2 ounces light rum
> 2 drops curaçao
> ½ ounce lime juice
> 1 ounce pineapple juice
> ¼ cup crushed or cracked ice
> **Pineapple slice for garnish**

Mix all the ingredients except the pineapple slice with crushed or cracked ice in a shaker or blender, pour into a chilled cocktail glass, and garnish with the pineapple slice.

GUANÁBANA COCKTAIL *cóctel de guanábana*

The *guanábana* (soursop) is similar to the better-known cherimoya. It can grow to the size of a grapefruit, and the skin is marked with a fingerprint-like pattern, making the fruit look like a green pinecone. The flesh when ripe is soft, creamy, and very fragrant. The *guanábana* nectar in this recipe can be found frozen or canned at your Latin market or in the Latino section of your local supermarket.

1 DRINK

> 2 ounces white or light rum
> 1 ounce *guanábana* (soursop) nectar
> 1 teaspoon lime juice
> ¼ cup crushed or cracked ice

Mix all the ingredients with crushed or cracked ice in a shaker or blender, and strain into a chilled cocktail glass.

HAVANA BANDANNA *Pañuelo habanero*

1 DRINK

> 2 ounces white rum
> ½ ounce lime juice
> 1 overripe banana, peeled and sliced
> ¼ cup crushed or cracked ice
> Banana liqueur, if available and to your taste

Mix all the ingredients except the banana liqueur with cracked or crushed ice in a blender until completely smooth, and pour into a chilled old-fashioned glass. If you'd like, float a dash of the banana liqueur on top.

BACARDI SOLO *sólo Bacardi*

1 DRINK

> 1½ ounces light or white rum, preferably the namesake
> ½ ounce lime juice
> 1 teaspoon grenadine
> ¼ cup crushed or cracked ice

Mix all the ingredients with cracked or crushed ice in a shaker or blender. Pour into a chilled cocktail glass.

BACARDI SPECTACULAR *Bacardi espectacular*

1 DRINK

> 1½ ounces light or white rum, preferably the namesake
> ¾ ounce gin
> 1 ounce lime juice
> 1 teaspoon grenadine
> ½ cup crushed or cracked ice

Mix all the ingredients with crushed or cracked ice in a shaker or blender, and strain into a chilled cocktail glass.

HAVANA CLUB

Havana Club is another famous brand of Cuban rum still alive on the island today.

1 DRINK

1½ ounces white or light rum
½ ounce dry vermouth
¼ cup cracked ice
1 mint sprig, if available, for garnish

Mix all the ingredients except the mint with cracked ice in a shaker or blender, and strain into a chilled cocktail glass. Garnish with the mint sprig.

CUBAN EGGNOG *crema de vie*

This drink is much sweeter and thicker and served in smaller portions than its American counterpart! This was my mom's staple item to bring to all our celebrations, in hot or cold weather! The name literally means "cream of life." It is sweet and velvety and makes a wonderful present when bottled.

8 DRINKS

2 cups sugar
1 cup water
½ teaspoon ground cinnamon
6 egg yolks
One 14-ounce can sweetened condensed milk
One 5-ounce can evaporated milk
1 teaspoon vanilla extract
1 cup white or light rum
1 cinnamon stick per drink for garnish

Mix the sugar, water, and ground cinnamon with the lemon rind in a saucepan over very low heat, stirring until the sugar dissolves.

Put the egg yolks in a blender, and mix with the condensed milk, evaporated milk, and vanilla. Continue beating until well combined.

Pour the egg-yolk mixture into the sugar water, and mix together.

Add the rum, and be sure to chill for at least 24 hours. Serve in shot glasses, each garnished with a cinnamon stick.

VARADERO WATERMELON COOLER
melón de Varadero

Varadero Beach is the stuff of legends. So many Cuban stories are about this magical beach. Some say that the sand is whiter and finer than on any other beach, that the ocean is unrealistically blue, and that the water is the exact warm temperature of your body. Varadero to this day is one of the Caribbean's top beach resorts, but its heyday was in the 1950s, when the very rich built their mansions and sprawling beach houses. Since then, this watermelon cocktail has become popular with sunbathers and fishermen alike.

1 DRINK

> 2 ounces white rum
> 1 ounce melon liqueur
> ½ ounce lime juice
> ½ ounce sugar syrup (see page 340)
> 1 cup peeled, seeded, and diced watermelon
> 1 lime slice for garnish

Mix all the ingredients except the lime slice with cracked or crushed ice in a blender, at slow speed, for 20 seconds, and pour into a small chilled tumbler glass. Garnish with the lime slice.

CUBAN DRINKS WITHOUT RUM

Despite our love for rum, amazingly enough, we do have some cocktails without it. Cuban sangria, the jai alai, and the *doncellita* all offer a refreshing change from the rum drinks so traditional in our culture.

CUBAN SANGRIA *sangría tropical*

Sangria is forever linked to Spain. This version features tropical fruits that make it refreshing and light.

8 DRINKS

> **1 bottle red wine**
> **¼ cup brown sugar**
> **1 cup fresh orange juice**
> **1 orange, thinly sliced and seeded**
> **1 ounce lemon juice**
> **1 mango, peeled, seeded, and diced**
> **1 cup guava juice or nectar**
> **2 cups club soda**
> **½ cup diced tropical fruit of your choice**

In a pitcher, mix the wine and sugar and stir until the sugar dissolves. Stir in the rest of the ingredients except for the club soda and diced fruit. Store in the refrigerator, covered, for at least 45 minutes before serving. Just before serving, stir in the club soda and throw in some diced tropical fruit.

secrets of a Cuban cook

HOW TO PEEL AND PREPARE MANGOES

To peel mangoes, cut lengthwise on either side of the large seed in the center, and curve the cut slightly to follow the shape of the seed. Cut the peeled flesh according to the recipe.

JAI ALAI *jai alai*

Jai alai was a very popular sport brought to Cuba by the Spaniards. This cocktail has been a favorite of professional jai-alai players since colonial times. My grandfather Sacramento, a Chinese Cuban, was an avid amateur player.

1 DRINK

> **Juice of 1 lime**
> **1 teaspoon sugar**
> **1 spearmint leaf**
> **½ cup crushed ice**
> **1 ounce gin**
> **1 ounce vermouth**
> **1 ounce sparkling mineral water**

Mix the lime juice, the sugar, and the spearmint leaf in a cocktail shaker, and shake vigorously for 10 seconds. Add the ice, gin, vermouth, and mineral water, shake again, and serve in a cocktail glass.

DONCELLITA *doncellita*

Doncellita is what the Cubans call a young debutante. This milky coffee-liqueur drink, with its maraschino cherry garnish, was the preferred drink among the young society ladies of Cuba in the 1950s.

1 DRINK

> **1 ounce coffee liqueur**
> **½ ounce evaporated milk, chilled**
> **1 maraschino cherry for garnish**

Pour the coffee liqueur into a clear shot glass. Very slowly add the evaporated milk in a thin stream; the drink should separate into two layers, with the milk on top. Gently add the cherry, and serve immediately.

CUBAN CHAMPAGNE COCKTAILS

As in many other cultural traditions, Cubans reserve champagne for very special occasions. We prefer to celebrate with the traditional *sidra*, which is a hard-tasting Spanish apple cider with an almost nonexistent alcohol content, a drink suitable for the youngest and oldest in a crowd. As a kid in a big Cuban family, when you have *sidra* you think you are drinking champagne! Sometimes the best things in life are the simplest. For more grown-up fun, try these tropical sparkling wonders.

PINEAPPLE MIMOSA *mimosa de piña*

1 DRINK

> **1 sugar cube (for maximum fizz)**
> **3 dashes Angostura bitters**
> **½ cup fresh pineapple juice**
> **½ cup champagne or sparkling wine, chilled**
> **Lemon peel or mint sprig for garnish**

Put the sugar cube in a chilled champagne glass, and saturate it with the bitters. Pour in the pineapple juice. Fill with very cold champagne, and stir gently. Garnish with lemon peel or a mint sprig.

GUAVA CHAMPAGNE COCKTAIL
cóctel de guayaba

Guavas are a beloved part of Cuban cooking; they even gave their name to one of our distinctive national fashions. *Guayaberas* are linen shirts worn by Cuban men and women so that they can feel comfortable in the hot weather. Cuban legend says the name comes from a poor country seamstress who sewed large pockets in her husband's shirts so that he could carry *guayabas*—guavas—home from the field. *Guayaberas* are distinguished by several details: two or four patch pockets and two vertical rows of tiny pleats sewn closely together running along the front and back of the shirt. The shirts are usually white or pastel-colored to help fight off the heat, and they have become

(continued on next page)

(continued from previous page)

very popular in tropical climates. *Guayaberas* are elegant and cooling, and so is this cocktail.

1 DRINK

> **1 sugar cube (for maximum fizz)**
> **3 drops Angostura bitters**
> **½ cup guava nectar or juice**
> **½ cup champagne or sparkling wine, chilled**
> **Mint sprig for garnish**

Put the sugar cube in a chilled champagne glass, and saturate it with the bitters. Pour in the guava nectar or juice. Fill with very cold champagne, and stir gently. Garnish with the mint sprig.

MANGO CHAMPAGNE COCKTAIL
cóctel de mango

1 DRINK

> **1 sugar cube (for maximum fizz)**
> **3 drops Angostura bitters**
> **½ cup fresh mango juice or nectar**
> **½ cup champagne or sparkling wine, chilled**
> **Lemon peel or mint sprig for garnish**

Put the sugar cube in a chilled champagne glass, and saturate it with the bitters. Pour in the mango juice or nectar. Fill with very cold champagne, and stir gently. Garnish with lemon peel or a mint sprig.

CUBAN BEER
la fría

A word about *la fría* . . .

We call a beer a *fría*—a "cold one"—and Cubans love a good beer. There are actually two outstanding Cuban beers with history on the island.

Hatuey beer, part of the Bacardi brand, was launched in 1927 in Cuba. The beer is named for a Dominican Indian chief who fought hard and gave his life for the struggle for Cuban independence from the Spanish. This beer took on a life of its own, and by the 1940s had been immortalized in Ernest Hemingway's *For Whom the Bell Tolls*.

Cerveza Tropical, which claims to be Cuba's first beer, was founded in the 1880s as a small family brewery business. It soon became one of Cuba's largest breweries but was confiscated by the Castro regime in 1960. The beer wasn't available until, in 1998, the brand came back under the leadership of the original owner's grandson. It is made with the original Cuban recipe.

Both beers are readily available in supermarkets, ethnic markets, and bodegas, and on the Internet.

You can also have a lot of fun with a beer-infused cocktail. Simply add mint and a sweet-and-sour drink mix to any Cuban beer, and shake it; you'll have a true beach mojito.

BATIDOS:
Milkshakes and juice
drinks the Cuban way
batidos y jugos tropicales

SOMETIMES we all just need a *batido*!

If you have been out in the sun and you're hot and tired, you need a *batido*!

If you overslept and have to rush breakfast for the whole family, you need a *batido*!

Cubans consider *batidos* to be an integral part of their daily diet. At least one a day is recommended by most grandmothers, and two a day is just perfect. Our Cuban *batidos* can wake you up in the morning with a big energy boost and can also lull you into sleep at night. They do differ from their American counterparts in distinct ways: Cuban *batidos* are more like smoothies, because they are actually based on fresh fruit and ice rather than on a combination of ice cream and dairy products. They are lighter than your regular shake, and the taste is much more intense and refreshing. The best part of these shakes is that they may actually contain few calories, since they are not made from ice cream. And if you are really calorie-conscious or battling diabetes, you could use Splenda or some other sugar substitute, and the *batido* will be just as good. On the other hand, many Cuban *batido* aficionados replace the whole milk with a combination of condensed, evaporated, and whole milk. Oh—and always add a pinch of salt before you put it in the blender.

The array of *batidos* is never-ending. Most markets now have the frozen pulps for virtually any tropical-fruit *batido*. Don't be afraid to mix and experiment.

PAPAYA MILKSHAKE *batido de fruta bomba*

The papaya—or *fruta bomba* (bomb·fruit), as we call it in Cuba—is a pear-shaped green-skinned fruit that grows in tropical climates all over the Americas and the Caribbean. It can be found fresh, so look for a fruit that yields to gentle pressure in the hand and feels heavy for its size. It is delicious ripe and raw with just a squeeze of lime juice. Reserve some for this great *batido*—or you can always use the frozen pulp.

2 BATIDOS

> **1 cup ripe papaya, or 4 ounces frozen papaya pulp**
> **3 tablespoons sweetened condensed milk**
> **½ cup evaporated milk**
> **½ cup whole milk**
> **1 cup crushed ice**
> **Pinch of salt**
> **Sugar to taste**

Mix all ingredients in a blender, and blend until smooth and creamy but light. Taste for sweetness, adding sugar if necessary. Pour into tall glasses.

MANGO MILKSHAKE   *batido de mango*

The mango, though native to India and Southeast Asia, arrived in the tropical Americas many centuries ago and has been at home ever since. The fruit can be eaten at all stages of ripeness, but it is best when the skin is soft and just the right shade of orange. Use it in your recipes or eat it before black spots begin to appear on the skin. For *batidos*, the riper the better. You may also, of course, substitute frozen mango pulp.

2 BATIDOS

> 1 cup diced ripe mango (see page 21) or 4 ounces
>   frozen mango pulp
> 3 tablespoons sweetened condensed milk
> ½ cup evaporated milk
> ½ cup whole milk
> 1 cup crushed ice
> Pinch of salt
> Sugar to taste

Mix all ingredients in a blender, and blend until smooth and creamy but light. Taste for sweetness, adding sugar if necessary. Pour into tall glasses.

MAMEY MILKSHAKE   *batido de mamey*

The mamey is a fruit similar to the sapote that is native to Mexico but known and sold throughout the world. The fruits are oval with reddish skins, and the flesh has a sweet banana/pineapple/vanilla fragrance and flavor, if you can imagine that! The skins and seeds in this fruit are not used. You can always substitute frozen mamey pulp for the fresh fruit; I actually find it easier to use frozen mamey pulp.

2 BATIDOS

> 1 cup diced ripe mamey, or 4 ounces frozen mamey pulp
> 3 tablespoons sweetened condensed milk
> ½ cup evaporated milk
> ½ cup whole milk
> 1 cup crushed ice
> Pinch of salt
> Sugar to taste

Mix all ingredients in a blender, and blend until smooth and creamy but light. Taste for sweetness, adding sugar if necessary. Pour into tall glasses.

PUFFED WHEAT MILKSHAKE *batido de trigo*

This is it—the breakfast of champions for kids who have any Cuban heritage. This is another *batido* that is not heavy but is filling. If you are into nutrition, you may add any supplement to this one for an extra early-morning boost. At home, we like it just like this.

2 BATIDOS

> 1 cup puffed-wheat cereal, preferably a generic brand
> ¾ cup whole milk
> ¼ cup sweetened condensed milk
> ¼ cup water
> 1 cup crushed ice
> 2 tablespoons sugar, plus more to taste
> Pinch of salt, or to taste

Mix all ingredients in a blender, and blend until smooth and creamy but light. Taste for sweetness, adding more sugar if necessary. Pour into tall glasses.

CUBAN COCONUT MILK *leche de coco*

The coconut is the fruit of the coconut palm, a plant that is a primary food source throughout the Tropics. Caribbean cooking uses coconut often, and coconut milk is delicious in rice puddings and milky desserts, as well as in all types of Brazilian and Colombian cuisine. When buying a whole mature coconut, shake it: You should hear a sloshing sound, which tells you it has plenty of liquid and is fresh. To learn how to crack a fresh coconut, refer to the Secrets of a Cuban Cook sidebar on page 356. Fresh is great if you have the time and inclination; if not, just buy frozen or canned coconut pulp.

2 BATIDOS

1 cup diced fresh coconut, or 4 ounces frozen coconut pulp
½ cup sweetened condensed milk
1 cup crushed ice
1 cup water
Sugar to taste

Mix all ingredients in a blender, and blend until smooth and creamy but light. Taste for sweetness, adding sugar if necessary. Pour into tall glasses.

MALTED-MILK MILKSHAKE *leche malteada*

This milkshake is so easy to prepare. It was often my after-school snack, both in Cuba and, later on, in the United States.

2 BATIDOS

3 tablespoons malted milk powder
1 cup whole milk
2 tablespoons sugar, plus more to taste
1 cup crushed ice
Pinch of salt, or to taste

Mix all ingredients in a blender, and blend until smooth and creamy but light. Taste for sweetness, adding more sugar if necessary. Pour into tall glasses.

CARROT AND ORANGE JUICE
jugo de naranja y zanahoria

A sunny and even healthier alternative to your morning OJ.

2 JUGOS

> 1 cup diced carrots
> 1 cup orange juice
> 3 tablespoons sugar
> 1 cup crushed ice

First put the carrots through the blender with a little water. Then add the rest of the ingredients, and blend for a few minutes, until smooth but creamy and light. Pour into tall glasses.

PINEAPPLE JUICE *jugo de piña*

Pineapples are great in many recipes, including fruit salads and drinks. The interior of this oddly constructed fruit is chewy but tender, juicy, and very fragrant. It is sweet balanced by sour. It will thrill your palate in this refreshing and nutritional juice.

2 JUGOS

> 1 cup diced fresh pineapple
> 1 cup water
> 3 tablespoons sugar, plus more to taste
> 1 cup crushed ice

Mix all ingredients in a blender, and blend until smooth and creamy but light. Taste for sweetness, adding more sugar if necessary. Pour into tall glasses.

secrets of a Cuban cook

HOW TO PEEL AND PREPARE PINEAPPLE

To peel and trim the pineapple, cut off the leafy crown. Cut a slice from the base, and set the pineapple upright. With a sharp knife, cut off the peel lengthwise, cutting thickly to remove the brown "eyes." For chunks, cut the peeled fruit into spears and remove the core. Cut across each spear into chunks.

MALTA AND CONDENSED MILK
malta con leche condensada

Malta is a type of soft drink, a carbonated malt beverage brewed from barley. It is very sweet, like molasses. There are various brands in the Latino section of your supermarket.

As kids, we always enjoyed this milkshake, and our moms thought it was the easiest and most fun way to make us fat! This is great for birthday parties.

2 SERVINGS

½ cup sweetened condensed milk
One 7-ounce bottle *malta* soft drink
1 cup crushed ice
Sugar to taste

Mix all ingredients in a blender, and blend until smooth and creamy but light. Taste for sweetness, adding sugar if necessary. Pour into tall glasses.

THE GREAT GUARAPO   *el guarapo cubano*

Sugarcane was a treat I used to enjoy as a child. My mom would bring in the fresh cane in short lengths, peel back the green skin, and let us suck the fibers to extract the juices. This delivered the ultimate energy buzz. I still often stop at fruit stands and eat it this way. But the majority of people I know continue to think that the great *guarapo*, or sugarcane juice, is the best way to enjoy sugarcane. It is easier and better to enjoy *guarapo* at your local Latin food market or fruit stand, because they have an industrial machine called a *trapiche* that quickly extracts the juice and processes the tough sugarcane. But if you want to prepare it at home, use your food processor or blender.

2 GUARAPOS

3 pieces sugarcane, each about 1 foot in length
1 cup water
1 cup crushed ice

Peel the pieces of sugarcane, cut up the inside meat, and put it in a food processor as you slowly add water and ice, blending until smooth and liquid.

BANANA MILKSHAKE *batido de plátano*

2 BATIDOS

> 1 cup diced bananas
> 3 tablespoons sweetened condensed milk
> ½ cup evaporated milk
> ½ cup whole milk
> 1 cup crushed ice
> Pinch of salt
> Sugar to taste

Mix all ingredients in a blender, and blend until smooth and creamy but light. Taste for sweetness, adding sugar if necessary. Pour into tall glasses.

TAMARIND JUICE *jugo de tamarindo*

The tamarind tree grows throughout the Caribbean. If you live anywhere with a Hispanic population, you will find tamarind pulp in the freezer of your local market. If you use fresh pods, you will need to break the pulp into small pieces.

2 JUGOS

> ½ cup diced tamarind, or 4 ounces frozen tamarind pulp
> ¼ cup sugar
> 3 cups water
> 1 cup crushed ice
> Sugar to taste

Mix all ingredients in a blender, and blend until smooth and creamy but light. Taste for sweetness, adding sugar if necessary. Pour into tall glasses.

TUTTI-FRUTTI SMOOTHIE *batido de frutas*

2 BATIDOS

½ cup diced fresh pineapple (see page 31)
½ cup diced bananas
2 tablespoons frozen mamey pulp
2 tablespoons frozen papaya pulp
Juice of 1 orange
3 fresh strawberries, diced
½ cup crushed ice
Sugar to taste

Mix all ingredients in a blender, and blend until smooth and creamy but light. Taste for sweetness, adding sugar if necessary. Pour into tall glasses.

PINEAPPLE BANANA SMOOTHIE
batido de piña y plátano

2 BATIDOS

1 cup diced fresh pineapple (see page 31)
½ cup diced bananas
1 cup crushed ice
½ cup water
¼ cup sugar, plus more to taste

Mix all ingredients in a blender, and blend until smooth and creamy but light. Taste for sweetness, adding more sugar if necessary. Pour into tall glasses.

APPETIZERS:
Croquettes, empanadas, and fritters

aperitivos: croquetas, empanadas, y frituras

CROQUETTES

croquetas

IT IS WIDELY KNOWN that Cubans will turn just about any food into fritters, from salt cod to corn to rice to black-eyed peas! But our national fritter is the *croqueta,* or croquette, a favorite Cuban specialty. We are really *croqueta* addicts at just about any time of the day. How can you not fall for their great taste and texture? They are crisp on the outside and creamy and semi-liquid on the inside. They can be made from leftover dinner meat—ham, pork, or whatever you have available. Typical Cuban croquettes are cylinder-shaped and about 2 inches long and 1 inch in diameter. But bear in mind that the size can easily be adapted to party portions—that is what makes them a perfect appetizer. Croquettes are definitely on every party menu list, from baptisms to *velorios* (wakes). The signature of the Cuban croquette is the béchamel sauce, which is a thick milk-butter-and-flour sauce to which you add your favorite minced or shredded filling. Make sure you chill this paste mixture well before forming the croquette cylinders. They are then dipped in batter and fried. What a delicacy. Almost every single Cuban in Miami (at least the ones whom I know) eats one or more croquettes a day. I will give you a basic recipe for the perennial ham croquette, as well as some lesser-known but equally delicious variations. And if you have meat or rice leftovers, you can always use them in these recipes. It's less work, too.

HAM CROQUETTES—BASIC RECIPE
croquetas de jamón—receta básica

12 CROQUETTES

> 4 teaspoons butter
> 1 onion, peeled and minced
> 1 cup whole milk, plus more to taste
> ³/₄ cup all-purpose flour
> ½ teaspoon salt
> 1 teaspoon black pepper
> 1 tablespoon dry white wine
> 1 cup ground, fully baked sweet ham
> 2 eggs, beaten
> 2 cups cracker meal or bread crumbs
> 2 cups corn oil, or enough for 3 or 4 inches in skillet

In a frying pan, melt butter over low heat and lightly sauté minced onion.

Blend milk with flour, salt, and pepper, and add to pan.

Stirring constantly over low heat, add wine and ground ham, and combine well. The consistency should be creamy. If not, slowly add a little more milk.

Pour the mixture into a shallow dish, and allow to cool before placing in the refrigerator for at least 2 hours, more if possible. It is very important that you allow the paste mixture to cool.

Form your croquettes into a cylinder, whatever size you desire. Typical Cuban croquettes are about 2 inches long and 1 inch in diameter.

Dip each croquette twice in the beaten eggs, and then coat with the cracker meal. Let them stand for a while at room temperature before frying.

Heat 3 or 4 inches of corn oil in a heavy skillet over medium heat to 350 degrees. Add the croquettes and fry for 5 to 7 minutes, until golden, turning them frequently so they brown evenly. Drain on paper towels and serve.

NOTE For an equally delicious variation, you can substitute 1 cup fully cooked ground sirloin or pork, or a combination of the two, for the ham in this recipe.

COJIMAR FISH CROQUETTES
croquetas de pescado Cojimar

The Cojimar we remember is a seaside town of cranky old fishermen and happy-go-lucky kids running into each other on streets that flank the ocean, where the delicious aromas of Cuban cuisine combine with the salty sea air. Cojimar inspired the setting for Ernest Hemingway's novel *The Old Man and the Sea*. More important to fishing aficionados around the world, Cojimar is also where Hemingway kept his beloved fishing vessel, *Pilar*. This recipe makes a great addition to a large appetizer platter of fried green plantain chips (see page 152) and fried shrimp.

12 CROQUETTES

> 1 pound fish fillets, boned
> 1 tablespoon butter
> 1 onion, peeled and minced
> 1 cup milk
> 3 tablespoons all-purpose flour
> 2 egg yolks
> ¼ teaspoon salt
> ¼ teaspoon black pepper
> 2 eggs, beaten
> 2 cups cracker meal or bread crumbs
> 2 cups corn oil, or enough for 3 or 4 inches in skillet
> Juice of 1 lime

In a medium pot, bring 2 cups water to a boil over medium heat. Add the fish fillets and poach for about 10 minutes, or steam them for about 15 minutes. Drain, cool, and shred.

In a frying pan, heat butter, and lightly sauté minced onion.

Blend milk with the flour, egg yolks, salt, and pepper, and add to onion in pan. Stir constantly over low heat. Add shredded fish, and combine well. You should get a creamy consistency.

Pour the mixture into a shallow dish, and allow to cool before placing in the refrigerator for at least 2 hours, more if possible. It is very important that you allow the paste mixture to cool.

Form your croquettes into a cylinder, whatever size you desire. Typical Cuban croquettes are about 2 inches long and 1 inch in diameter.

(continued on next page)

(continued from previous page)

Dip each croquette twice in the beaten eggs, and then coat with the cracker meal. Let them stand for a while at room temperature before frying.

Heat 3 or 4 inches of corn oil in a heavy skillet over medium heat to 350 degrees. Add the croquettes and fry for 5 to 7 minutes, until golden, turning them frequently so they brown evenly. Drain on paper towels. Just before serving, sprinkle the lime juice over the croquettes.

BISHOP STREET CHICKEN CROQUETTES
croquetas de pollo Calle Obispo

Calle Obispo, or Bishop Street, is perhaps Havana's most vibrant and famous thoroughfare, even today. In its heyday, Calle Obispo was *the* happening street for music, culture, and definitely food. The site of El Floridita, the most famous bar and restaurant in the city, Calle Obispo used to throng with the evening pulse and beat of the music and people. These Calle Obispo croquettes are perfect with mojitos (see page 14).

12 CROQUETTES

> 1 pound boneless and skinless chicken breast
> 1 tablespoon butter
> 1 onion, peeled and minced
> 1 cup whole milk
> ¾ cup all-purpose flour
> ½ teaspoon salt
> 1 teaspoon black pepper
> 1 teaspoon grated nutmeg
> 3 eggs, beaten
> 2 cups cracker meal or bread crumbs
> 2 cups corn oil, or enough for 3 or 4 inches in skillet

In a medium pot, bring 2 cups water to a boil over medium-high heat. Add the chicken breast. Cook over medium heat for about 15 minutes. When cooked, drain, cool, and shred, or grind in food processor if you prefer a lighter, creamier texture.

In a frying pan, melt butter over low heat and lightly sauté the minced onion. Blend milk with flour, salt, and pepper, and add to pan.

Stirring constantly over low heat, add chicken and nutmeg, and combine well. You should get a creamy consistency.

Pour the mixture into a shallow dish, and allow to cool before placing in the refrigerator for at least 2 hours, more if possible. It is very important that you allow the paste mixture to cool.

Form your croquettes into a cylinder, whatever size you desire. Typical Cuban croquettes are about 2 inches long and 1 inch in diameter.

Dip each croquette twice in the beaten eggs, and then coat with the cracker meal. Let them stand for a while at room temperature before frying.

Heat 3 or 4 inches of corn oil in a heavy skillet over medium heat to 350 degrees. Add the croquettes and fry for 5 to 7 minutes, until golden, turning them frequently so they brown evenly. Drain on paper towels and serve.

RICE CROQUETTES *croquetas de arroz*
12 CROQUETTES

> 4 teaspoons butter
> 1 onion, peeled and minced
> 1 cup whole milk
> ¾ cup all-purpose flour
> ½ teaspoon salt
> 1 teaspoon black pepper
> ¼ cup dry white wine
> 1 cup cooked white (see page 160), yellow (saffron), or brown rice
> 2 eggs, beaten
> 2 cups cracker meal or bread crumbs
> 2 cups corn oil, or enough for 3 or 4 inches in skillet

In a frying pan, melt butter over medium heat and lightly sauté minced onion.

Blend milk with the flour, salt, and pepper, and add to pan.

Stirring constantly over low heat, add wine and cooked rice, and combine well. You should get a creamy consistency.

Pour the mixture into a shallow dish, and allow to cool before placing in the refrigerator for at least 2 hours, more if possible. It is very important that you allow the paste mixture to cool.

(continued on next page)

(continued from previous page)

Form your croquettes into a cylinder, whatever size you desire. Typical Cuban croquettes are about 2 inches long and 1 inch in diameter.

Dip each croquette twice in the beaten eggs, and then coat with the cracker meal. Let them stand for a while at room temperature before frying.

Heat 3 or 4 inches of corn oil in a heavy skillet over medium heat. Add the croquettes and fry for 5 to 7 minutes, until golden, turning them frequently so they brown evenly. Drain on paper towels and serve.

CUBAN TURNOVERS
empanadas

Empanadas go way back in history and may have originated in the Middle East. They were carried to the rest of the world by travelers and traders, as they are now by cooks and chefs. *Empanadas* are thought to have been made very popular in Spain, where even today they have an Empanada Festival as part of the Galician Culture Series. The name *empanada* comes from *empanar,* which means to coat with bread crumbs. It is the original pocket food for when you're on the go, a portable meal. Every cuisine has its form of *empanada,* but for our recipes please remember that the shape is that of the eternal turnover. After sealing with a fork, the turnover should have the shape of a half-moon.

Empanadas are usually fried (though sometimes baked) and contain the most delicious fillings and combinations of the best of Cuban cooking. The traditional Cuban turnover is filled with beef *picadillo* (such as the one on page 280), so whenever you make *picadillo* think of leftovers as fillings for delicious *empanadas* the very next day. Another of my favorite combinations is guava paste and cheese, which makes the ultimate sweet *empanada.* Do not limit yourself—experiment with fillings!

EMPANADA DOUGH *masa para empanadas*
The principal difference between croquettes and *empanadas* is that, while croquettes are based on a béchamel sauce, *empanadas* are made with flour dough. The form is also different: croquettes are cylindrical, but *empanadas* are turnovers formed from

about a 3-inch circle. The dough is turned over the filling like a half-moon, and the edges are sealed by pressing a fork into them.

The great thing about *empanadas* is the infinite variety of fillings. My favorites range from the traditional ham and cheese to *picadillo* (see pages 280–281), *ropa vieja* (see page 278), *vaca frita* (see page 279), guava and cheese, chicken fricassee, spinach, and shrimp *enchilados* (see page 234). But the very best fillings are always born out of some great leftovers, such as *arroz con pollo* (see pages 163–168).

10 EMPANADAS

> **3 cups all-purpose flour, plus more for the board**
> **1 teaspoon salt**
> **½ teaspoon baking powder**
> **2 tablespoons vegetable shortening**
> **1 teaspoon butter**
> **1 tablespoon sugar**
> **¼ cup boiling water**
> **1 teaspoon cinnamon powder**
> **2 eggs, beaten**
> **2 cups corn oil**

Prepare the dough: If using a food processor, place the flour, salt, and baking powder in a food processor, and cut in the shortening. (See Secrets of a Cuban Cook, page 248, for how to cut in shortening.) Then add the butter, sugar, water, and cinnamon powder. The mixture should appear and feel sandy. If you are doing it manually, spread the flour and baking powder on a cutting board or on the kitchen counter. Make a well in the middle, and place the vegetable shortening, salt, butter, sugar, water, and cinnamon stick inside. Add the beaten eggs. Stir and knead until well combined.

Take a portion of the mixture and roll out very thin on a floured board or countertop, into a ⅛-inch-thick layer.

Cut the dough into 3-inch-diameter circles with round cookie or biscuit cutter, and place your desired filling right smack in the center of the circle.

Carefully fold over the dough to make a semicircle around the filling. Crimp down the edges with a damp fork.

Fry in hot oil (about 350 degrees) until golden, about 7 to 10 minutes.

Soak up excess oil on paper towels before serving.

PICADILLO FILLING *relleno de picadillo*

Prepare the recipe on page 280. You can make the *picadillo* with chicken, turkey, lean meat, or pork. Chilled *picadillo* makes stuffing the *empanadas* easier.

3 cups *picadillo*, fully cooked, chilled

Place a spoonful of *picadillo*, about ¼ cup, in each *empanada* circle. Carefully fold over the dough to make a semicircle around the filling. Crimp down the edges with a damp fork. Fry, and enjoy.

VACA FRITA FILLING *relleno de vaca frita*

Prepare the recipe on page 279. Make sure there are onions in the leftovers to be used for the *empanada* filling. Again, if the *vaca frita* is chilled it makes stuffing the *empanadas* easier.

3 cups *vaca frita*, cooked but not refried, chilled

Place a spoonful, about ¼ cup, of *vaca frita* in each *empanada* circle. Carefully fold over the dough to make a semicircle around the filling. Crimp down the edges with a damp fork. You can also add a few strips of your favorite cheese to this one. Fry, and enjoy.

GUAVA AND CHEESE FILLING
relleno de guayaba y queso

For this recipe, cut your guava and cheese strips very thin. Authentic *queso blanco* is preferred, but you may opt for any white cheese, or even cream cheese, as long as it is completely chilled. Guava paste can be found in the Hispanic aisle of your supermarket.

10 strips white cheese, no more than 1 inch in length or width, well chilled
10 strips guava paste, no more than 1 inch in length or width, well chilled

Place a strip of chilled cheese and a strip of chilled guava paste in each *empanada* circle. Carefully fold over the dough to make a semicircle around the filling. Crimp down the edges with a damp fork. Fry, and enjoy.

CHICKEN FRICASSEE FILLING
relleno de fricasé de pollo

3 cups *bohío* chicken fricassee (see page 245), cooked but not refried, chilled

Before you begin, shred the chicken pieces with a fork, carefully removing any bones. Try to use only the chicken pieces, not the potatoes. Place a spoonful of chicken fricassee, about ¼ cup, in each *empanada* circle. Carefully fold over the dough to make a semicircle around the filling. Crimp down the edges with a damp fork. You can also add a few strips of your favorite cheese to this one. Fry, and enjoy.

SHRIMP ENCHILADOS FILLING
relleno de camarones enchilados

You could use the smallest shrimp and dedicate this *enchilado* strictly to *empanada* filling. This delicacy can easily become a main dish when accompanied by a salad. Chilling the *enchilados* makes it easier to stuff the *empanadas*.

3 cups shrimp *enchilados* (see page 234), cooked and chilled
Lemon juice

Place a spoonful, about ¼ cup, of the shrimp in each *empanada* circle. Carefully fold over the dough to make a semicircle around the filling. Crimp down the edges with a damp fork. Fry, sprinkle with lemon juice, and enjoy.

FRITTERS
frituras

Fritters are very popular in Cuba and essential in a Cuban menu. Deep-frying is easy; just make sure that your oil is not too cool, or you will have soggy *frituras*. Cook fritters in small batches, and be sure to soak up any excess oil by setting them on paper towels. The variety of Cuban fritters is endless. You can have tropical-fruit fritters, or root-vegetable fritters, or seafood or even bean fritters! Sprinkle some lemon juice on your fritters, or decide to splurge and drench them in a thick tropical sauce. Wow. And always remember that fritters taste best when served immediately!

secrets of a Cuban cook

TIPS FOR THE CRISPIEST FRITURAS

To get the most crispy and juicy fritters it is best to deep-fry them. There are certain rules to follow for ideal results. The first thing is to gauge the temperature of your oil. You do not want it too hot, because it can burn your food and make it taste bitter, but it should be hot enough so that the oil does not seep into the fritters, making them soggy and unhealthful. If you want to test the temperature to be sure the oil is ready, you can invest in a candy thermometer, available at most houseware stores (the oil temperature should be around 350 degrees Fahrenheit). If you do not have a thermometer, then dip a fork, chopstick, or vegetable into the oil. If bubbles form around the utensil or food, the oil is ready to fry fritters. Alternatively, throw a drop of water in; if it sizzles immediately, start frying. Don't slam-dunk the fritters into the hot oil, which will cause your oil to splatter. And always use clean oil—this is very important!

RICE FRITTERS *frituras de arroz*

12 FRITURAS

> 1 ½ cups cooked rice
> 1 cup water
> 1 cup milk
> 1 teaspoon melted butter
> Salt and pepper to taste
> 1 tablespoon sugar
> 5 eggs, beaten
> 1 cup bread crumbs or cracker meal
> 4 cups vegetable oil

In a large mixing bowl, combine the cooked rice with the water, milk, butter, salt, pepper, and sugar. Add half of the beaten eggs, and mix together to make a sticky batter.

Form 1-inch balls of this mixture with your hands, and set aside. If you can, chill the batter balls for about 5 minutes in a covered pan in the refrigerator.

Dip each fritter twice in the remaining beaten eggs, and then coat with the bread crumbs. Allow fritters to stand for a while at room temperature before frying.

Fry at medium heat (350 degrees) until golden, about 7 minutes. Soak up excess oil on paper towels.

CODFISH FRITTERS *frituras de bacalao*

A platter of these fritters is possibly the best reason to enjoy a nice cold beer.

12 FRITURAS

> 3 large potatoes, peeled, diced, and boiled until fully tender
> 4 ounces dried salt cod, already soaked per package instructions
> 5 eggs, beaten
> Salt and pepper to taste
> ½ cup chopped fresh parsley
> 1 cup bread crumbs or cracker meal
> 4 cups vegetable oil

(continued on next page)

(continued from previous page)

In a food processor or blender, purée the potatoes. Set aside.

In a clean saucepan, boil the salt cod in 3 cups water for 25 minutes. Remove from heat when tender, and allow to cool to room temperature. When cool, shred the salt cod and add to the puréed potatoes. Add half of the beaten eggs, and mix together to make a sticky batter.

Form 1-inch balls of this mixture with your hands, and set aside. If you can, chill the batter balls for about 5 minutes in a covered pan in the refrigerator.

Dip each fritter twice in mixture of the remaining beaten eggs, salt, pepper, and parsley, and then coat with the bread crumbs. Allow fritters to stand for a while at room temperature before frying.

Fry at medium heat (350 degrees) until golden, about 7 minutes. Soak up excess oil on paper towels.

CORN FRITTERS *frituras de maíz tierno*
12 FRITURAS

>1 cup prepared cornmeal, medium grind
>4 eggs
>1 teaspoon milk or heavy cream
>Salt and pepper to taste
>½ cup chopped fresh parsley
>1 cup bread crumbs or cracker meal
>4 cups vegetable oil

Combine the cornmeal, one egg, milk, salt, and pepper in a mixing bowl to make a sticky batter.

Form 1-inch balls of this mixture with your hands, and set aside. If you can, chill the batter balls for about 5 minutes in a covered pan in the refrigerator.

Beat the eggs and add chopped fresh parsley before you dip the fritters for a nice color and flavor. Dip each fritter twice in the beaten eggs, and then coat with the bread crumbs. Allow fritters to stand for a while at room temperature before frying.

Fry at medium heat (350 degrees) until golden, about 7 minutes. Soak up excess oil on paper towels.

MALANGA FRITTERS *frituras de malanga*

12 FRITURAS

> 2 cups mashed *malanga* (see page 134), chilled
> Salt and pepper to taste
> 5 eggs, beaten
> 1 cup bread crumbs or cracker meal
> 4 cups vegetable oil

In a large mixing bowl, mix the mashed *malanga,* salt, and pepper with half of the beaten eggs to make a sticky batter.

Form 1-inch balls of this mixture, and set aside. If you can, chill the batter balls for about 5 minutes in a covered pan in the refrigerator.

Dip each fritter twice in the remaining beaten eggs, and then coat with the bread crumbs. Allow fritters to stand for a while at room temperature before frying.

Fry at medium heat (350 degrees) until golden, about 7 minutes. Soak up excess oil on paper towels.

ÑAME FRITTERS *frituras de ñame*

12 FRITURAS

> 2 cups boiled *ñame* (see page 132), chilled
> Salt and pepper to taste
> 5 eggs, beaten
> 1 cup bread crumbs or cracker meal
> 4 cups vegetable oil

In a large mixing bowl, mash the boiled *ñame* and mix with salt, pepper, and half of the beaten eggs to make a sticky batter.

Form 1-inch balls of this mixture, and set aside. If you can, chill the batter balls for about 5 minutes in a covered pan in the refrigerator.

Dip each fritter twice in the remaining beaten eggs, and then coat with the bread crumbs. Allow fritters to stand for a while at room temperature before frying.

Fry at medium heat (350 degrees) until golden, about 7 minutes. Soak up excess oil on paper towels.

CASSAVA FRITTERS *frituras de yuca*

12 FRITURAS

> 2 cups boiled cassava (see page 133), chilled
> 1 cup milk
> 1 teaspoon butter
> Salt and pepper to taste
> 1 tablespoon sugar
> 5 eggs, beaten
> 1 cup bread crumbs or cracker meal
> 4 cups vegetable oil

Mash the cassava by hand in a large mixing bowl, or purée in a food processor. Mix in the milk, butter, salt, pepper, and sugar. Add half of the beaten eggs, and mix together to make a sticky batter.

Form 1-inch balls of this mixture, and set aside. If you can, chill the batter balls for about 5 minutes in a covered pan in the refrigerator.

Dip each fritter twice in the remaining beaten eggs, and then coat with the bread crumbs. Allow fritters to stand for a while at room temperature before frying.

Fry at medium heat (350 degrees) until golden, about 7 minutes. Soak up excess oil on paper towels.

CASSAVA AND CHEESE FRITTERS

frituras de yuca y queso

12 FRITTERS

> 2 cups boiled cassava (see page 133), chilled
> ¼ cup grated Parmesan cheese
> 1 cup milk
> 1 teaspoon butter
> Salt and pepper to taste
> 1 tablespoon sugar
> 5 eggs, beaten
> 1 cup bread crumbs or cracker meal
> 4 cups vegetable oil

Mash the cassava by hand in a large mixing bowl, or purée in a food processor. Add the cheese. Mix in the milk, butter, salt, pepper, and sugar. Add half of the beaten eggs, and mix together to make a sticky batter.

Form 1-inch balls of this mixture, and set aside. If you can, chill the batter balls for about 5 minutes in a covered pan in the refrigerator.

Dip each fritter twice in the remaining beaten eggs, and then coat with the bread crumbs. Allow fritters to stand for a while at room temperature before frying.

Fry at medium heat (350 degrees) until golden, about 7 minutes. Soak up excess oil on paper towels.

CASSAVA FRIES *yuca frita*

Not exactly fritters, these fries are wonderful with green parsley sauce (page 117), cilantro sauce, or green mayonnaise (see page 118). A true treat.

4 SERVINGS

> **4 cups vegetable oil**
> **3 cups boiled cassava (see page 133), chilled and cut into 1-inch strips**
> **Salt to taste**
> **Juice of 1 lemon**

Pour the oil to a depth of at least 1 inch in a medium skillet, and heat to 350 degrees. Salt the cassava, and fry until golden, about 7 minutes. Soak up excess oil on paper towels. Sprinkle with lemon juice, and serve immediately.

BLACK-EYED PEA FRITTERS *bollitos de carita*

Just saying the Spanish name for these black-eyed pea fritters is enough to make you blush and go to confession. If the name *bollito* (look it up) is naughty, the taste of the fritters is just as sinfully delicious.

12 BOLLITOS

> 1 cup dried black-eyed peas, soaked overnight in the refrigerator
> 5 garlic cloves, minced
> ¼ cup water
> 2 eggs
> Salt and pepper to taste
> 2 cups vegetable oil
> Juice of 1 lemon

Drain the soaked peas in a colander, and process with garlic, water, and eggs in a food processor to make a smooth purée. Purée again for 2 or 3 minutes after you scrape the sides of the bowl, to achieve a smooth paste. Season with salt and pepper.

Form 1-inch balls of this mixture with your hands, and set aside. If you can, chill the balls for about 5 minutes in a covered pan in the refrigerator.

Pour the oil to a depth of at least 1 inch in a medium skillet, and heat to 350 degrees. Fry your fritters until golden, about 7 minutes. Soak up excess oil on paper towels. Serve immediately, and sprinkle with lemon juice.

BROTHS, SOUPS, AND CREAMS CUBAN STYLE

*caldos, sopas,
y cremas al estilo cubano*

BROTHS AND CONSOMMÉS

los caldos y los consomés

THESE BASIC BOUILLONS, the result of cooking vegetables, poultry, meat, or fish in water, can form the base for soups, sauces, and many stews and potages. They can all be prepared in advance and kept frozen for up to two months. Remember, homemade broths are always the most flavorful.

WAJAY · HAVANA

VEDADO DISTRICT BASIC BROTH *caldo básico*

This very simple recipe was usually served as the first appetizer during family dinners at upscale residences in El Vedado. During the 1950s, the Vedado District was home to the most sophisticated and posh hotels, clubs, and cabarets, as well as to rich and famous people. Its proximity to the equally rich and even more beautiful Miramar was also a plus for the countless natives and tourists in that epoch. It was definitely the place to be seen (and heard) in exciting Havana.

6 SERVINGS

½ pound beef brisket (*falda* in Spanish), cubed
½ pound beef soup bones (not necessary, but they give authentic and deep flavor)
1 onion, peeled and chopped
6 medium tomatoes, peeled and chopped
1 green bell pepper, seeded and chopped
3 garlic cloves, minced
1 bay leaf
1 teaspoon salt
8 cups water
Saffron (optional)

Place all ingredients in a large, heavy pot and allow to stand for ½ hour, covered with cloth or paper towel.

Bring all ingredients to a boil over medium heat, reduce the heat, and simmer, partially covered, for 40 minutes.

Strain broth to make a very light and fine consommé. Serve hot or chilled.

NOTE For a tasty variation of this broth, add 2 cups of peeled and chopped carrots when you put the other ingredients in the pot to soak.

CUBAN VEGETABLE CONSOMMÉ
caldo de vegetales

This is so replete with necessary nutrients that it makes a perfect digestive first course for the babies in the family. This is usually served hot, but some like it chilled.

6 SERVINGS

> 1 onion, peeled and chopped
> 2 cups peeled and chopped carrots
> 4 cups peeled and chopped potatoes
> 2 cups cooked rice, or ¾ cup uncooked rice (make sure uncooked rice is tender by the end of cooking time)
> 3 garlic cloves
> 6 medium tomatoes, peeled and chopped
> 1 green bell pepper, seeded and chopped
> 1 bay leaf
> 2 cups peeled and chopped pumpkin
> 1 teaspoon black pepper
> 1 teaspoon salt
> 8 cups water
> 3 cups corn kernels—fresh, frozen, or canned

Place all ingredients in a large, heavy pot and allow to stand for ½ hour, covered with cloth or paper towel.

Bring all ingredients to a boil over medium heat, reduce the heat, and simmer, partially covered, for 40 minutes.

Strain broth to make a very light and fine consommé.

CHICKEN CONSOMMÉ *consomé de pollo*

This is usually served hot, but some like it chilled.

6 SERVINGS

> One 2- to 3-pound chicken, cut into 6 pieces, plus giblets
> 1 onion, peeled and chopped
> 2 cups peeled and chopped carrots
> 3 garlic cloves
> 6 medium tomatoes, peeled and chopped
> 1 green bell pepper, seeded and chopped
> 1 teaspoon freshly ground black pepper
> 1 teaspoon salt
> 8 cups water
> Pinch of paprika, or 1 chicken bouillon cube, for coloring

Place all ingredients in a large, heavy pot and allow to stand for ½ hour, covered with cloth or paper towel.

Bring all ingredients to a boil over medium heat, reduce the heat, and simmer, partially covered, for 40 minutes.

Strain broth to make a very light and fine consommé.

CELERY CONSOMMÉ *consomé de apio*

This consommé is made elegant by the combination of egg whites and lemon juice. The secret is to let it simmer slowly. Usually served hot, this one is really wonderful chilled.

6 SERVINGS

> 1 onion, peeled and chopped
> 10 celery stalks, chopped
> ½ pound beef brisket (*falda* in Spanish), cubed
> 4 medium tomatoes, peeled and chopped
> 1 green bell pepper, seeded and chopped
> 1 bay leaf
> 3 garlic cloves, minced
> 1 teaspoon freshly ground black pepper

> **1 teaspoon salt**
> **8 cups water**
> **2 egg whites, beaten**
> **Juice of 1 lemon**

Place all ingredients except egg whites and lemon juice in a large, heavy pot and allow to stand for ½ hour, covered with cloth or paper towel.

Bring all ingredients to a boil over medium heat, reduce the heat, and simmer, partially covered, for 50 minutes.

Strain broth to make a very light and fine consommé. Then add the beaten egg whites, and boil again, for another 10 minutes.

Add the lemon juice and serve.

FISH STOCK *caldo de pescado*

This is usually served hot, but some people like it chilled.

6 SERVINGS

> **1 pound fish bones with heads on but gills removed**
> NOTE The best fish bones are those from flounder, snapper, and grouper.
> **1 onion, peeled and chopped**
> **2 cups peeled, chopped carrots**
> **3 garlic cloves**
> **6 medium tomatoes, peeled and chopped**
> **1 green bell pepper, seeded and chopped**
> **1 teaspoon freshly ground black pepper**
> **1 teaspoon salt**
> **8 cups water**
> **1 fish or vegetable bouillon cube**

Place all ingredients in a large, heavy pot and allow to stand for ½ hour covered with cloth or paper towel.

Bring to a boil over medium heat. Reduce the heat, and simmer, partially covered, for 40 minutes.

Strain broth to make a very light and fine consommé.

SOUPS IN THE CUBAN STYLE
sopas a la cubana

The curative and comforting effects of soups are known in most cultures. Many people in the Northern Hemisphere think of soup only during the colder months, but people in the Tropics enjoy soup all year long. Soups are the perfect comfort food—wouldn't it be great if every meal started with one! My mother's family was very big, and all my uncles and aunts were wonderful cooks and had their own personal favorite soup recipes. I am including these family favorites here. Serve these great soups with a loaf of Cuban bread (see page 78) and a small dinner salad for a perfect light meal.

CREOLE GARLIC SOUP *sopa de ajo a la criolla*
4 SERVINGS

> 4 tablespoons butter
> 7 garlic cloves, peeled
> ½ loaf Cuban bread (see page 78) or your favorite store-bought
>   bread, cut into small cubes
> 4 cups water
> Salt to taste
> 4 eggs, beaten
> 1 tablespoon chopped fresh parsley

Melt the butter in a large, heavy pot over low heat. Add the garlic cloves and cook until they are tender; mash them while stirring. Remove the garlic and reserve.

Add the bread cubes to the melted butter.

Add the water and salt. Bring to a boil over medium heat, reduce heat, and simmer, partially covered, for about 20 minutes. Halfway through, put the smashed garlic cloves back in, and continue heating.

Add the beaten eggs and parsley. Stir and heat for another 5 minutes. Remove from heat, and serve immediately.

CLASSICALLY CUBAN ONION SOUP

sopa de cebolla a la francesita

I am always amazed by the wonderful taste of onion soup. This classic French staple was featured in restaurants in Cuba in the 1950s and is also one of the most popular items in many Cuban restaurants and cafeterias in South Florida today. This variation is lighter and uses less cheese than its French counterpart. Combine this soup with chicken salad and Cuban bread for a delicious meal (see pages 197 and 78).

4 SERVINGS

> 4 tablespoons butter
>
> 2 large yellow onions, peeled and thinly sliced (slices should be almost transparent)
>
> 6 cups vegetable consommé (see page 53) or Vedado District basic broth (see page 52)
>
> 4 cups bread cubes
>
> 4 slices Gruyère cheese

Melt the butter in a medium pot over low heat, add the onions, and cook, stirring occasionally, until the onions are very soft but not brown.

Add the consommé, bring to a boil, and continue simmering over low heat for about 15 minutes.

In the oven, toast the bread cubes. Add them to the soup. Set the oven for 425 degrees.

Pour the soup into individual ovenproof bowls or soup crocks. Top each bowl with cheese. Bake for 5 minutes, and serve immediately.

SAN IGNACIO MUSHROOM SOUP
sopa de champiñones San Ignacio

San Ignacio Street, in a beautiful and ornate part of town, housed an important Cuban Jewish community. Cuban Jews have a rich traditional heritage to preserve. Their recipes reflect this. Today a very important segment of the Cuban Jewish immigrant community is in Puerto Rico, as well as in the mainland United States. Cuban Jews have worked hard and prospered in exile, and many families figure prominently among those who have attained the American Dream. Philanthropic and community-oriented, they preserve their Cuban and their Jewish roots. This recipe pays tribute to that brilliant diaspora.

4 SERVINGS

> **4 cups béchamel sauce (see page 109)**
> **3 cups fresh mushrooms, cut into thick slices**
> NOTE You may also use portobello mushrooms, or even substitute asparagus.
> **2 cups water**
> **2 egg yolks, beaten**
> **1 cup diced cooked chicken breast**
> **½ cup heavy cream**

Combine the béchamel sauce, mushrooms, and water in a saucepan. Bring to a boil over medium heat, reduce the heat, and simmer, stirring constantly for about ten minutes.

Add the beaten egg yolks, and keep stirring, so they are completely integrated into the soup.

Add the chicken, and simmer slowly for ten minutes.

Stir in the heavy cream, and serve immediately.

BLACK BEAN SOUP AT VICTOR'S CAFÉ
sopa de frijoles negros de Victor's Café

Victor's Café is the most famous Cuban restaurant in New York City. Ever since the del Corral family opened the doors of this Cuban outpost back in 1963, Cubans and non-Cubans have been savoring traditionally Cuban dishes and consistently coming back for more. Victor's Café is a place to return to again and again for generous portions of fresh, authentic Cuban cuisine and good old-fashioned Cuban American hospitality. This is their signature black bean soup.

4 SERVINGS

> 1 pound dried black beans
> 1 green bell pepper, seeded and halved
> 10 cups water
> ¼ cup olive oil, plus a drizzle for serving
> 4 garlic cloves, minced
> 1 medium onion, peeled and chopped
> 1 teaspoon ground bay leaf
> Salt to taste
> 1 tablespoon sugar
> 2 tablespoons dry red or white wine

Wash the beans with cold water, drain, and place in a large bowl with the green pepper. Soak the beans and pepper in 10 cups water overnight, or for at least 6 hours.

When the beans have swollen, cook them in the same water until soft, approximately 45 minutes.

Remove the green pepper and chop it.

In another large pot, heat the oil, and fry the garlic, onion, and the pepper, adding the bay leaf as you cook.

Add the cooked black beans with water to the mixture, and stir well to mix.

Add the salt, sugar, and wine, and continue to simmer for another 30 minutes.

Serve with a drizzle of olive oil.

ZOILA'S EGG DROP SOUP CUBAN STYLE

sopa de huevos Tía Zoila

My aunt Zoila made the absolute best Cuban-style egg drop soup. Our family is very proud of its Chinese Cuban heritage, and this soup was Aunt Zoila's way of helping us all remember that very special part of our background—and, of course, our grandfather, whom we called *el chino de Santo Suárez.*

4 SERVINGS

> **4 eggs**
> **1½ cups all-purpose flour**
> **1 teaspoon grated nutmeg**
> **1½ cups basic broth, or more to taste**
> NOTE The Vedado District basic broth (see page 52) and the vegetable and celery consommés (see pages 53 and 54) are all great bases for this recipe.

Beat the eggs, then add the flour and nutmeg slowly. Keep stirring and swirling until you have a smooth paste. Let this sit for 2 to 3 hours.

Pour the broth into a large, heavy saucepan. Strain the egg paste into the broth, making sure that you achieve a smooth consistency throughout. Keep mashing the paste into the broth to get the consistency you like. Add more broth if needed.

Stir, simmer for about 20 minutes over low to medium heat, and serve.

ULTIMATE CUBAN POTATO SOUP
sopa de papas Tía Berta

My *madrina* (godmother) made a mean potato soup. Well, she was really my brother's godmother, not mine, but we both called her *madrina*. I remember there were very few cold days during my childhood in Cuba, but whenever the weather turned a bit nippy, my aunt and *madrina* Berta had this soup on the table for us, to keep all of us cozy and nourished. My dad, who was of Spanish descent and never considered a meal to be complete without potatoes, loved this soup.

4 SERVINGS

> 3 cups basic broth or consommé
> ½ pound of potatoes, peeled and diced
> NOTE The Vedado District basic broth (see page 52) and the vegetable and celery consommés (see pages 53 and 54) are all great bases for this recipe.

Prepare the broth according to the recipe.

Add the potatoes, and bring to a boil over medium heat. Reduce the heat, and simmer, partially covered, for another 20 minutes. Serve and enjoy!

UNCLE NENO'S FISH SOUP
sopa de pescado Tío Neno

My uncle Neno was a bus driver in Cuba, going from province to province on long road trips. The Cuban fish stew—or *sopa de pescado,* as we call it—was served in most bus rest stops along his route, varying from place to place, but always boasting fresh island fish. Grouper or snapper is normally used in this soup.

6 SERVINGS

> 10 cups water
> 2 fish heads (preferably grouper or snapper)
> 1 cup sofrito (see page 119)
> 2 cups peeled and diced potatoes
> 4 slices bread (preferably Cuban bread; see page 78), toasted

Over medium heat, boil the fish heads for about 20 minutes in the water. Reserve and strain the broth; reserve the fish heads.

(continued on next page)

(continued from previous page)

When the fish heads have cooled, remove as much flesh as possible from the bones, breaking it into small pieces.

Prepare and sauté the sofrito over low heat, and add the fish pieces, strained broth, and diced potatoes. Simmer for about 15 minutes over low to medium heat to blend the flavors and cook the potatoes until tender.

Dish into individual soup bowls and top with the slices of toasted bread before serving.

LUCILA'S TARTAR SOUP *sopa tártara*

My aunt Lucila was quite a character, the rebel without a cause, and the one who stayed at home with my grandmother. This was one of her favorite recipes, and she made it often for our family. It was eccentric, and she was eccentric. For that very reason, as a child I loved both Aunt Lucila and her soup.

4 SERVINGS

> 6 cups water
> 2 boneless and skinless chicken breasts
> 3 garlic cloves, minced
> 4 tomatoes, peeled and diced
> 1 medium onion, peeled and chopped
> 1 green bell pepper, seeded and chopped
> 4 slices bread (preferably Cuban bread; see page 78), cubed in
>   ½-inch pieces
> Salt to taste
> Black pepper to taste
> 4 egg yolks

Pour water into a medium soup pot and add the chicken breasts, garlic, tomatoes, onion, and pepper. Let the chicken poach slowly. Cook over medium heat until liquid starts boiling. Reduce heat.

Add the bread cubes and simmer over low heat until the liquid reduces to about half the volume. Remove from heat.

Remove your chicken breasts, and run them through a food processor or grinder. Return chicken to soup, and continue heating over low heat, letting the flavors and ingredients blend. Taste, and add seasonings while simmering.

Put an egg yolk in the bottom of each individual soup bowl and ladle the piping hot soup over it. Serve immediately.

CORN CHOWDER *guiso de maíz tierno*
4 SERVINGS

> ¼ cup olive oil
> ¼ pound ham, diced
> ¼ pound chorizo sausage, chopped
> 1 onion, peeled and chopped
> 3 garlic cloves, minced
> 1 green bell pepper, seeded and chopped
> ½ cup tomato sauce
> Salt and pepper to taste
> 3 cups chicken consommé (see page 54)
> 1 cup water
> 1 cup peeled and diced potatoes
> 1 cup peeled, seeded, and diced pumpkin (*calabaza*)
> 2 cups corn kernels, frozen or fresh

In a large saucepan, heat the olive oil over medium heat. Add the ham and sausage, and sauté for 2 or 3 minutes. Add the onion, garlic, and green pepper, and sauté for another 5 to 7 minutes, until the onion becomes translucent.

Reduce the heat; add the tomato sauce, salt, pepper, chicken consommé, water, and potatoes; simmer, covered, over medium-low heat for another 10 to 12 minutes. Add the *calabaza* and the corn, and continue to cook for another 30 minutes, stirring occasionally, until all vegetables are tender and chowder is thick. Taste, and correct seasonings if necessary. Serve with a dollop of sour cream.

CUBAN CREAM SOUPS
cremas

CREAM OF SPINACH SOUP   *crema de espinacas*

Spinach is full of vitamins and minerals, and this cream soup is very easy to prepare. Serve with croutons made from Cuban bread (see page 78).

4 SERVINGS

> 2 cups white sauce (see page 110)
> Salt and pepper to taste
> 2 cups chopped spinach, fresh or frozen

Heat the sauce through, and season with salt and pepper.

Add the spinach, and simmer over very low heat for 15 minutes. Season along the way with salt and pepper to taste.

NOTE It is wonderful if you have the white sauce already prepared. If not, remember this very basic rule for cream soups: To start your cream base, use butter, flour, milk, and salt, and cook over low heat until liquid begins to bubble and thicken.

CREAM OF TOMATO SOUP *crema de tomates*

This delicious soup is full of vitamins and minerals. If you add crabmeat or lobster, it can become a whole meal the entire family will like. Just serve with Cuban croutons.

4 SERVINGS

> **2 cups water**
> **4 cups peeled and diced tomatoes**
> **1 medium onion, peeled and chopped**
> **Salt and pepper to taste**
> **1 teaspoon sugar**
> **2 cups béchamel sauce (see page 109)**

Pour water into a medium pot, and add the tomatoes, onion, salt, pepper, and sugar. Simmer over medium heat for about 10 minutes.

Purée this mixture in a food processor or blender, and return to the heat. Add the béchamel sauce, and cook over low heat for another 5 minutes, until all flavors are blended. Serve immediately, or chill.

NUTRITIOUS POTAGES

potajes más nutritivos

POTAJES, THE THICK STEWS that all Cubans are accustomed to, come from the Galician and northern-Spanish cooking tradition that is prevalent on the island of Cuba. For the many Cuban households in which there is still an *abuelita* at home, the custom of two *potajes* a day still sticks—one for lunch and one for dinner. These stews are great to take to work for lunch, or to pop into the microwave for a complete, nutritious, and inexpensive meal. I also remember our own family tradition of having Lugo Galician *potaje* (see page 69) with a glass of milk early on Sunday evenings. What a treat. Serve with a loaf of homemade Cuban bread (see page 78) and you have a delectable version of Sunday stew.

TRADITIONAL BEEF AND VEGETABLE STEW
ajiaco criollo

This is it! After all, it is our Cuban national dish, and we can trace its origins back to the Taíno and Ciboney Indians, who inhabited the island in the fifteenth century, before the Spanish arrived. The *ajiaco* can be started early in the morning and can be kept continuously simmering. You may vary the recipe by adding fresh ingredients, including anything that your guests or family desire. The original version uses *tasajo* (see page 305), which is salt-dried beef (or, traditionally, horsemeat), also used in Italian cooking and available in most markets. If you are at all squeamish about *tasajo* made with horsemeat, you can substitute flank steak. But the original *ajiaco* with *tasajo* is still the best (in my humble opinion). You can also double up ingredients and make this recipe for a crowd.

Please remember that your ingredients make your stew. In the *ajiaco criollo*, each vegetable has a role to play to enhance the flavor, consistency, or color.

8 SERVINGS

> 12 cups water
> 2 cups Vedado District basic broth (see page 52)
> ½ pound sweet cassava (*yuca*), peeled and diced
> ½ pound *malanga*, peeled and diced
> ½ pound boniato (Cuban sweet potato; see page 126), peeled and diced
> ½ pound *ñame*, peeled and diced
> NOTE You may find *ñame* in a Hispanic market; if not, substitute another root vegetable, such as turnip.
> 1½ cups sofrito (see page 119)
> 1 pound boneless pork shoulder, cubed
> ½ pound *tasajo* (salt-dried beef; see headnote)
> ½ lb pumpkin (*calabaza*) or winter squash, peeled, seeded, and diced
> 2 green plantains, peeled and cut
> 2 ripe sweet plantains, peeled and cut
> Salt to taste
> 4 corn ears cut into bite-sized pieces
> ¼ cup lemon juice

Bring the water and broth to a boil over high heat in a very large, heavy pot. Then reduce the heat to low, and add the root vegetables: cassava, *malanga,*

(continued on next page)

(continued from previous page)

boniato, and *ñame*. Simmer over low heat until the root vegetables have cooked, about 20 minutes.

Meanwhile, make the sofrito in a skillet. Add the pork and *tasajo,* and sauté for 5 to 7 minutes. Add the sofrito to the vegetable broth, and add the pumpkin; cook until pumpkin is tender, about 10 minutes.

In another saucepan, boil the green and sweet plantains—plantains tend to darken the broth. Then, when tender, add them to the broth as well.

Simmer very slowly for as long as you like, adding broth, other liquids, or other ingredients as you see fit. This should take an additional 15 to 18 minutes. Taste, and add salt, blending the flavors. Add the corn. When everything has reached the right consistency, add the lemon juice and remove from heat. Serve immediately, by spooning stew into soup bowls.

MY MAMA'S RED BEANS *potaje de frijoles colorados*

It's a macho thing. Every Cuban guy thinks *his* mother makes the best red beans. Sitting at a lunch counter in downtown Miami, David Torres, in his crisp white *guayabera,* gave me his Cuban mother's recipe for this wonderful red bean stew—or, better yet, as he called it, "my mama's red beans!" After testing this recipe (and many other contenders), I have to agree that this guy might just be right that his mother makes *the* best red bean stew.

4 SERVINGS

1 pound dried red beans
1 green bell pepper, seeded and halved
10 cups water
2 cups peeled and diced potatoes
½ cup chunks of peeled pumpkin (*calabaza*) or butternut squash
¼ cup olive oil, plus a dash for serving
1 chorizo sausage, peeled and sliced
4 garlic cloves, minced
1 medium onion, peeled and chopped
1 teaspoon ground bay leaf
Salt to taste
1 tablespoon sugar
2 tablespoons dry white wine

Wash the red beans with cold water, drain, and place in a large bowl with the green pepper. Soak the beans in 10 cups water overnight, or for at least 6 hours.

When the beans have swollen, cook the beans in the same water until soft, approximately 45 minutes. Add the potatoes and pumpkin in the last 20 minutes, and simmer until vegetables are tender.

Remove the green pepper and chop it.

In another large pot, heat the oil and fry the chorizo with garlic, onion, and pepper, adding the ground bay leaf as you cook for 5 to 7 minues.

Add to the beans, and stir well to mix.

Add the salt, sugar, and wine, and continue to simmer for another 20 minutes.

Serve with a drizzle of olive oil.

LUGO GALICIAN STEW *caldo gallego de Lugo*

Lugo is a beautiful city in the north of Spain. This is where my father's Spanish ancestors come from. This stew recipe has been handed down through the generations, and you will see why after tasting it.

4 SERVINGS

> 1 cup dried white beans
> 1 green bell pepper, seeded and halved
> 8 cups water
> 2 teaspoons olive oil, plus a dash for serving
> 1 potato, peeled and diced
> 1 chorizo sausage cut in 8 pieces (about 1 cup)
> 1 cup cubed cooked ham
> 1 onion, peeled and chopped
> 2 garlic cloves, minced
> 2 teaspoons tomato purée
> 1 cup chopped collard greens
> ¼ cup chopped turnip greens
> ½ cup chopped cabbage
> Salt to taste

(continued on next page)

(continued from previous page)

Wash the white beans with cold water, drain, and place in a large bowl with the green pepper. Soak the beans in 8 cups water overnight, or for at least 6 hours.

When the beans have swollen, cook them in the same water until soft, approximately 45 minutes. Add the potato in the last 15 minutes of cooking.

Remove the green pepper and chop it.

In another large pot, heat the oil and fry the chorizo with the ham, onion, garlic, and pepper, adding the tomato sauce as you cook, for 5 to 7 minutes. Add the collard greens, turnip greens, and cabbage, and cook over low heat for an additional 3 to 5 minutes.

Add to the beans, and stir well to mix.

Taste, and season with salt if needed. Continue to simmer for another 10 to 15 minutes.

Serve with a dash of olive oil.

CHICKPEA STEW *potaje de garbanzos*

My uncle Guillermo has always been called Garbanzo by his family. I am sure it goes back to his fondness for this stew at lunchtime.

4 SERVINGS

> 1 cup dried chickpeas (garbanzo beans)
> 1 green bell pepper, seeded and halved
> 8 cups water
> 1 potato, peeled and diced
> 2 teaspoons olive oil, plus a dash for serving
> 1 chorizo sausage cut in 8 pieces (about 1 cup)
> 1 cup cubed cooked ham
> 2 garlic cloves, minced
> 1 onion, peeled and chopped
> 2 teaspoons tomato purée
> ½ cup chopped cabbage
> Salt and pepper to taste

Wash the chickpeas with cold water, drain, and place in a large bowl with the green pepper. Soak the beans in 8 cups water overnight, or for at least 6 hours.

When the chickpeas have swollen, cook them in the same water until soft, approximately 45 minutes. Add the potato in the last 15 minutes of cooking.

Remove the green pepper and chop it.

In another large pot, heat the oil and fry the chorizo with the ham, garlic, onion, and pepper, adding the tomato purée as you cook, for 5 to 7 minutes. Add cabbage, and cook over low heat for an additional 3 to 5 minutes.

Add to the chickpeas, and stir well to mix.

Taste, and season with salt and pepper if needed. Continue to simmer for another 10 to 15 minutes.

Serve with a dash of olive oil.

LENTIL STEW *potaje de lentejas*

Lentils are small, round, flat beans that melt in your mouth. Try this earthy stew and you will appreciate them.

4 SERVINGS

> 1 cup lentils
> 1 green bell pepper, seeded and halved
> 8 cups water
> 1 potato, peeled and diced
> 2 teaspoons olive oil, plus a dash for serving (optional)
> 1 strip bacon
> 1 cup cubed cooked ham
> 2 garlic cloves, minced
> 1 onion, peeled and chopped
> 2 teaspoons tomato purée
> ½ cup chopped cabbage
> Salt and pepper to taste
> Sour cream for serving (optional)

Wash the lentils with cold water. Drain and place the beans in a large bowl with the green pepper.

Cook them in 8 cups water until soft, approximately 30 minutes. Add the potato in the last 15 minutes of cooking.

Remove the green pepper and chop it.

(continued on next page)

(continued from previous page)

In another large pot, heat the oil and fry the bacon with the ham, garlic, onion, and pepper, adding the tomato purée as you cook, for 5 to 7 minutes. Add cabbage, and cook over low heat for an additional 3 to 5 minutes.

Add to the lentils, and stir well to mix.

Taste, and season with salt and pepper if needed. Continue to simmer for another 10 to 15 minutes.

Serve with a dash of olive oil or with a dollop of sour cream.

BUTTER BEAN STEW *potaje de judías*

This great, filling stew has its origins in Afro-Cuban cooking. A one-dish meal!

4 SERVINGS

> 1 cup dried butter beans or lima beans
> 1 green bell pepper, seeded and halved
> 8 cups water
> 1 potato, peeled and diced
> 2 teaspoons olive oil, plus a dash for serving
> 1 chorizo sausage, peeled and sliced
> 2 garlic cloves, minced
> 1 onion, peeled and chopped
> 1 celery stalk, chopped
> 1 carrot, grated
> 2 teaspoons tomato purée
> ½ cup chopped cabbage
> Salt and pepper to taste

Wash the butter beans with cold water, drain, and place in a large bowl with the green pepper. Soak the beans in 8 cups water overnight, or for at least 6 hours.

When the lima beans have swollen, cook them in the same water until soft, approximately 1 hour. Add the potato in the last 15 minutes of cooking.

Remove the green pepper and chop it.

In another large pot, heat the oil and fry chorizo sausage with the garlic, onion, pepper, celery, and carrot, adding the tomato purée as you cook, for 5 to 7 minutes. Add cabbage, and cook over low heat for an additional 3 to 5 minutes.

Add to the butter or lima beans, and stir well to mix.

Taste, and season with salt and pepper if needed. Continue to simmer for another 10 to 15 minutes.

Serve with a dash of olive oil.

SPLIT PEA STEW *potage de chícharos*

It is nice to make a *chícharo* stew early Sunday morning and keep it going all day long.

4 SERVINGS

> 1 cup dried split peas, green, yellow, or combination
> 1 green bell pepper, seeded and halved
> 8 cups water
> 1 potato, peeled and diced
> 2 teaspoons olive oil
> 1 chorizo sausage, peeled and sliced
> 1 cup diced smoked ham
> 2 garlic cloves, minced
> 1 onion, peeled and chopped
> 1 celery stalk, chopped
> 1 carrot, grated
> 1 cup chopped tomatoes
> ½ cup chopped cabbage
> Salt and pepper to taste
> Dash of lemon juice for serving

Wash the split peas with cold water, drain, and place in a large bowl with the green pepper. Soak the peas in 8 cups water overnight, or for at least 6 hours.

When the split peas have swollen, cook them in the same water until soft, approximately 45 minutes. Add the potato in the last 15 minutes of cooking.

Remove the green pepper and chop it.

In another large pot, heat the oil and fry chorizo sausage with the ham, garlic, onion, pepper, celery, and carrot, adding the chopped tomatoes as you cook, for 5 to 7 minutes. Add cabbage, and cook over low heat for an additional 3 to 5 minutes.

Add to the split peas, and stir well to mix.

(continued on next page)

(continued from previous page)

Taste, and season with salt and pepper if needed. Continue to simmer for another 10 to 15 minutes.

Serve with a dash of lemon juice.

CORN STEW *guiso de maíz*

4 SERVINGS

> 8 cups water
> 3 corn ears, cut into quarters
> 1 cup peeled and diced potato
> ⅔ cup vegetable oil for frying
> 1 chorizo sausage, peeled and sliced
> 2 garlic cloves, minced
> 1 onion, peeled and chopped
> 1 green bell pepper, seeded and halved
> 1 celery stalk, chopped
> 2 cups chopped tomatoes
> 1 cup chicken consommé (see page 54) or canned chicken broth
> 2 teaspoons olive oil
> 1 cup diced butternut squash
> Salt and pepper to taste
> Dash of lemon juice for serving
> Cuban bread (see page 78) for serving

In a large saucepan, bring the water to a boil, add the corn and potato, and cook for approximately 20 minutes. Drain, set aside, and discard the water.

In another large pot, heat the vegetable oil and fry chorizo sausage with the garlic, onion, green pepper, and celery, adding the chopped tomatoes as you cook, for 5 to 7 minutes. Add chicken consommé, butternut squash, and olive oil, and cook over low heat for an additional 5 to 7 minutes.

Add the corn-and-potato mixture, and stir well to mix.

Taste, and season with salt and pepper if needed. Continue to simmer for another 10 to 15 minutes.

Serve with a dash of lemon juice and a chunk of Cuban bread.

CUBAN SEAFOOD STEW *potaje de pescadero*

4 SERVINGS

> 1 cup dried pinto beans
> 1 green bell pepper, seeded and halved
> 8 cups water
> 1 potato, peeled and diced
> 2 teaspoons olive oil
> 1 cup crabmeat
> 1 cup small shrimp, peeled and deveined
> 2 garlic cloves, minced
> 1 onion, peeled and chopped
> 1 celery stalk, chopped
> 1 carrot, grated
> 2 cups chopped tomatoes
> 1 cup dry white wine
> 1 cup fish stock (see page 55) or store-bought fish stock
> Salt and pepper to taste
> Dash of lemon juice for serving

Wash the pinto beans with cold water, drain, and place in a large bowl with the green pepper. Soak the beans in 8 cups water overnight, or for at least 6 hours.

When the pinto beans have swollen, cook them in the same water until soft, approximately 1½ hours. Add the potato in the last 15 minutes of cooking.

Remove the green pepper and chop it.

In another large pot, heat the oil and fry the crabmeat and shrimp with the garlic, onion, pepper, celery, and carrot, adding the chopped tomatoes as you cook, for 5 to 7 minutes. Add the wine and fish stock, and simmer over low heat for an additional 3 to 5 minutes.

Add to the pinto beans, and stir well to mix.

Taste, and season with salt and pepper if needed. Continue to cook over low heat another 10 to 15 minutes.

Serve with a dash of lemon juice.

ASTURIAN FABADA STEW *fabada asturiana*

Asturias is another famous part of Spain with a rich heritage passed on to the island of Cuba. The *fabada* takes advantage of the almost sweet taste of white beans; it is always considered a main dish at dinner.

4 SERVINGS

> 1 cup dried white beans (Great Northern or navy beans)
> 1 green bell pepper, seeded and halved
> 8 cups water
> 1 potato, peeled and diced
> 2 teaspoons olive oil
> 1 chorizo sausage, peeled and sliced
> 1 cup diced smoked ham
> 1 strip bacon, chopped
> 2 garlic cloves, minced
> 1 onion, peeled and chopped
> 1 celery stalk, chopped
> 1 carrot, grated
> 2 cups chopped tomatoes
> ½ cup chopped cabbage
> ½ cup chopped collard greens
> Salt and pepper to taste

Wash the white beans with cold water, drain, and place in a large bowl with the green pepper. Soak the beans in 8 cups water overnight, or for at least 6 hours.

When the beans have swollen, cook them in the same water until soft, approximately 1½ hours. Add the potato in the last 15 minutes of cooking.

Remove the green pepper and chop it.

In another large pot, heat the oil and fry chorizo sausage with the ham, bacon, garlic, onion, pepper, celery, and carrot, adding the chopped tomatoes as you cook, for 5 to 7 minutes. Add cabbage and collard greens, and cook over low heat for an additional 3 to 5 minutes.

Add to the white-bean mixture, and stir well to mix.

Taste, and season with salt and pepper if needed. Continue to simmer for another 10 to 15 minutes. Serve immediately.

CUBAN SANDWICHES, WRAPS, AND CHOPS

sándwiches y bocaditos

MOST OF THE SANDWICHES in this chapter use the famous "Cuban bread." So that there is no confusion: Cuban bread is not a French baguette, but a softer and larger loaf that is often baked in the bodegas and left on top of the oven for the customers to grab. Make sure that the loaf you buy or make and serve is hot and soft. If you cannot find any authentic *pan cubano,* then substitute any long, soft, not-too-crusty Italian or French bread you find at the supermarket. I am including a fast and easy recipe for my homemade Cuban bread. There is nothing better than the smell of fresh Cuban bread in the mornings, to make *tostadas cubanas,* or Cuban toast, with butter. Some of the other sand-

wiches use the equally famous *medianoche*, or midnight bread. You can usually buy these rolls in the ethnic or Hispanic aisle at your local supermarket, in a Cuban bodega or grocery store, or even on the Internet. If you cannot find *medianoche*, opt for egg bread or Jewish challah. *Medianoche* bread is sweet and also soft.

When you are talking about a Cuban sandwich, a *medianoche* sandwich, an Elena Ruth, or a *pan con lechón*, picture a Latin-style panino. It is great to use a flat-plate sandwich grill, which presses your sandwiches so the cheese melts and the flavors of the meats blend. If not, use the tried-and-true method of a frying pan with a weight. I like to order and make my sandwiches *bien plancha-ditos*. This translates as "well ironed," but everyone knows it is the perfect catchphrase to describe the most traditional Cuban sandwich.

CUBAN BREAD *pan cubano*

Cuban bread is, of course, ideal for all sandwiches. It is also wonderful with a small slab of guava paste or your favorite marmalade or jelly, and with cream cheese. My grandfather would have it with olive oil, minced garlic, and salt and pepper just before lunchtime. This was my favorite treat. My kids eat it hot out of the oven with nothing on it. My mother dunks it in her *café con leche,* which I highly recommend. Day-old Cuban can make great bread pudding, and it's just perfect for making croutons.

2 LOAVES

> 2 cups warm water
> 1½ packages active dry yeast
> 1 tablespoon sugar
> 1 teaspoon salt
> 6 cups all-purpose flour, plus more for dusting
> 1 egg white, lightly beaten

Mix the 2 cups warm water with the yeast, and add the sugar and salt, stirring thoroughly.

Add the flour slowly, 1 cup at a time, and beat the mixture manually with a spoon, or with an electric mixer at low speed, until the dough is pretty stiff and consistent.

Turn the dough out on a floured surface and roll for 3 minutes. Knead for about 10 minutes, and shape it into a ball.

Place the dough in a greased bowl, cover it, and leave it to double in size. This usually takes about 2 hours, but it can be left longer.

Preheat oven to 400 degrees.

Turn the dough once again onto a floured surface, and shape it into two loaves about 18 inches long and 4 inches wide.

Paint the top of the loaves with the egg white.

Bake in the oven for about 35 minutes, until loaves turn golden.

MIDNIGHT BREAD *medianoche*

This bread is sweet and soft, very similar to challah.

8 ROLLS

> 1½ packages active dry yeast
> 1 cup warm water
> ¾ cup sugar
> 3 tablespoons vegetable oil
> 2 eggs, beaten
> 2 teaspoons salt, plus more for glaze
> 6 cups all-purpose flour, plus more for dusting
> Butter, melted (optional)

Mix the yeast with the warm water, and add the sugar slowly. Stir thoroughly to mix. When the mixture is foamy, add the oil and eggs, reserving 1 tablespoon of beaten egg for the glaze.

Stir in the salt and flour slowly, and beat the mixture manually with a spoon, or with an electric mixer at a low speed, until the dough is stiff and consistent but still soft enough for handling.

Turn the dough out on a floured surface and roll for 3 minutes. Knead for about 10 minutes, and then cover it and leave it to rise. This usually takes about 1½ hours.

Preheat oven to 375 degrees.

Turn the dough once again onto a floured surface, and shape it into eight rolls that are about 5 inches long and 2½ inches wide, with tapered edges.

Beat the remaining tablespoon of egg with salt, and brush the rolls with the egg glaze.

Bake in the oven for about 35 minutes, until golden brown. Brush with butter if you desire.

MIDNIGHT SANDWICH *sándwich de medianoche*

Just as the name implies, this is the sandwich that most Cubans have as a late-evening snack, after a night of dancing or an evening at the movies. It is sometimes served cold, but most often grilled. It is smaller than the Cuban sandwich, but the big difference between a traditional Cuban sandwich and its cousin the *medianoche* is, of course, the egg bread used for *medianoches,* which is sweet and yellow in color. Just like the *sándwich cubano,* however (see page 81), the *medianoche* has no mayonnaise, or tomato or lettuce—it is a pure sandwich.

1 SANDWICH

> 1 *medianoche* roll (see preceding recipe)
> Mustard to taste
> 3 slices sweet Virginia ham
> 3 slices roast pork (preferably home-cooked, with mojo sauce,
>   page 121)
> 3 slices Swiss cheese
> 4 slices sweet pickle

Split the roll lengthwise, and spread the mustard on both sides.
   Place the slices of ham, pork, Swiss cheese, and pickle on the bread.
   Place the sandwich on the press grill, and cook until it is hot and melted.
   Halve diagonally, and serve.

ELENA RUTH SANDWICH *sándwich Elena Ruth*

When I started researching the Elena Ruth, I asked many Cubans (mostly members of my immediate family) how the sandwich got its name. The stories were varied and got wilder as the storyteller's age increased. Well, here it goes—the urban legend that I like the most about Elena Ruth.

   Elena Ruth was a single woman—heaven forbid!—a *solterona,* living in the middle of Havana in the 1950s (though, since it's a legend, it could have been in the 1940s). Her parents were American journalists, so she was, by Cuban standards, considered eccentric. She even liked to attend the ballet by herself! Across the street from the theater was a famous café called El Carmelo. Elena would always go there afterward, again by herself, and custom-order her sandwich. She would give the waiter strict instructions; he would then run to the kitchen and yell these out to the chef. Other diners who heard the loud instructions started following Elena's trend. Soon the novelty became a tradition, and Elena Ruth was famous all over Havana for having created the sweetest sandwich.

1 SANDWICH

1 *medianoche* roll (see page 79), or 2 thick slices challah, or egg
    bread
1 rounded tablespoon strawberry preserves
3 rounded tablespoons cream cheese
3 thick slices roast turkey

Slice the bread lengthwise, and spread the preserves and cream cheese on one side of the bread. On the other side place the slices of turkey.

Place the sandwich on the press grill, and wait for the bread to toast a bit and the cream cheese to melt.

CUBAN SANDWICH *sándwich cubano*

In Cuba and now in Miami, we simply call it *el sándwich*. The Cuban sandwich has been a tradition since the 1930s, when it became a typical *merienda*, or snack, in the cosmopolitan cafés of Havana. Even though there are many variations on the Cuban sandwich, every Cuban follows a few unspoken rules: Never put mayonnaise, tomatoes, lettuce, onions, or bell peppers on your Cuban sandwich. For an authentic Cuban sandwich try not to use a panini grill—a real Cuban sandwich doesn't have little lines grilled into it. When finished grilling, slice the sandwich diagonally across the middle, to make triangle-shaped wedges, and enjoy.

1 SANDWICH

⅓ loaf Cuban bread (see page 78)
Yellow mustard to taste
3 slices sweet Virginia ham
3 slices roast pork, preferably home-cooked with mojo sauce (see
    page 121)
3 slices Swiss cheese
4 slices sweet pickle

(continued on next page)

(continued from previous page)

Slice the bread lengthwise, and spread mustard on both halves.

Place the slices of ham, pork, and cheese on bread, and follow with the pickle.

Place the sandwich on the press grill, and cook until it is hot and melted.

Slice diagonally across the middle, and serve.

VEGETARIAN CUBAN SANDWICH
sándwich cubano vegetariano
1 SANDWICH

> ⅓ loaf Cuban bread (see page 78)
> Yellow mustard to taste
> 1 roasted red or green bell pepper
> 1 cup fried spinach Sacramento (see page 131)
> 5 Spanish green olives, pitted and thinly sliced
> 4 slices *queso blanco* or Swiss cheese
> 4 slices sweet pickle

Slice the bread lengthwise, and spread mustard on it.

Place the roasted bell pepper on top, layer with spinach, olives, and cheese, and follow with the pickle.

secrets of a Cuban cook

HOW TO ROAST AND PEEL A PEPPER

There are several methods for peeling peppers. The most basic is to shave off the skin with a vegetable peeler. But roasting the pepper will heighten the sweet flavor of the flesh, as well as making it easy to peel. Just wash the pepper, slice it in half, cut out the stem, and scrape out the seeds. Place on foil or a cookie sheet, skin side up. Heat the oven to broil and place peppers under the broiler for 5 to 8 minutes; allow to broil until skin bubbles, wrinkles, and then chars. Remove, and when the peppers are cool enough to handle, peel with the help of a small knife.

Place the sandwich on the press grill and cook until it is hot and melted. Slice diagonally across the middle and serve

CUBAN FLYING SAUCER *platillo volador*

When I was a kid growing up in Cuba, my favorite snack was something we called *platillos voladores,* or "flying saucers." Not only was I fascinated with their shape and name, but everyone in the neighborhood loved to use the flying-saucer sandwich press or toasting iron to make these great grilled sandwiches, stuffed with basically anything we wanted at the time. This is still a favorite snack for Cuban American children after school.

1 SANDWICH

> **2 slices white bread, crusts removed**
> **Your favorite filling**
> **Butter for grill**

Spread both slices of bread with your favorite filling.

Close the sandwich, place the entire thing over the buttered cavity of the sandwich grill or special press, and bring down the top, in order to crimp the sandwich and give it a great shape. Toast, and then trim any excess bread.

If I had to choose one filling, it would have to be guava and cream cheese, but try these combinations, too: ham and Swiss cheese, pork and provolone cheese, cooked ground beef and cheddar, and turkey and mozzarella. Also great with plain peanut butter and jelly.

NOTE The flying-saucer sandwich press is inexpensive and available on the Internet, or at most Cuban pharmacies and grocery stores. If you do not have one handy, then use a sandwich grill or a simple frying pan.

SANDWICH TOO MUCH *sándwich demasiado*

In Spanish, when something pleases us immensely it is *demasiado*, or just too much. The honey in this sandwich makes it *demasiado rico!* Just too much and too good. This is a Caprese-type sandwich, with tomato and cheese.

1 SANDWICH

> 1 teaspoon butter
> 2 slices whole-wheat or pumpernickel bread
> 1 teaspoon honey
> 3 slices tomato
> 2 slices fresh mozzarella cheese or *queso blanco*
> 3 teaspoons basic Cuban dressing (see page 106)

Spread butter on slices of bread. Drizzle with honey.

Add the slices of tomato, and follow with the cheese. Drizzle on Cuban dressing. Top with other bread slice.

Place the sandwich on the grill and press if you want it hot and melted. For a cold sandwich, just slice diagonally across the middle and serve.

PRESSED CUBAN HAM AND PINEAPPLE SANDWICHES *sándwiches cubanos de jamón y piña*

This throwback to the good old grilled cheese sandwich is a great way to revive the lunch routine. Make these sandwiches for a pool party, an office lunch, or for your family to eat on the run. They are great served with a tossed salad and a chilled pitcher of orange juice, wine, or sangria (see page 21).

4 SANDWICHES

> ½ cup (4 ounces) cream cheese, softened
> 8 slices whole-wheat bread, cinnamon bread, or pumpernickel
> One 8-ounce can pineapple rings, drained
> 12 slices cooked ham (baked, sweet, or honey)
> 2 teaspoons butter

Spread cream cheese on four slices of bread. Layer each with a pineapple ring, and pile high with thinly sliced ham. Top with the remaining bread slice.

Heat the butter in a large skillet over medium heat until it bubbles slightly.

Place the sandwiches in the skillet, and press with a clean, heavy smaller skillet, spatula, or plate. Turn over to brown the other side, and continue to cook for about 4 minutes. Remove from skillet with spatula, and serve immediately.

UPSCALE CUBAN PANINIS
paninis cubanos elegantes

The panini trend caught on strong in our household. This recipe is fancy enough for visiting relatives on a lazy summer day. We use Cuban bread instead of an artisan baguette; your favorite challah will do as well. Serve with slices of fresh fruit.

4 SANDWICHES

> ¼ stick (4 tablespoons) butter, plus more (optional) for grill
> 2 baguettes, cut into 6-inch lengths and halved
> ¼ cup green mayonnaise (see page 118)
> 4 teaspoons sweet pickle relish
> 8 slices roast pork
> 8 slices sweet ham
> One 14-ounce wheel of Brie, sliced into ¼-inch-thick strips across the diameter
> 2 teaspoons Dijon mustard
> Vegetable oil for grill (optional)

Spread butter on one side of each baguette slice. Reserve.

Spread each unbuttered side with mayonnaise and with the sweet pickle relish. Place pork and ham slices on top of the relish. Top with the Brie and mustard.

Preheat panini grill to medium heat. Brush the grill with butter, and place the sandwiches on it. Press down and heat for about 4 minutes, until golden brown on both sides. Remove from grill, and cut in half. Serve immediately.

NOTE If you do not have a panini grill, use the skillet method. Heat the butter in a large skillet over medium heat until it bubbles slightly. Place the sandwiches on the skillet, and press with a clean, heavy small skillet, spatula, or plate. Turn over to brown the other side, and continue to cook for about 4 minutes. Remove from skillet with spatula and serve immediately.

CUBAN STEAK SANDWICH *pan con bistec*

The secret of this great hearty sandwich, which simply must be enjoyed with a cold tropical milkshake or juice, is that Cubans like their steaks cut very thin. It makes for fast cooking, and when marinated offers a burst of taste in every bite. *Palomilla* steaks (see page 261) are ideal for the Cuban steak sandwich; with tomatoes, lettuce, onions, potato sticks, and plenty of mayonnaise, the Cuban steak sandwich is one heck of a hearty meal, served in all Cuban households. Sprinkle ketchup with a trickle of olive oil on your *pan con bistec* for a delicious variation.

1 SANDWICH

½ cup cooked onions (marinated, overnight if possible, in mojo
     sauce; see page 121)
⅓ loaf Cuban bread (see page 78)
1 tablespoon mayonnaise or ketchup
One 6- to 8-ounce beef sirloin steak, sliced thin, marinated ahead
     of time in mojo sauce (see page 121), and cooked
1 cup potato sticks or very thin French fries
3 slices tomato
2 lettuce leaves

Slice the bread in half lengthwise, and spread the mayonnaise or ketchup on both cut surfaces of the bread.

Place the steak on top of one half, then the cooked onions, and cover with the potato sticks.

On the other half, place the tomato slices and lettuce leaves. Place this half on top of the other to make the sandwich.

FISH-FRY SANDWICH *pan con minuta*

In the heart of Miami, there is a little eccentric spot called La Camaronera where it is literally standing room only (there are no chairs to sit on, so wear comfortable shoes), which is known for its *pan con minuta*, or fish-fry sandwich *a la cubana*. The only requirement is that the fish be fresh.

Follow this mouth-watering recipe and you, too, will feel transported to La Camaronera.

1 SANDWICH

> **1 onion, sliced (retain 1 slice whole for optional garnish)**
> **¼ cup ketchup**
> **¼ cup tomato juice**
> **1 tablespoon lemon juice**
> **½ teaspoon Worcestershire sauce**
> **½ teaspoon salt**
> **¼ teaspoon pepper**
> **½ pound fresh fish fillets, cut into 1-inch pieces**
> **2 eggs, beaten**
> **1½ cups cracker crumbs**
> **3 cups vegetable oil**
> **1 bread roll—Cuban, *medianoche,* or hamburger**
> **Mayonnaise, tartar sauce, or cocktail sauce**
> **Lettuce leaves**
> **1 slice tomato (optional)**

Grind together onion, ketchup, tomato juice, lemon juice, Worcestershire sauce, salt, and pepper in a food processor. Heat this mixture for a few minutes, and then cover the raw fish with it in a casserole. Cover casserole, and refrigerate for 5 hours to marinate.

Drain fish, then dip first in beaten eggs and then in cracker crumbs. Fry in hot oil. Remove fish from oil and drain off excess.

Slice the roll lengthwise, and spread mayonnaise, tartar sauce, or cocktail sauce on both halves.

Place the fish piece on top of one half. Place lettuce leaves and tomato slice or onion slice (if desired) on the other half, and assemble the sandwich.

MANOLITO'S PORK SANDWICH *pan con lechón*

Every Cuban has a favorite recipe for *pan con lechón,* or pork sandwich. My brother Manolito (diminutive of "Manolo," which is short for "José Manuel," a name he shared with our dad and his dad, *his* dad, and so on) says the secret to a great *pan con lechón* is Manolito's mojo sauce—which turns out to be the mojo recipe on page 121, though my brother doubles up on the garlic. Be careful whom you kiss after enjoying this sandwich!

1 SANDWICH

> ½ loaf Cuban bread (see page 78)
> 3 or 4 slices or chunks roast pork, or ½ cup shredded roast pork
> 1 cup sliced cooked or raw onion
> 1 teaspoon mojo sauce (see page 121)

Slice the bread lengthwise, and place the pork and the onion on one half. Sprinkle with the mojo sauce.

Put together into a sandwich, and cook on a sandwich grill. If you do not have a sandwich grill, then just prepare it in an oven at 350 degrees, with the top buttered and an iron skillet placed over the sandwich to weigh it down. Bake until crisp.

PREPARED CRACKER FULANA *galletita preparada a la fulana*

When my grandmother forgot the name of one of her friends, she would call her *fulana,* and if she forgot the first and last names she would call her *fulana de tal,* the equivalent of "Jane Doe." This is one mean prepared cracker, like the ones you find on the menus of many Cuban restaurants. You must double up on the saltines so your creation stays strong and sturdy as you pile on the ham and cheese.

1 SERVING

> 4 saltine crackers
> 2 slices sweet Virginia ham
> 2 slices Swiss cheese
> 2 slices sweet pickle
> Mustard to taste

Stack two saltines as each side of the sandwich. Place the slices of ham, cheese, and pickle on the crackers as you would on a slice of bread. Spread the mustard to your taste.

CROQUETTE SANDWICH A LA MENGANA
croqueta preparada a la mengana

You guessed it! *Mengana* was what my grandmother called the *other* friend whose name she did not remember. My grandmother was a great sandwich-maker, since kids and other famly members were in and out of her house all day long. The *croqueta* sandwich is made up of the Cuban's perfect food dream team: ham, spiced pork, two ham or chicken croquettes, Swiss cheese, mustard, and pickles pressed on fresh Cuban bread.

You can, of course, put on as many slices of meat and cheese and as many *croquetas* as you can handle. This is my *croqueta preparada* "in moderation." My mom always said: Cubans need to learn to do things in *moderación*.

1 SANDWICH

> ⅓ loaf Cuban bread (see page 78)
> 3 slices sweet Virginia ham
> 3 slices Swiss cheese
> 3 slices roast pork
> 4 slices sweet pickle
> 2 or 3 ham or chicken *croquetas* (see pages 36 and 38)

Slice the bread lengthwise, and place the slices of ham, cheese, pork, and pickle on one side. Then place your *croquetas* on top, and press them in a little with a knife or fork. Place the sandwich on a press grill, and cook until the cheese is melted and the bread is golden brown.

CHORIPÁN (BREAD AND CHORIZO)
choripán

This very simple and delicious sandwich originated in Argentina, where it is served as an appetizer to their famous *asados*. Cubans adopted it as an entire meal, however. A *choripán* is a combination of a grilled chorizo and crusty, preferably Cuban, bread. The chorizo may be used whole or split in half lengthwise, butterfly style. Sauces can be added, such as *chimichurri* (see page 111) or my special *salsa cubana* (see page 112). In Miami, *choripanes* are made to order at Cuban lunch counters all over the city, sometimes topped with fried onions and accompanied by a tropical juice or milkshake. On the other hand, *choripanes* are perfect for get-togethers in which friends dine alfresco, with some cheese and wine or sangria. Accompany them with some tango music from Carlos Gardel and a little romantic dancing to the Cuban *son* and you have a great party.

1 SANDWICH

> **1 chorizo sausage**
> **⅓ loaf Cuban bread (see page 78), split lengthwise**
> **Your favorite sauce for topping**

Grill the chorizo. Before cooking, prick to let out any extra fat or grease.
   Place on the Cuban bread, and top with your favorite sauce.

FRITA CALLE PROGRESO   *frita Calle Progreso*

A Cuban *frita* is something amazing. Just bite into one of these small, sweet, yet spicy hamburgers with crunchy but light-as-angel's-hair shoestring potatoes. Progreso was one of the most famous streets in Havana, where there were little stands serving *fritas*, like our own American hot-dog vendors. In the 1950s, when people were out all evening in Havana, crowds would gather around the *frita* stands and talk politics, movies, and culture. People would sometimes eat three or four delectable *fritas*. The secret to the *frita*, and what makes it completely different from the hamburger, is that the ground meat is a combination of beef sirloin and pork. A little ground chorizo is recommended for a spicier *frita*. Make sure that your meat is ground well and that you have the right combination for your taste.

When in Miami, try a *frita* at the landmark restaurant Rey de las Fritas (King of the Fritas).

4 SANDWICHES

> ¼ **cup milk**
> 1 **egg, beaten**
> 1 **teaspoon grated onion**
> 1 **teaspoon ketchup**
> 2 **teaspoons salt**
> ½ **teaspoon pepper**
> ½ **teaspoon Worcestershire sauce**
> ½ **cup bread crumbs**
> 1 **pound ground meat, half ground sirloin and half ground pork**
>   **(you can also add ¼ pound ground chorizo)**
> 1 **tablespoon vegetable shortening or butter**
> 4 **hamburger buns**
> 1 **cup potato sticks**

Combine the milk, beaten egg, onion, ketchup, salt, pepper, and Worcestershire sauce, and soak the bread crumbs in the mixture.

Add the meat to the bread-crumb mixture, and form into four patties.

Let the patties set in the refrigerator for about 2 hours.

Grease a skillet with the vegetable shortening, and fry the patties in it.

Place each patty on a bottom hamburger bun; top with potato sticks or homemade French fries cut very thin, and put on the tops of the buns.

NOTE You can make a larger quantity, form it into patties, and freeze for up to 2 months for future use.

CUBAN WRAPS

The new generation is always on the go, so they need food that travels well, too. These wraps and the following chops (see pages 100–103) are what young urban Cuban Americans eat today. They stress healthy, active living, but they still want to enjoy many traditional ingredients and flavors. My children and their friends have collected and used many of these recipes, and it is very interesting to see how beloved recipes have evolved and been adapted to the twenty-first century.

PORK WRAPS *wraps de puerco*

An apple a day . . . What a great mixture: cheese, apples, and Cuban pork in a tortilla wrap! Serve with plantain chips.

4 WRAPS

> **4 flour tortillas, steamed**
> **4 slices cheddar cheese or American cheese**
> **12 very thin slices roast pork loin**
> **1 apple, unpeeled, cored, and thinly sliced**
> **4 teaspoons mustard**
> **8 slices sweet pickle**

Spread out the tortillas on a work surface. Arrange the cheese slices on the tortillas. Stack with pork slices. Add about three apple slices per tortilla. Dot with mustard, and layer with the pickle slices.

Tuck in sides of each tortilla, and roll up like a cigar or a jelly roll to form a wrap. Slice in half on a diagonal, and serve immediately.

CHICKEN AND RICE WRAPS *arroz con pollo wraps*

This is for the day after the big chicken-and-rice meal. It can be eaten cold or heated up in the microwave. Leftover *arroz con pollo* can go to school with your child in a wrap! For this dish you must have boneless chicken; if there were bones in your *arroz con pollo*, remove them all before preparing the wraps.

4 WRAPS

> **4 flour tortillas, steamed**
> **4 teaspoons olive oil**
> **2 cups leftover chicken and rice (see pages 163–168)**
> **4 teaspoons sour cream**

Spread the tortillas on a work surface. Drizzle each tortilla with olive oil. Divide the chicken-and-rice mixture evenly among the tortillas.

Top with sour cream.

Tuck in sides of each tortilla, and roll up like a cigar or a jelly roll to form a wrap. Heat in microwave for 1 to 1½ minutes. Remove from microwave, slice in half on a diagonal, and serve immediately.

PULLED PORK WRAPS *wraps de puerco demenuzado*

The *pernil* includes the rump, or butt, and the shanks of a pig. *Pernil* is meatier and tastier than the *paleta,* which is the shoulder (picnic and butt) of a pig. Your local butcher or supermarket should have both of these cuts available.

6 WRAPS

FOR PERNIL OR PALETA

> **One 2- to 3-pound boneless pork *pernil* (rump) or**
> **   *paleta* (shoulder)**
> **2 cups mojo marinade (see page 120)**
> **2 onions, peeled and thinly sliced**
> **2 cups barbecue sauce**
> **2 cups water**

(continued on next page)

(continued from previous page)

FOR WRAPS

> **6 flour tortillas, steamed**
> **½ cup mojo sauce (see page 121)**
> **2 onions, peeled and thinly sliced**

To make the roast pork: Make shallow slits all over the pork with the tip of a knife, and place in a heavy pan. Pour the mojo marinade all over the pork and refrigerate for at least 2 hours, covered, and preferably overnight.

Preheat oven to 350 degrees.

Remove the meat from the refrigerator, drain, and reserve the marinade. Place in a baking pan and cook for 1 hour, turning it over a couple of times so it browns evenly.

Reduce the heat to 300 degrees, pour the reserved marinade over the roast, and place the sliced onions on top. Cover with aluminum foil, and continue cooking, basting occasionally, for 1 more hour. Add liquid if pork becomes dry. At the end of the cooking time, remove the foil and cook uncovered for 30 minutes.

Remove from heat, and set aside. When pork is cool enough to handle, use a fork or your fingers to pull it apart until the entire roast is shredded.

Place pulled pork in a large saucepan, and cover with the barbecue sauce and 2 cups water. Stir. Simmer over medium-low heat for 35 to 40 minutes, until the flavors are thoroughly mixed.

To make the wraps: Spread the tortillas on a work surface. Drizzle each tortilla with a little mojo sauce. Arrange the onion slices on the tortillas. Divide the pulled pork evenly among them. Tuck in sides of each tortilla, and roll up like a cigar or a jelly roll to form a wrap. Heat in microwave for 1 to 1½ minutes. Remove from microwave, slice in half on a diagonal, and serve immediately.

NOTE For a great twist, you can add shredded Swiss cheese to the wrap before you roll it.

AVOCADO POCKET PITAS *pitas de aguacate*

A wonderful avocado salad made with cucumber, olives, tomatoes, and *queso blanco* overflows from pita bread.

6 PITAS

> 2 ripe avocados, peeled, pitted, halved, and cubed
> 1 large cucumber, peeled and diced
> 2 tomatoes, diced
> 10 green olives, pitted and chopped
> 1 cup *queso blanco*, cubed, or crumbled feta cheese
> 1 cup basic Cuban dressing (see page 106)
> Salt and pepper to taste
> 6 oval pita breads, cut in half crosswise

In a mixing bowl, combine the avocados, cucumber, tomatoes, olives, and cheese.

Pour the dressing over the salad, and toss all ingredients together. Season with salt and pepper.

Gently open the pita bread halves. Fill the pockets with the salad, and serve immediately.

BLT AND GUACAMOLE WRAPS
wraps de bacón, lechuga, tomate y guacamole

4 WRAPS

> 4 flour tortillas, steamed
> 1 cup (8 ounces) cream cheese, softened
> ½ cup pica-pica sauce (see page 115)
> 1 cup shredded lettuce
> 12 strips bacon, cooked
> ½ cup guacamole

Place the tortillas on a work surface. Spread one side of each tortilla with cream cheese. Add the pica-pica sauce and lettuce, making sure all ingredients are evenly distributed.

(continued on next page)

(continued from previous page)

Put three strips of bacon on each tortilla, and top off with guacamole. Tuck in sides of each tortilla, and roll up like a cigar or a jelly roll to form a wrap. Slice in half on a diagonal, and serve cold.

secrets of a Cuban cook

COOKING BACON

For perfect bacon every time, place the strips on a baking sheet covered with aluminum foil. Bake in a 350-degree oven for about 5 minutes. Turn the strips and bake for another 2 minutes. Can't miss.

CUBAN HAM WRAPS *wraps cubanos de jamón*

This recipe is great for those with special dietary needs—low-carb, no bread or tortilla, just a delicious combination. They also make wonderful appetizers if they are simply sliced into 1-inch pieces.

4 WRAPS

1 cup (8 ounces) cream cheese, softened
½ cup sour cream
½ onion, peeled and minced
2 teaspoons minced fresh chives
4 teaspoons sweet pickle relish
1 teaspoon garlic powder
1 pound sweet ham, thinly sliced
4 lettuce leaves

Process the cream cheese, sour cream, onion, chives, pickle relish, and garlic powder in a blender or food processor until smooth. For a sturdier wrap, layer 3 ham slices per serving, and spread cheese mixture on the slices. Roll up like a cigar or a jelly roll to form a wrap.

Place on a plate and cover with an aluminum-foil tent. Refrigerate for about 2 hours. Remove, and slice in half on a diagonal. For an easy sandwich, wrap each uncut ham roll in a lettuce leaf. Serve immediately.

CUBAN SHRIMP WRAPS
wraps cubanos de camarones
4 WRAPS

> **2 teaspoons olive oil**
> **1½ pounds raw shrimp, peeled and deveined**
> **1 cup sofrito (see page 119)**
> **½ cup chopped fresh parsley**
> **Salt and pepper to taste**
> **1 teaspoon dry white wine**
> **2 teaspoons lemon juice**
> **4 flour tortillas, steamed**

In a large skillet over low heat, heat the olive oil. Add the shrimp, and sauté for about 2 minutes without browning.

Increase the heat slightly, and add the sofrito. Cook until the shrimp are done, about 5 minutes. Reduce heat, add the parsley, season with salt and pepper, and add the wine; simmer for 2 minutes. Remove from heat, and transfer to a mixing bowl.

Toss the shrimp with the lemon juice. Place the shrimp down the center of each tortilla; divide evenly for equal servings. Tuck in sides of each tortilla, and roll up like a cigar or a jelly roll to form a wrap. Heat in microwave for 1 to 1½ minutes. Remove from microwave, slice in half on a diagonal, and serve immediately.

NOTE For a great twist, you can add shredded Swiss cheese to the wrap before you roll it.

CUBAN BURRITOS *burritos cubanos*

Why not make a simple burrito using leftover white rice, beans, and cheese? Here is the basic recipe to start with. Add whatever extra ingredients you like, such as chopped *palomilla* steak (see page 261), *ropa vieja* (see page 278), *vaca frita* (see page 279), or fried ripe plantains (see page 142). What makes it Cuban and not Mexican? It is not spicy!

4 SERVINGS

> 1½ cups mostly drained cooked black bean soup (see page 59)
> 2 cups cooked white rice (see page 160)
> 4 tortillas, steamed
> 1 cup shredded iceberg lettuce
> 1 cup chopped tomatoes
> 1 cup grated cheddar cheese
> ½ cup sour cream

In a large skillet over low heat, combine the black bean soup and white rice, and allow to mix thoroughly and cook without browning for just about 2 to 3 minutes.

Place the tortillas on a work surface. Spoon the rice-and-beans mixture onto the tortillas, dividing evenly. Top tortillas with equal amounts of iceberg lettuce, chopped tomatoes, grated cheese, and sour cream.

Tuck in sides of each tortilla, and roll up like a cigar or a jelly roll to form a burrito. Heat in microwave for 1 to 1½ minutes. Remove from microwave, slice in half on a diagonal, and serve immediately.

BLACK BEAN HUMMUS ON PITA BREAD
pita con hummus de frijoles negros

This hummus makes a great sandwich on pita bread, but it's also good with whole-wheat Cuban crackers. If you spread it on crackers, top with fresh watercress and shaved Parmesan cheese.

4 SERVINGS

2 cups drained black bean soup (see page 59)
1 tablespoon tahini
NOTE Tahini, a paste of Middle Eastern origin made from ground sesame seeds, is available in most supermarkets.
1 tablespoon olive oil
1 teaspoon lime juice
1 garlic clove, minced
4 oval pita breads
4 slices cheese of your choice (optional)

In a food processor, combine all the ingredients and process until thoroughly mixed and smooth.

Cover, and chill for about 15 minutes. Remove hummus from the refrigerator and spread on the pita breads. You may want to add a slice of your favorite cheese and grill for a few minutes, until melted.

LOBSTER PITAS *pitas de langosta*

4 PITAS

> 2 uncooked lobster tails, split down the back and deveined (see
>   page 195)
> 1 cup mayonnaise
> Roasted sweet red peppers, drained, cut into julienne strips
> 1 small onion, peeled and minced
> Salt and pepper to taste
> 4 teaspoons lemon juice
> 4 oval pita breads
> 1 cup coarsely chopped watercress
> Olive oil for drizzling

In a large saucepan, boil the lobster tails in water for 10 minutes. Remove
from heat, drain the lobster tails, and cool to room temperature. (Watch
carefully—lobster becomes dry and tough when overcooked.)

Remove the lobster meat from the shells and tear into chunks, removing
any bits of shell. In a mixing bowl, combine lobster, mayonnaise, sweet red
peppers, and onion. Season with salt and pepper, add lemon juice, and toss
lightly.

Cut off the top third of the pita breads. Stuff pitas with lobster mixture by
dividing evenly and spooning into pockets. Tuck watercress on top, and tightly
wrap in wax paper. Refrigerate for about 1 hour. Drizzle with olive oil before
serving.

THE CUBAN CHOP SCENE

Chops have become part of the young urban Latin American menu. It all started
with chains like Chicken Kitchen, Natural Chicken Grill, and the homegrown
Pollo Tropical. College students needed to have their favorite home comfort
foods all mixed together in one quick dish to gulp down while they crammed
for exams. That is why all over Florida you will find these "chop" restaurants
very near institutions of higher learning. It is not a difficult concept to imitate,
and the core ingredients are much better when homemade: rice, beans, chicken

or beef, and vegetables. The secret is that all the ingredients are chopped up and mixed in one dish and topped off by a wonderful sauce. This is just a small roundup of the most popular Cuban chops.

DAX ROQUE'S CHICKEN CHOP
el pollo picado de Dax Roque

My older son was the one who introduced me to Cuban chops. His favorite is this Cuban chicken chop.

1 SERVING

> 1 teaspoon butter
> 1 boneless chicken breast, marinated in mojo marinade (see page 120)
> 1 cup cooked white (see page 160) or yellow (saffron) rice
> ½ cup mostly drained black bean soup (see page 59)
> ½ cup shredded lettuce
> ½ tomato, chopped
> ¼ cup Dax's honey-mustard sauce (see below)

In a large skillet over medium-high heat, heat the butter until hot but not browning. Add the chicken breast, and sauté, turning over on both sides, until brown, about 5 minutes. Remove from heat, chop into bite-sized pieces, and reserve.

In the microwave or on the stovetop, heat the cooked rice and cooked black bean soup.

Now you are ready to assemble your chop: In a rimmed soup bowl, layer the rice, the beans, then the chicken pieces. Arrange the lettuce and tomato on top, and drizzle with the honey-mustard sauce. Do not drown it in sauce, or dress it too far in advance. Toss, and enjoy your quick chop.

NOTE For a great honey-mustard sauce, mix 2 parts mayonnaise with 1 part Dijon mustard, ½ part sugar, and ½ part honey.

ALY ROQUE'S PALOMILLA CHOP
la palomilla picada de Aly Roque

When my daughter started community college in downtown Miami, she would dictate this recipe to the cooks at random Cuban lunch counters between classes. She soon began making it at home.

1 SERVING

> 1 teaspoon olive oil
> 1 sirloin or top-round steak, pounded to ¼-inch thickness and marinated with ¼ cup mojo marinade (see page 120)
> ½ cup onion, peeled and chopped
> 1 cup cooked white or yellow (saffron) rice
> ½ cup mostly drained black bean soup (see page 59)
> ½ cup shredded lettuce
> ½ tomato, chopped
> ¼ cup Aly's *chimichurri* sauce (see below)
> 1 lemon wedge

Heat oil in a large skillet over medium-high heat, and drop the steak into the hot oil. Cook each side for 1 or 2 minutes and set aside. Sauté the onion in the oil until tender.

Chop the steak into bite-sized pieces and reserve.

In the microwave or on the stovetop, heat the cooked rice and black bean soup separately.

Now you are ready to assemble your chop: In a rimmed soup bowl, layer the rice, the beans, then the steak pieces. Arrange the lettuce and tomato on top, and drizzle on *chimichurri* sauce. Remember not to drown it or dress it too far in advance. Squeeze a little lemon juice on top of the creation. Toss, and enjoy your quick chop.

NOTE For Aly's great *chimichurri* sauce, combine in a blender ¼ cup minced parsley, 1 minced garlic clove, 2 teaspoons olive oil, 1 teaspoon fresh lemon juice, and salt and pepper to taste.

KYLE ROQUE'S VACA FRITA CHOP
la vaca frita picada de Kyle Roque

Kyle is our youngest, and the gourmet in the family. He will go far to get that special Serrano-ham–and–cheese-sandwich, and shares my passion for Cuban coffee and *cortaditos*. He is definitely my food buddy and will try any dish at least once. This is his perfect chop combination, one he makes often with leftover *vaca frita*. His secret is that he refries the "fried cow."

1 SERVING

> **2 teaspoons olive oil**
> **1 cup cooked *vaca frita* (see page 279)**
> **½ onion, peeled and sliced**
> **1½ cups *moros y cristianos* (see page 161)**
> **½ cup shredded lettuce**
> **½ tomato, chopped**
> **¼ cup shredded cheddar cheese**
> **1 lemon wedge**
> **1 tablespoon sour cream**

Heat the oil in a large skillet over medium-high heat, and sauté the *vaca frita* once again. Cook for 1 or 2 minutes and set aside. Sauté the onion in the oil until tender.

In the microwave or on the stovetop, reheat the *moros y cristianos*.

Now you are ready to assemble your chop: In a rimmed soup bowl, layer the rice, then the *vaca frita,* and the onion. Arrrange the lettuce, tomato, and cheese on top. Squeeze a little lemon over the chop, and toss before you serve, with a dollop of sour cream.

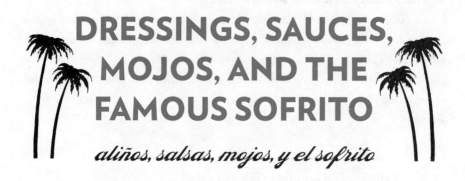

DRESSINGS, SAUCES, MOJOS, AND THE FAMOUS SOFRITO

aliños, salsas, mojos, y el sofrito

SALADS MADE FROM CRISP GREENS are on everyone's plate these days. All they need is the perfect dressing from the collection below. Sauces or *salsas* turn up with grilled meats, chicken, and fish and accompany many Cuban dishes. Included here, to make your vegetables come really alive, are the basic white sauce, béchamel sauce, and hollandaise sauce for novice and not-so-novice cooks.

The mojo, both as a marinade for raw food and as a sauce for cooked food, is a constant in all Latin cuisines. Bodegas and supermarkets are crammed with bottled commercial mojo, but in our world, you make your own. And what can I say about the famous sofrito, the base for most Cuban cooking? You need to have it, and you need to have it homemade.

secrets of a Cuban cook

MARINADES AND MARINATING

Most foods taste better marinated. It is one of the best ways to add flavor to vegetables, meat, poultry, and fish. If you master these simple dos and don'ts of marinating, you will be good to go:

- Do marinate ahead of time.
- Do marinate food in the refrigerator rather than at room temperature.
- Do marinate in resealable plastic bags. It is more effective, and you are sure to marinate all the food evenly.
- Do cover anything you marinate.
- Do not marinate fish for more than 50 minutes, because the flesh might get mushy; marinate your steaks as long as you want.
- Do not marinate in aluminum containers or foil, because a chemical reaction could spoil your food.

These are some of the foods you might want to marinate:

Chicken
Steak
Pork
Tofu
Fish
Broccoli
Cauliflower
Mushrooms
Eggplant
Red or green bell peppers
Zucchini

BASIC CUBAN DRESSING *aliño básico*

This is perfect for greens and vegetables—it is the most popular dressing. It is important that you use high-quality olive oil, preferably from Spain, Italy, or California, with a pronounced flavor. Vinegars also come in a wonderful variety: distilled, wine, cider, fruit, or herb. Still, most Cuban salads require only Spanish olive oil and white vinegar.

4 SERVINGS (¾ CUP)

> 3 tablespoons white vinegar
> ½ teaspoon salt
> ¼ teaspoon freshly ground black pepper
> ½ cup olive oil

Whisk the vinegar, salt, and pepper together in a small bowl. Slowly drizzle in the oil, and whisk until thickened and mixed. Taste, and, if needed, adjust salt and pepper.

Store, covered, or pour over salad immediately.

CUBAN FRENCH DRESSING *aliño francés*

This dressing is great for salads with hard-boiled eggs and for any cooked vegetables.

4 SERVINGS (¾ CUP)

> 3 tablespoons white vinegar
> ½ teaspoon salt
> 1 teaspoon sugar, preferably superfine
> ¼ teaspoon freshly ground black pepper
> ½ teaspoon paprika
> ½ cup olive oil

Whisk the vinegar, salt, sugar, pepper, and paprika in a small bowl. Slowly drizzle in the oil, and whisk until thickened and mixed. Taste, and adjust seasonings as you see fit.

Store, covered, or pour over salad immediately.

TROPICAL VINAIGRETTES *vinagretas tropicales*

Vinaigrettes go well with grilled seafood, fish, and meats. They are equally wonderful on light mixed green salads or coating a wedge of iceberg lettuce. Use your imagination, and add exotic tropical fruits or the ingredients that you have available. Just carefully balance the acidity of the vinegar.

BASIC VINAIGRETTE *salsa vinagreta básica*
4 SERVINGS (1 CUP)

> 4 tablespoons white vinegar
> 1 teaspoon Dijon or yellow mustard
> Salt and pepper to taste
> Sugar to taste
> 1 teaspoon onion powder
> 1 teaspoon parsley flakes
> ¾ cup olive oil

In a large bowl, combine the vinegar, mustard, salt, pepper, sugar, onion powder, and parsley flakes. Whisk the mixture for 1 to 2 minutes, and continue to whisk while slowly dribbling in the olive oil until the mixture thickens.

Taste and correct the seasonings. Refrigerate, covered, for about 30 minutes. Remove from refrigerator, and transfer to a gravy or sauce boat to serve immediately on the side or pour over food, or store, covered, in the refrigerator for future use.

CUBAN CITRUS VINAIGRETTE *vinagreta de cítricos a la cubana*

Before combining ingredients, bring ¾ cup orange juice, tangerine juice, or lemon juice (or, even better, a combination) to a boil in a nonreactive saucepan. Cook until you have reduced it to about 3 tablespoons. Allow to cool. Then follow the steps for basic vinaigrette (preceding recipe). Refrigerate, covered, for about 30 minutes. Remove from refrigerator, and transfer to a gravy or sauce boat to serve immediately on the side, or pour over food, or store, covered, in the refrigerator for future use.

BLACK BEAN VINAIGRETTE *vinagreta de frijoles negros*

After adding the olive oil, whisk in ½ cup cooked black beans and ¼ cup finely chopped fresh cilantro leaves. Then process in food processor or blender for about 1 minute. Refrigerate, covered, for about 30 minutes. Remove from refrigerator, and transfer to a gravy or sauce boat to serve immediately on the side or pour over food, or store, covered, in the refrigerator for future use.

GUAVA-MINT VINAIGRETTE *vinagreta de guayaba con menta*

After adding the olive oil, whisk in ½ cup diced guava and ¼ cup finely chopped fresh mint leaves. Then process in food processor or blender for about 1 minute. Refrigerate, covered, for about 30 minutes. Remove from refrigerator, and transfer to a gravy or sauce boat to serve immediately on the side or pour over food, or store, covered, in the refrigerator for future use.

AVOCADO SAUCE *salsa de aguacate*

This is great as a salad dressing or over cooked vegetables, and it's also delicious and different over a plain grilled chicken breast. The olives give it a very Mediterranean flavor, and the capers add a finishing touch. Besides using it in salads or pouring over vegetables or main dishes, I personally also love serving this with potatoes. Try it!

4 SERVINGS (2 CUPS)

> 2 avocados, peeled, pitted, and diced
> 2 hard-boiled eggs (see page 201)
> 1 tablespoon capers
> 1 cup olive oil
> ¼ cup white vinegar
> 10 Spanish green olives, pitted and chopped
> Salt and pepper to taste

Place the diced avocado pieces in a food processor, and process for about 2 minutes, until puréed.

Cut the hard-boiled eggs in half, and separate yolks from whites. Chop the whites and reserve.

Add the cooked egg yolks and the capers to the avocado mixture, and process for about 30 seconds longer. Leave the motor running, and dribble in the oil in a slow, steady stream. Do the same with the vinegar, and mix until all is thoroughly combined.

Transfer to a sauce or gravy boat, and top with chopped olives and egg whites. Season with salt and pepper.

BÉCHAMEL SAUCE CUBAN STYLE
salsa béchamel a la cubana

The béchamel sauce is one of the four original "mother sauces" that are the base for so many recipes. What makes this milk-based sauce a little different in Cuban cooking is that we add chopped onions and chopped parsley to the original French recipe. We also make it a little thinner by adding chicken stock or consommé. This sauce is also used in the preparation of Cuban croquettes.

4 SERVINGS (2 CUPS)

> 1 cup chicken consommé (see page 54)
> 1 onion, peeled and chopped
> 1 parsley sprig, chopped
> ¼ teaspoon pepper
> ½ stick (4 tablespoons) butter
> 6 tablespoons all-purpose flour
> 1½ cups hot milk
> Salt to taste
> Grated nutmeg to taste

In a saucepan, heat the chicken consommé with the onion, parsley, and pepper. Bring to a boil, and quickly remove from heat. Pour through a strainer. You should have about 1 cup.

Melt the butter in a heavy saucepan over low heat. Sprinkle in the flour, and continue to cook gently for about 5 minutes, stirring constantly. Be sure not to overheat or brown. Remove from heat.

Meanwhile, in another saucepan, bring the milk to the boiling point. Pour the boiling milk all at once into the butter-and-flour mixture. As it bubbles, whisk it constantly. Stir in the consommé.

Return the pan to medium heat, and once again bring the béchamel sauce to a boil, and cook, stirring constantly, for an additional 5 minutes or so.

(continued on next page)

(continued from previous page)

Season with salt and nutmeg to taste. Use at once in a recipe, pour over food, or store, covered, in refrigerator.

AURORA SAUCE *salsa aurora*

This sauce gives any dish an explosion of pink color. It tastes great with pasta or any fish or chicken dish. Also try it over tomatoes.

4 SERVINGS (2 CUPS)

> 1½ cups béchamel sauce (see page 109)
> ½ cup tomato sauce

Whisk the béchamel sauce and the tomato sauce together in a bowl until thoroughly combined.

Transfer to a medium saucepan, and simmer over low heat for about 5 minutes, whisking and stirring occasionally. Serve immediately on the side, pour over food, or store, covered, in refrigerator.

WHITE SAUCE *salsa blanca*

A very simple sauce that is lighter than the béchamel.

4 SERVINGS (2 CUPS)

> ½ stick (4 tablespoons) butter
> 6 tablespoons all-purpose flour
> 2 cups chicken consommé (see page 54) or milk
> 1 teaspoon salt, or to taste

Melt the butter in a heavy saucepan over low heat. Add the flour, and continue to cook gently for about 5 minutes, stirring constantly. Be sure not to overheat or brown.

Reduce the heat, and add the broth or milk slowly while whisking constantly. Bring to a simmer, and continue to cook, stirring constantly, for about 3 to 5 minutes, or until sauce thickens and is thoroughly smooth. Add salt to taste, and serve immediately on the side, pour over food, or store, covered, in refrigerator.

LOBSTER SAUCE *salsa cardenal*

What could be better than grilled shrimp coated in lobster sauce served over a bed of *moros y cristianos* (see page 161)? This sauce makes a simple meal luxurious.

4 SERVINGS (2 CUPS)

> 2 cups *salsa blanca* made with chicken consommé (see page 110)
> ½ cup cooked lobster meat, ground or diced
> ½ stick (4 tablespoons) butter
> 1 parsley sprig, chopped
> ½ teaspoon red food coloring (optional)
> Salt and pepper to taste

Combine all the ingredients, and cook over low heat in a medium saucepan for about 20 minutes. Stir occasionally. When thoroughly cooked, remove from heat.

Taste and correct the seasonings. Transfer to a food processor, and process for 1 to 2 minutes to purée. Pour into a gravy or sauce boat and serve immediately on the side or pour over food, or store, covered, in refrigerator.

CHIMICHURRI SAUCE *chimichurri*

This is a Latin pesto sauce. Always served in Argentinean households, it is also popular in many Cuban recipes. Try *chimichurri* sauce on a Cuban *choripán* (see page 90).

4 SERVINGS (2 CUPS)

> 2 cups chopped fresh parsley
> 8 garlic cloves, minced
> 3 tablespoons lemon juice
> 1 cup olive oil
> Salt and pepper to taste

(continued on next page)

(continued from previous page)

Combine the parsley, garlic, and lemon juice in a food processor, and process for about 1 minute.

With the motor running, add the oil slowly in a steady stream. Process for an additional 15 seconds. Taste and add salt and pepper. Transfer to a gravy or sauce boat and serve immediately on the side or pour over food, or store, covered, in refrigerator.

CUBAN SALSA *salsa cubana*

Unlike Mexican salsa, this Cuban sauce is not spicy or hot. It is a mixture of vivid colors and flavors and yet light to the palate, perfect to pour over tamales (see page 138).

4 SERVINGS (2 CUPS)

> ½ stick (4 tablespoons) butter
> ½ teaspoon paprika
> 1 large onion, peeled and chopped
> 1 medium green bell pepper, seeded and chopped
> 1 garlic clove, minced
> 1½ cups canned chopped tomatoes
> Salt and pepper to taste

Melt the butter in a heavy saucepan over low heat. Add the paprika, onion, green pepper, and garlic. Stirring constantly, add the canned tomatoes, and continue cooking over medium-low heat for about 5 to 7 minutes. Season with salt and pepper to taste, and remove from heat. Cool to room temperature.

Transfer to a food processor, and process for about 1 minute to purée. Taste and correct the seasonings. Transfer to a gravy or sauce boat and serve immediately on the side or pour over food, or store, covered, in refrigerator.

SEAFOOD COCKTAIL SAUCE *salsa de mariscos*

This is not the usual "cocktail sauce" served in the States, but it *is* great for shrimp cocktails when chilled. If served warm, it is best paired with baked or grilled fish.

4 SERVINGS (2 CUPS)

> 1½ cups béchamel sauce (see page 109)
> 1 garlic clove, minced
> ½ cup ketchup
> 5 tablespoons Worcestershire sauce
> Salt and pepper to taste

Heat the béchamel sauce over low heat, and add the minced garlic. Stirring constantly, simmer for about 3 to 5 minutes, making sure garlic is completely mixed in. Remove from heat.

Add the ketchup and the Worcestershire sauce, taste, and add salt and pepper if needed. Refrigerate, covered, for 25 to 30 minutes if serving chilled. Transfer to a gravy or sauce boat and serve on the side.

CHEESE SAUCE *salsa de queso*

Serve over pasta—or even rice, for a risotto effect.

4 SERVINGS (2 CUPS)

> 2 cups béchamel sauce (see page 109)
> 1 cup freshly grated or shaved Parmesan cheese

Heat the béchamel sauce in a medium saucepan over medium heat. Just before the boiling point, add the cheese, reduce heat, and, stirring constantly, continue to simmer over very low heat for 3 to 5 minutes, until sauce reaches a creamy but light consistency.

Transfer to a gravy or sauce boat and serve immediately on the side or pour over food, or store, covered, in refrigerator.

NOTE You can substitute cheddar or American cheese for the Parmesan, to please the little ones in the family.

HOLLANDAISE SAUCE CUBAN STYLE
salsa holandesa

A Cuban twist on your run-of-the-mill hollandaise sauce.

4 SERVINGS (1½ CUPS)

> 3 egg yolks
> 1 tablespoon lemon juice, or more to taste
> 1 tablespoon white vinegar, or more to taste
> Salt and pepper to taste
> 2 sticks (8 ounces) butter, melted

Whisk the egg yolks and lemon juice together in a double boiler. Add the vinegar, salt, and pepper, and continue to whisk until the sauce is thick and creamy.

Place over very low heat, and continue to stir and whisk until the egg mixture begins to thicken. Remove from heat, and slowly pour the melted butter in a very fine stream into the mixture.

Taste and correct the seasonings, adding a few more drops of lemon or vinegar if you like. Transfer to a gravy or sauce boat and serve immediately on the side or pour over food, or store, covered, in refrigerator.

MIXED SAUCE   *salsa mixta*

This full-bodied sauce can be served over Cuban bread slices to make a great appetizer. It's also wonderful over pork and ham.

4 SERVINGS (1½ CUPS)

> 1 cup mayonnaise
> 2 hard-boiled eggs (see page 201)
> 1 tablespoon capers
> 1 cucumber, peeled and chopped
> Salt and pepper to taste

Combine the mayonnaise, hard-boiled eggs, capers, and cucumber in a food processor, and process for about 1 minute.

Taste and season with salt and pepper if needed. Refrigerate, covered, for about 30 minutes. Remove from refrigerator and transfer to a gravy or sauce boat and serve immediately on the side or pour over food, or store, covered, in the refrigerator for future use.

PICA-PICA SAUCE *salsa pica-pica*

This slightly piquant sauce is great over root vegetables. Also try it over slices of toasted Cuban bread for a very Cuban bruschetta!

4 SERVINGS (3 CUPS)

> **2 large onions, chopped**
> **1 cup white vinegar**
> **2 garlic cloves, minced**
> **Salt and pepper to taste**
> **3 tablespoons all-purpose flour**
> **2 cups chicken consommé (see page 54)**
> **Grated nutmeg to taste**
> **1 cucumber, peeled and chopped**

In a saucepan, cook the onions in the vinegar over low heat for about 3 to 5 minutes. Add the garlic, season to taste with salt and pepper, and continue to simmer for an additional 1 to 2 minutes.

Add the flour, chicken consommé, nutmeg, and cucumber and bring to a boil. Continue to cook over medium heat for an additional 3 to 5 minutes. Remove from heat, and set aside, allowing to cool to room temperature.

Transfer mixture to a food processor or blender, and process to a smooth purée, for about 1 minute. Taste and correct the seasonings. Refrigerate, covered, for about 30 minutes. Remove from refrigerator, and transfer to a gravy or sauce boat to serve immediately on the side or pour over food, or store, covered, in the refrigerator for future use. If you want a warm sauce, just heat in a saucepan over very low heat for 2 to 3 minutes before serving.

TARTAR SAUCE *salsa tártara*

Some people love to eat every single bite of their fish with a bit of tartar sauce. For those people, here is the best homemade recipe.

4 SERVINGS (2 CUPS)

> 3 hard-boiled eggs (see page 201), chopped
> 1 tablespoon Dijon or yellow mustard
> 1 onion, peeled and chopped
> 1 cup mayonnaise
> 1 teaspoon white vinegar
> 1 parsley sprig, chopped
> 1 cucumber, peeled and chopped
> Salt and pepper to taste

Combine the eggs, mustard, onion, mayonnaise, vinegar, parsley, and cucumber in a food processor. Process until smooth and creamy, pausing a couple of times to scrape down the sides with a spatula.

Taste and season with salt and pepper if needed. Refrigerate, covered, for about 30 minutes. Remove from refrigerator, and transfer to a gravy or sauce boat to serve immediately on the side or pour over food, or store, covered, in the refrigerator for future use.

CUBAN VEGETARIAN SAUCE *salsa vegetariana*

So quick and easy, it takes less effort than going to the store and buying a jar. Serve with mushrooms, and then use leftovers of this combination as an omelette filling.

4 SERVINGS (1½ CUPS)

> 1 cup mayonnaise
> 1 sweet pickle, chopped
> ¼ cup canned beets, chopped
> 1 tablespoon mustard, Dijon or yellow
> 1 tablespoon parsley flakes
> Salt and pepper to taste

Combine the mayonnaise, pickle, beets, mustard, and parsley in a food processor. Process until smooth and creamy, pausing a couple of times to scrape down the sides with a spatula.

Taste and season with salt and pepper. Refrigerate, covered, for about 30 minutes. Remove from refrigerator, and transfer to a gravy or sauce boat to serve immediately on the side or pour over food, or store, covered, in the refrigerator for future use.

GREEN PARSLEY SAUCE *salsa verde*

This sauce is fantastic over fish. It can also be served with meat and egg dishes, with boiled potatoes, and with pasta (see page 189).

4 SERVINGS (1½ CUPS)

> 1 garlic clove, minced
> 1 medium onion, peeled and chopped
> 1 cup finely chopped fresh parsley
> Salt and pepper to taste
> 1 cup olive oil
> 2 tablespoons white vinegar
> ¼ cup dry white wine

Combine the garlic, onion, and parsley in a food processor or blender, and pulse to chop. Season with salt and pepper to taste.

Leave the motor running, and add the olive oil in a steady stream. Do the same with the vinegar and wine. Process briefly to purée. Reserve until ready to use. Taste and correct the seasonings, and transfer to a gravy or sauce boat to serve immediately on the side or pour over food, or store, covered, in the refrigerator for future use.

GREEN MAYONNAISE *mayonesa verde*

This is great to serve on the side with any fritters or croquettes. You can use 2 to 3 cups of store-bought mayonnaise as a shortcut. Or you can follow the homemade recipe below, which is ready in just a few minutes. This recipe contains raw eggs, so children, the elderly, pregnant women, and people with weak immune systems should forgo it.

4 SERVINGS (2 CUPS)

1 egg yolk
1 whole egg
1½ teaspoons Dijon mustard
Salt and pepper to taste
2 teaspoons lemon juice
1½ cups corn or vegetable oil
1 cup chopped fresh parsley

Combine the egg yolk, whole egg, mustard, salt, pepper, and 2 teaspoons of the lemon juice in a food processor, and process for about 1 minute, until mixture is smooth and thoroughly combined.

Leave the motor running, and add the oil slowly, in a steady stream. Continue to process, pausing a couple of times to scrape down the sides with a spatula. Add the fresh parsley, and process for an additional 1 to 2 minutes.

NOTE You can also substitute watercress for the parsley, to make a very light herbal mayonnaise.

THE FAMOUS SOFRITO FONTANAR
el famoso sofrito Fontanar

Now at last we come to the basis for all Cuban cooking: the famous sofrito. A sofrito is the aromatic preparation of fresh vegetables and herbs in a light sauté. It is all about building layers and layers of flavors in our foods. The secret to a good sofrito is to let the flavors marry. You can improve any recipe as long as you have a good sofrito. My mom always made the quickest sofrito, which would turn a can of black beans into a true gourmet Cuban delicacy. In Fontanar, our neighborhood in Havana, the kids would always know when it was time to come home for lunch or dinner. We could actually identify our own mom's sofrito. I named this recipe for a quick and easy sofrito after my neighborhood, and thus my mother's creation. Of course, you can buy sofrito in a can or bottle—but don't!

6 SERVINGS (1½ CUPS)

> **2 garlic cloves, minced**
> **Salt and pepper to taste**
> **1 tablespoon olive oil**
> **1 large onion, peeled and chopped**
> **1 green bell pepper, seeded and chopped**
> **½ cup tomato purée**
> **2 teaspoons white vinegar**
> **1 bay leaf**

Grind and press garlic with the salt and pepper, to mix. (This is the perfect time to use a mortar and pestle if you have them.)

In a skillet, heat olive oil, then sauté the onion, green pepper, and the garlic mixture for 5 to 7 minutes.

Add the tomato purée, vinegar, and bay leaf, and simmer, covered, over very low heat for an additional 10 minutes. Remove from heat, and remove bay leaf.

THE MOJOS

A mojo (not to be confused with the mojito cocktail) is a Cuban garlic-citrus sauce that is the authentic marinade for raw meats, chicken, and fish, and can also be used as a sauce for cooked vegetables and side dishes. Mojos are always cooked. The citrus fruits used in authentic mojos are sour or bitter oranges, the best known of which is the Seville orange. Bitter or sour oranges are exactly that: too sour to eat raw, and almost always used in food preparation. Outside of Miami, it is difficult to find these oranges, but you can always substitute two parts lemon or lime juice to one part orange juice. Here are two very simple mojos.

MOJO MARINADE *mojo para carnes crudas*

This one is for raw meat, fish, and chicken.

4 SERVINGS (1³⁄₄ CUPS)

> 6 garlic cloves, thinly sliced or minced
> Salt and pepper to taste
> ³⁄₄ cup olive oil
> 1 cup sour or bitter orange juice, or ²⁄₃ cup lemon juice and ¹⁄₃ cup
>   orange juice
> 1 teaspoon ground oregano
> ¹⁄₂ teaspoon ground cumin
> 1 bay leaf

Grind and press garlic with the salt and pepper, to mix. (This is the perfect time to use a mortar and pestle if you have them.)

Heat the oil in a skillet over medium heat. Add the garlic mixture, and cook for 2 to 3 minutes. Add the citrus juice, and remove from heat. Add the oregano, cumin, and bay leaf. You can store it, or use immediately.

Marinate your meat, chicken, or fish with this mojo, and refrigerate, covered, for 2 to 3 hours or longer.

MOJO SAUCE *mojo para viandas y carnes cocidas*

This one is for cooked meat, fish, chicken, or vegetables.

4 SERVINGS (2 CUPS)

> **6 garlic cloves, thinly sliced or minced**
> **Salt and pepper to taste**
> **1½ cups olive oil**
> **½ cup sour or bitter orange juice, or ⅓ cup lemon juice and**
>   **2 tablespoons plus 2 teaspoons orange juice**

Grind and press garlic with the salt and pepper, to mix. (This is the perfect time to use a mortar and pestle if you have them.)

Heat the oil in a skillet over medium heat. Add the garlic mixture, and cook for 2 to 3 minutes. Add the citrus juice, and remove from heat. Transfer to a gravy or sauce boat and serve immediately on the side or pour over food.

VEGETABLES AND ROOT VEGETABLES

vegetales y viandas

CUBAN CUISINE is not really known for its vegetable dishes. Yet in fact Cubans devour root vegetables at nearly every meal. Our meals thrive on boniato, *malanga,* and cassava (*yuca*), nourishing root vegetables that have always been part of the geography of the Caribbean land. And every lunch counter in Miami boasts the best *tamal en cazuela* (cornmeal casserole—see my version on page 140)—a throwback to the 1930s, when, in the midst of the Depression, Cubans ate cornmeal daily. Still, many vegetables today remain relatively unexplored by Cuban cooks. Allow yourself some creative freedom to experiment with vegetables and sauces.

GRILLED CORN ON THE COB WITH QUESO BLANCO AND LIME

mazorca de maíz con queso blanco y limón a la parilla

This was a favorite of mine on the streets of Mexico City when I was eleven years old. My family came to the United States via Mexico, where we had stayed for about five months. I remember the street food of Mexico City as if it were yesterday. We gravitated toward the corn on the cob, because it seemed less foreign. It was 1965; Mexico City was prosperous and overcrowded at the beginning of our exile. This was the first time I tasted chili powder and freshly squeezed lime sprinkled on a vegetable, and, most important, the time when I began to understand that food was an adventure.

4 SERVINGS

> 1 tablespoon salt
> 4 corn ears in husks, silk removed
> 2 teaspoons chili powder
> 1 teaspoon paprika
> ¾ stick (6 tablespoons) butter
> ½ cup *queso blanco*, finely grated
> **NOTE** The secret to this recipe is the Cuban or Mexican *queso blanco*. Look for it in the Hispanic section of your supermarket, or anywhere with a good cheese selection.
> 1 lime, cut in quarters

Fill a large saucepan with 10 cups water, add 2 teaspoons of the salt, and bring to a boil. Add corn in husks, and boil for about 8 minutes. Remove from heat and set aside, discarding the water. Meanwhile, in a small bowl, mix the chili powder, paprika, and the remaining 1 teaspoon of salt.

On a medium grill or in the broiler, grill corn just until the charred marks are visible on the husks. Remove from heat, and allow to cool. Pull back husks and rub corn with butter, roll in cheese, and sprinkle with paprika mixture. Serve with lime wedges.

STUFFED GREEN PEPPERS WITH RICE
AND HAM *pimientos verdes rellenos de arroz y jamón*

Stuffed peppers are a favorite among Cubans and Greeks. Rice is nice and light, and the ham makes it a main dish.

4 SERVINGS

> ½ pound ground ham
> 1 tablespoon olive oil
> ½ onion, peeled and chopped
> ¼ teaspoon garlic salt
> ½ cup tomato sauce
> 1 tablespoon dry white wine
> 1 teaspoon white vinegar
> 2 cups cooked white rice (see page 160)
> 2 eggs, beaten
> Salt and pepper to taste
> 4 large green bell peppers, tops removed, seeded
> ¼ cup grated Parmesan cheese
> ¼ cup bread crumbs or cracker meal
> 4 tablespoons (½ stick) butter, melted, for basting

In a skillet over medium heat, sauté the ham in the oil for 2 to 3 minutes, stirring occasionally. Add the onion and garlic salt, and continue to sauté for an additional 5 to 7 minutes, until onion becomes translucent.

Reduce the heat, and add the tomato sauce, wine, vinegar, and rice. Simmer over medium-low heat for around 5 minutes, stirring constantly.

Remove from heat, and stir in the beaten eggs. Season with salt and pepper to taste.

Preheat the oven to 350 degrees. Place the peppers in a shallow greased baking pan, and stuff, filling them to the very top with the rice mixture, using a spoon. Layer the top with the Parmesan cheese and bread crumbs. Cover the pan tightly with aluminum foil, and bake in the middle rack of the oven for 45 to 55 minutes. Baste with butter every 10 minutes. Remove foil and place under the broiler to brown the crust for about 45 seconds. Serve immediately.

STUFFED EGGPLANTS *berenjenas rellenas*

Just like the Italians, Cubans eat eggplant as an entrée. Accompany the stuffed egg-plant with Cuban salsa (see page 112) for a perfect combination.

4 SERVINGS

> **4 or 5 baby or small eggplants**
> **3 cups *picadillo al guapo* (see page 281)**
> **3 eggs, beaten**
> **Salt and pepper to taste**
> **¼ cup shaved or grated Parmesan cheese**
> **½ cup bread crumbs or cracker meal**
> **4 tablespoons (½ stick) butter, melted, for basting**

Bring 10 cups water to a boil in a large pot, and boil the eggplants for about 10 minutes over medium heat. Remove from heat, drain eggplants, and allow them to cool to room temperature. Discard water.

Halve the eggplants lengthwise. Scoop out the flesh, and transfer to a food processor to process for about 30 seconds. Add the *picadillo,* and process for an additional 30 seconds. Add in the beaten eggs, and season with salt and pepper to taste.

Preheat the oven to 350 degrees. Place the eggplant shells in a shallow greased baking pan, and stuff, filling them to the very top with the *picadillo,* using a spoon. Layer the top with the Parmesan cheese and bread crumbs. Cover the pan tightly with aluminum foil, and bake on the middle rack of the oven for 45 to 55 minutes. Baste with butter every 10 minutes. Remove foil and place under the broiler to brown the crust for about 45 seconds. Serve immediately.

BAKED EGGPLANT *berenjenas al horno*
4 SERVINGS

> 6 baby eggplants, about 3 to 4 inches long
> 2 teaspoons olive oil
> 1 teaspoon white vinegar
> Salt to taste
> 1 teaspoon ground oregano or dried oregano leaves
> ¼ teaspoon pepper

Preheat the oven to 375 degrees. Wash and dry the eggplants, leaving stems intact. Arrange in a shallow baking pan in a single layer. Sprinkle with the olive oil and white vinegar, and season with salt, oregano, and pepper.

Place the pan on center rack of oven and bake for 25 to 30 minutes, or until golden brown. Cool to room temperature, and serve as a great side dish.

STUFFED BONIATO WITH TASAJO
boniatos rellenos con tasajo

Literally hundreds of sweet-potato or boniato varieties are grown, ranging from long and tubular to short and round. The Cuban boniato is less sweet than the American sweet potato, and its flesh is cream-colored. Look for hard boniatos in the Hispanic vegetable section of your local supermarket. If you can't find them, substitute sweet potatoes.

4 SERVINGS

> Salt to taste
> 2 pounds boniatos, peeled and diced
> 1 cup Cuban-style beef jerky (*tasajo;* see page 305)
> 3 eggs, beaten
> 2 cups bread crumbs or cracker meal
> 2 cups corn or vegetable oil, or enough for 3 to 4 inches in skillet

Boil the boniatos in 10 cups salted water until very tender, about 10 minutes. Drain the boniatos, discard the water, and transfer to a food processor to purée for about 30 seconds.

To stuff, first shape a spoonful of the mashed boniato into a 3-inch ball. Make an indentation at the center of the ball, and fill with about a tablespoon of *tasajo*. Seal the *tasajo* completely in the mashed-potato ball. Repeat this step, making all the *boniatos rellenos* as uniform as possible. Use all your mashed boniato. The amount of *tasajo* you put in the center of each ball is completely up to you. Just be sure to seal with the mashed boniato.

Roll the stuffed boniato balls in beaten egg and then in bread crumbs. Set aside. If you prefer very firm stuffed boniatos, refrigerate, covered in wax paper, for about 20 minutes.

Heat at least 3 to 4 inches of vegetable oil in a heavy skillet over medium heat. Add the boniato balls, and fry them for 5 to 7 minutes, turning them frequently so they brown evenly on all sides. Drain on paper towels, and serve immediately.

BONIATO CHIPS *boniato frito*

These are as delicious as sweet-potato fries. Serve with softened cream cheese and chopped parsley.

4 SERVINGS

> 2 cups vegetable oil
> 1 pound boniatos, peeled and cut in very thin lengthwise slices
>   (no more than $1/4$ inch thick)
> Salt to taste

In a large, heavy skillet, heat the oil over medium-high heat.

Once the oil is hot (test the temperature by dropping a small square of bread into it and making sure it turns golden brown in about 30 seconds), place the boniato slices in the hot oil, and fry for about 2 or 3 minutes, turning occasionally, until crispy but not brown.

Remove carefully, and drain on paper towels. Salt to taste, and serve immediately, on plates or in brown paper bags.

STUFFED POTATOES *papas rellenas*

These are fritters of a sort, meat-and-potatoes fritters in the shape of baseballs. A *papa rellena* is just plain awesome in a sandwich.

6 SERVINGS

> 3 pounds Yukon Gold potatoes, peeled and cubed
> ¼ cup evaporated milk, warm
> 4 teaspoons butter, melted
> ½ cup heavy cream
> 2 garlic cloves, minced
> Salt and pepper to taste (optional)
> 3 cups *picadillo al guapo* (see page 281)
> 4 large eggs, beaten
> 2 cups cracker meal
> 2 cups vegetable oil, or enough for 3 to 4 inches in skillet

Bring 8 cups water to a boil in a large, heavy pot. Reduce the heat, add the potato pieces, and cook for 25 to 30 minutes, or until very tender. When fully cooked, drain the potatoes in a colander and reserve in a large bowl, discarding the water.

In a small bowl, mix the milk, butter, cream, and minced garlic cloves. Add to the drained potatoes very slowly, and beat the potatoes with a handheld mixer. Don't overbeat. The potatoes should be firm and hold their shape. Season with salt and pepper, if needed.

To assemble the *papas rellenas:* First shape a spoonful of mashed potatoes into a 3-inch ball. Make an indentation at the center of the ball, and fill with about a tablespoon of *picadillo.* Seal the *picadillo* completely in the mashed-potato ball. Repeat this step, making all the *papas rellenas* as uniform as possible. Use all your mashed-potato mixture. The amount of *picadillo* you put in the center of each potato ball is completely up to you. Just be sure to seal with the mashed potato.

Roll the stuffed potato balls in beaten egg and then in cracker meal. Set aside. If you prefer very firm stuffed potatoes, refrigerate for about 20 minutes covered in wax paper.

Heat at least 3 or 4 inches of vegetable oil in a heavy skillet over medium heat. Add the potato balls, and fry them for 5 to 7 minutes, turning them frequently so they brown evenly on all sides. Drain on paper towels and serve immediately.

CAULIFLOWER AND CHEESE *coliflor con queso*

This is a great bake, just like a casserole. You will completely forget that it is cauliflower—food that is good for you.

4 SERVINGS

> 1 head cauliflower, cut into florets (approximately 4 cups)
> 3 tablespoons olive oil
> Salt and pepper to taste
> ½ cup grated mozzarella cheese
> ¼ cup bread crumbs

Bring 3 cups water to a slow boil in a saucepan over medium-high heat. Add the cauliflower florets, and return to a simmer, reduce heat, and cover. Continue to cook for about 10 minutes, or until tender. Drain.

Preheat oven to 350 degrees. In a round or rectangular baking dish, arrange the cauliflower, dress with a drizzle of olive oil, season with salt and pepper, top with cheese, and sprinkle with bread crumbs. Cover with aluminum foil, and bake for about 20 minutes. Remove the foil, and continue to bake for an additional 3 to 5 minutes, until the cheese and the bread crumbs are browned and bubbling.

CAULIFLOWER IN SAUCE *coliflor en salsa*

A simple way to dress up steamed cauliflower: Serve it with a sauce!

4 SERVINGS

> 1 head cauliflower, cut into florets (approximately 4 cups)
> 3 tablespoons olive oil
> Salt and pepper to taste

Bring 3 cups water to a slow boil in a saucepan over medium-high heat. Add the cauliflower florets, return to a simmer, reduce heat, and cover. Continue to cook for about 10 minutes, or until tender. Drain.

Dress with a few drops of olive oil, and season with salt and pepper. Set aside arranged on a platter. Serve with any of the following sauces, and enjoy the rave reviews.

AURORA SAUCE *salsa aurora*
See page 110. This sauce gives the cauliflower an explosion of pink color.

LOBSTER SAUCE *salsa cardenal*
See page 111. Serve this as a main dish.

CHIMICHURRI SAUCE *chimichurri*
Don't forget the power of this Latin pesto sauce. See page 111.

TWICE-BAKED CHAYOTES *chayotes rellenos*

The chayote is a summer squash from Mexico that looks like a pear with pale green skin and has crisp, firm flesh.

4 SERVINGS

> 4 medium chayotes
> 2 tablespoons butter, plus more for baking dish
> 1 cup milk, whole or skim
> 4 tablespoons cornstarch
> 1 cup sugar
> Salt and pepper to taste
> 4 egg yolks
> ¼ cup raisins
> 1 teaspoon vanilla extract
> 5 teaspoons bread crumbs or cracker meal

Bring water to a slow boil in a saucepan over medium-high heat. Place the chayotes in the water, return to a simmer, reduce heat, and cover. Continue to cook for 17 to 20 minutes, or until tender. Drain, and allow to cool to room temperature.

When cool, cut in half lengthwise. Scrape out and discard the seeds and flesh in the center. Scoop out most of the flesh, chop it, and reserve. Arrange the chayote shells in a buttered baking dish.

Process the flesh in a food processor for about 1 minute. Add the milk, 2 tablespoons butter, cornstarch, sugar, salt, pepper, and egg yolks. Process until thoroughly mixed.

Preheat oven to 350 degrees.

Transfer stuffing to a saucepan, and simmer over medium heat for 3 to 5 minutes, stirring continuously to prevent sticking. Add the raisins and vanilla extract.

Stuff the chayote shells in the baking dish, sprinkle with bread crumbs, and bake on center rack for 25 minutes.

FRIED SPINACH SACRAMENTO
espinacas fritas Sacramento

This recipe comes from the Chinese who immigrated to Cuba and is named after my Chinese Cuban grandfather, Sacramento.

4 SERVINGS

> 1 tablespoon butter
> 2 cups fresh spinach, chopped
> ½ cup evaporated milk
> Salt and pepper to taste
> ½ teaspoon all-purpose flour
> 6 slices bread, preferably Cuban bread
> 3 eggs, beaten
> 1 cup bread crumbs or cracker meal
> 1 cup vegetable oil
> 1 cup béchamel sauce (see page 109)

Melt butter in a skillet and sauté the spinach over medium heat for 2 or 3 minutes. Add the milk, bring to a simmer, reduce heat, cover, and cook for about 5 minutes over low heat.

When spinach is tender, season with salt and pepper and add the flour. Continue to cook over very low heat, stirring constantly until you get a very thick sauce. Remove from heat.

Spread this mixture on the bread slices, roll the slices up, and secure ends with toothpicks. Roll each slice in the beaten eggs, coat with the bread crumbs, and fry in hot oil in skillet for 2 or 3 minutes, until golden brown. Drain on paper towels, and serve immediately, smothered in béchamel sauce.

BOILED MALANGA *malanga sancochada*

Malanga is a root vegetable about the size and shape of a regular white potato. Easily found in Hispanic and Asian markets, it needs only a few drops of olive oil and a little salt and pepper, although it is even better with mojo sauce (see page 121).

4 SERVINGS

> 1 pound *malanga*, **peeled and cut into 3-inch pieces**
> **Salt and pepper to taste**

Bring 10 cups water to a slow boil in a saucepan over medium-high heat. Add the *malanga* pieces, return to a simmer, reduce heat, and cover. Continue to cook for 17 to 20 minutes, or until tender. Drain, and season with salt and pepper.

BOILED ÑAME *ñame sancochado*

Ñame is a starchy root vegetable like the boniato that is in the sweet-potato family. Look for it in the Hispanic-fruit section of your supermarket, or in your favorite bodega. If you can't find it, substitute cream-colored or white sweet potatoes. Drizzle with olive oil or try this one with mojo sauce (see page 121) or a tropical fruit vinaigrette (such as those on pages 107–108).

4 SERVINGS

> 1 pound *ñame*, **peeled and cut into 3-inch pieces**
> **Salt and pepper to taste**

Bring 10 cups water to a slow boil in a saucepan over medium-high heat. Add the *ñame* pieces, return to a simmer, reduce heat, and cover. Continue to cook for 17 to 20 minutes, or until tender. Drain, and season with salt and pepper.

BOILED POTATOES *papas sancochadas*

Use medium-sized potatoes for this recipe. Serve with olive oil, melted butter, or white sauce (see page 110). You could also pair it with black bean vinaigrette (see page 108) or mojo sauce (see page 121).

4 SERVINGS

> 1 pound potatoes, **peeled and cut into 3-inch pieces**
> **Salt and pepper to taste**

Bring 10 cups water to a slow boil in a saucepan over medium-high heat. Add the potato pieces, return to a simmer, reduce heat, and cover. Continue to cook for 17 to 20 minutes, or until tender. Drain, season with salt and pepper, and serve with olive oil.

BOILED CASSAVA *yuca sancochada*

Use small to medium-sized cassavas for this recipe. It must be served with the traditional mojo for cooked vegetables.

4 SERVINGS

> **1 pound cassava, peeled and cut into 3-inch pieces**
> **Salt and pepper to taste**
> **2 cups mojo sauce (see page 121)**

Bring 10 cups water to a slow boil in a saucepan over medium-high heat. Add the cassava, return to a simmer, reduce heat, and cover. Continue to cook for 17 to 20 minutes, or until tender. Drain, season, and serve with mojo sauce.

MASHED POTATOES *puré de papas*

4 SERVINGS

> **1 pound potatoes, peeled and cut into 3-inch pieces**
> **½ stick (4 tablespoons) butter**
> **¼ cup hot milk**
> **Salt and pepper to taste**

Bring 10 cups water to a slow boil in a saucepan over medium-high heat. Add the potato pieces, return to a simmer, reduce heat, and cover. Continue to cook for 17 to 20 minutes, or until tender.

Drain and mash the potatoes, and stir in the butter and hot milk. Beat the potatoes with a wire whisk until fluffy. Season with salt and pepper to taste, and serve immediately.

NOTE For duchess potatoes, add 2 beaten egg yolks to the mashed potatoes after adding milk and butter, and bake at 375 degrees until golden.

MASHED MALANGA *puré de malanga*

4 SERVINGS

> 1 pound *malanga*, peeled and cut into 3-inch pieces
> ½ stick (4 tablespoons) butter
> 2 teaspoons cream cheese, softened
> ¼ cup hot milk
> Salt and pepper to taste
> 1½ tablespoons olive oil (optional)

Bring 10 cups water to a slow boil in a saucepan over medium-high heat. Place the *malanga* pieces in the water, return to a simmer, reduce heat, and cover. Continue to cook for 17 to 20 minutes, or until tender.

Drain and mash the *malanga* pieces. Stir in the butter, cream cheese, and hot milk, and beat with a wire whisk until fluffy. Season with salt and pepper to taste, and serve immediately. Soften with olive oil if needed.

CUBAN OKRA *quimbombó a la cubana*

My friend Eric Price, a Southern cook and a connoisseur of all things wonderful, warned me about okra. He reminded me that even though okra recipes are wildly popular in the South, the taste really must be acquired, and the texture is somewhat slimy. Okra, often called "ladies' fingers," is a pod vegetable in the same family as hibiscus and was part of the ancient Egyptians' food feasts. It was later imported from Africa as part of the slave culture and established itself as an important vegetable in the Caribbean nations as early as the seventeenth century. When choosing okra, look for bright green pods with no sign of browning or withering; the seeds inside should be pale and pinkish for the freshest taste. Don't cook okra in iron or copper pots; it will turn black. Our Cuban take on okra is tasty, nutritious, and not at all slimy!

4 SERVINGS

> 1 pound fresh okra, washed, stemmed, and diced (2 cups)
> Salt and pepper to taste
> ½ pound bacon, cubed
> 1 onion, peeled and chopped
> 2 garlic cloves, minced
> 1 cup diced tomatoes
> 4 cups cooked white rice (see page 160)

Trim the ends off the okra.

Bring 6 cups water to a slow boil in a saucepan over medium-high heat. Add the okra, return to a simmer, reduce heat, and cover. Continue to cook for about 10 minutes, or until tender. Drain and reserve.

In a skillet over medium heat, sauté the bacon for 2 or 3 minutes, or until the bacon is cooked but still soft (not crisp). Add the onion and garlic, and continue to sauté over medium-low heat for 2 or 3 minutes, or until the meat is browned and the onion is translucent and tender.

Reduce heat; add the tomatoes and the boiled okra slices. Stir well, and simmer for 12 to 15 minutes over low heat, partially covered, stirring occasionally. Remove from heat, and spoon over a mound of white rice.

CREOLE ONION CASSEROLE
guiso criollo de cebolla

The caramelized onions on this great entrée are like bacon to the vegetarian world.

4 SERVINGS

> **2 large Spanish onions, thinly sliced**
> **4 teaspoons olive oil, plus more for greasing the pan**
> **Salt and pepper to taste**
> **½ cup tomato purée**
> **¼ cup dry white wine**
> **¼ cup water**
> **½ teaspoon dried thyme**
> **1 small green bell pepper, seeded and chopped**
> **1 garlic clove, minced**
> **4 cups cooked white rice (see page 160)**

Heat the oil in a medium saucepan over medium heat, sauté onions for 2 or 3 minutes, and transfer to a lightly greased baking pan. Season with salt and pepper.

Preheat oven to 375 degrees.

In the original pan, combine tomato purée, wine, water, and thyme, and stir well as you simmer for about 5 minutes. Remove from heat, and pour over the onions in the baking pan.

(continued on next page)

(continued from previous page)

Again in the original pan, sauté the green pepper and garlic until tender. Spoon this over onion mixture. Cover the baking pan with aluminum foil, and bake in oven for 30 to 35 minutes.

Remove from heat, and serve over rice.

GUESS AGAIN CARROTS *zanahorias diferentes*

This is not the same old carrot dish and makes a nice change of pace.

4 SERVINGS

> **2 pounds carrots, peeled and sliced**
> **2 tablespoons butter, plus more for greasing pan**
> **1 medium onion, peeled and chopped**
> **1½ cups grated cheddar cheese**
> **Salt and pepper to taste**
> **1 green bell pepper, seeded and chopped**
> **1 parsley sprig, chopped**
> **1 cup bread crumbs**

In a large saucepan, boil carrots in 8 cups water for about 20 minutes, or until very tender. Drain, and process in food processor or blender for about 1 minute. Add butter, onion, and cheese, and process for about 2 minutes, or until thoroughly mixed and puréed. Add salt and pepper if desired.

Preheat oven to 350 degrees.

Transfer to a greased baking pan, and top with chopped green pepper, parsley, and bread crumbs.

Bake in oven for about 30 minutes, or until bubbly and golden on top. Serve immediately.

CUBAN GARDEN SAUTÉ *saltaado a la jardinera*

4 SERVINGS

½ stick (4 tablespoons) butter
2 cups sliced zucchini
1 cup drained, canned whole-kernel corn
1 small green bell pepper, seeded and chopped
1 small onion, peeled and chopped
1 tablespoon sugar
Salt and pepper to taste
1 cup chopped tomatoes
4 cups cooked white rice (see page 160) or saffron rice

Melt butter in a large skillet over medum heat. Add zucchini, corn, green pepper, onion, and sugar. Season to taste. Sauté over medium heat, stirring frequently, until vegetables are tender and onion is translucent.

Gently add the tomatoes, and continue cooking until hot but still firm. Serve immediately over saffron rice or white rice.

TAMAL AND TAMALES
tamal y tamales

The tamal is a cornmeal dumpling, sometimes filled with a delicious stuffing and steamed or boiled until firm. The most widely known tamales are wrapped in corn husks and made with *masa harina,* a precooked yellow cornmeal.

Tamales in Cuba can be traced back to the Ciboney, the original native inhabitants of the island. Before 1959, street vendors in Cuba sold Mexican-style tamales wrapped in corn husks but made without any spicy seasoning, in order to accommodate the milder Cuban palate. The fact that Cuban tamales are identical in shape to Mexican tamales suggests the intense cultural exchange that these two nations have always shared. In the 1950s, a very famous Cuban song (actually a cha-cha) called "Los Tamalitos de Olga" celebrated the delicious tamales sold by street vendors all over Cuba. Close your eyes and envision street vendors dancing to the beat of the song while selling their tamales. The scene is animated—regulars buying, kids playing, and people talking all over the place. It is a chance to get together with friends and socialize. Inhale the exotic potpourri of grilling meat, steamed corn, and flowering trees. Tamales are street food at its best. They are designed for portability, so, for a real food rush, eat them straight from your hand.

Tamal en cazuela, or cornmeal casserole, is a thinned-down version of the fresh-corn-and-pork mixture used to make husk-wrapped tamales. It is a very simple dish, almost a soup, creamy in consistency (imagine polenta) and thickened with cornmeal. This casserole came straight from the African (Yoruba) meal *ekoh,* a thick creamy paste of water and cornstarch very similar to tamale dough.

STUFFED TAMALES IN THEIR HUSKS
tamales en hoja

Serve these cornmeal dumplings arranged on a platter with slices of sweet ham, pickles, and slices of roast pork. First choose your wrappers. Ready-prepared corn husks are available in ethnic departments of some supermarkets. Or use banana leaves, or even foil squares. Your stuffing should be as fresh as possible.

4 TAMALES

> 2 teaspoons olive oil, plus more for brushing wrappers
> 1 cup peeled and chopped chorizo sausage
> 1 small onion, peeled and chopped
> 1 small green bell pepper, seeded and chopped
> 2 garlic cloves, minced
> 2 tomatoes, chopped
> 2 cups ground pork
> Salt and pepper to taste
> 8 large ears fresh yellow corn, or 2 pounds frozen yellow corn
>   kernels
> 1 cup finely ground yellow cornmeal or *masa harina*
> 4 wrappers, if needed

In a skillet over medium heat (375 degrees), sauté the chorizo in olive oil, and add the onion, green pepper, and garlic. Continue to sauté for 5 to 7 minutes, or until the onion becomes translucent. Reduce heat, stir in the tomatoes, and add the pork; cook for an additional 12 minutes, stirring occasionally. Season with salt and pepper if desired. When everything is tender and meat is done, remove from heat.

Meanwhile, if using fresh corn, remove the husks and silk from corn ears. Discard the silk and reserve the husks for wrapping. Grate the corn off the cobs into a mixing bowl. Once you have that, process it in food processor until puréed. If you are using frozen corn kernels, simply process them in food processor until puréed.

Place the corn purée in a large saucepan, and cook over low heat for 4 or 5 minutes. Gradually start adding the cornmeal to form a thick mixture as it cooks. When the consistency is super-thick, remove from heat and set aside. Allow to cool to room temperature or in the refrigerator, to make a smooth, slightly sticky dough.

Now assemble the tamales. Lay out the corn husks or wrappers and brush lightly with oil. Arrange two corn husks with the wide ends overlapping. Place a smaller husk covering the overlap. Spoon in about ¼ of the corn mixture, or break off with your hands and spread as evenly as possible to make a rectangular mass. Make an indentation in the middle, stuff with the meat filling, and cover with the corn dough. Continue with each tamal until they are all done.

To wrap: Fold in the long sides to cover the filling. Fold up the two pointed ends to form a rectangular package and tie with string. Make sure they are completely secured and tied.

Bring 12 cups water to a boil in a large pot over medium-high heat. Place the tamales in the pot when the water starts to boil, and continue cooking gently over medium heat for 40 to 50 minutes. Serve immediately in the husk wrappings, and let your diners cut the strings and enjoy.

CORNMEAL CASSEROLE *tamal en cazuela*

This is a creamy cornmeal-based soup.

4 SERVINGS

> 1 tablespoon olive oil
> 1 cup peeled and chopped chorizo sausage
> ½ pound pork loin, cubed
> 1 onion, peeled and chopped
> 4 garlic cloves, minced
> 1 small green bell pepper, seeded and chopped
> ½ cup tomato purée
> 1 tablespoon dry white wine
> 10 cups water
> 1 pound frozen yellow corn kernels
> 1 cup yellow cornmeal
> Salt and pepper to taste

In a skillet, heat the olive oil to 375 degrees and sauté the chorizo for 2 or 3 minutes. Add the pork loin, onion, garlic, and green pepper, and continue to sauté for 3 to 5 minutes. Reduce heat, and add the tomato purée and the wine. Simmer for an additional 7 to 10 minutes over low heat, covered. Set aside.

Meanwhile, in a large saucepan, bring the water to a boil. Once it is boiling, add the corn kernels and the cornmeal in a slow, steady stream. Stir, and return to a simmer while stirring constantly. Reduce the heat to low, and continue to cook for another 30 minutes. Taste, and season with salt and pepper. Continue to cook until it reaches a thick, creamy consistency. Add the chorizo-and-pork mixture and stir well. Serve immediately—and you'll want to save any leftovers. They will stay good for up to 1 week refrigerated, or up to 2 months frozen.

PLANTAINS IN MANY VARIATIONS

los plátanos en variantes

IF I HAD TO PICK ONE INGREDIENT, one fruit, one vegetable, or one food that just shouts "Cuban cooking," it would have to be the plantain.

The plantain did not originate in Cuba, and even if Cubans have adopted it as their very own, it is also extremely popular in other parts of the Caribbean and Latin America, as well as in Africa, Asia, and India. The plantain is so versatile yet exotic that even the leaves, which are large and pliable, are used for cooking. If you are a true foodie, try this cooking method: Just wrap a piece of freshly caught fish in a plantain leaf and bake it or steam it. If you are an art expert, you know that plantain plants have been the subject of many fine works

of tropical art. Some artists actually paint on the delicate canvases of the plantain leaves themselves.

The plantain is not, as you might think, a separate species from our regular banana, but a very large, firm variety that is only eaten cooked. It may be cooked when either green or ripe. It can be fried, boiled, steamed, baked, pounded, stuffed, mashed, refried, battered, turned into a soup, and even transformed into a delicious dessert. The plantain has many lives, many nicknames, and many variations in a Cuban kitchen. I would say that we have an obsession with, and yes, an addiction to the plantain.

FRIED RIPE PLANTAINS *plátanos maduros fritos*

When you pick the plantains to make this recipe, choose the ripest ones you can find. They will be black, overripe, and to the rookie eye will seem spoiled. These are the best of the lot, and experienced Cuban cooks run to grab them first in the supermarket.

4 SERVINGS

3 extremely ripe plantains, peeled like bananas
1½ tablespoons vegetable oil

Cut the peeled plantains diagonally into ½-inch slices. Set aside.

Heat the oil in a skillet over medium heat to 375 degrees. (Do not overheat—if you do, the plantains will brown prematurely but remain uncooked inside.) When the oil is sizzling, place the plantain slices in it carefully to fry, a few at a time, until they are golden brown and caramelized, about 3 or 4 minutes. Turn once during cooking for even browning.

Remove the plantain slices carefully with a slotted spoon, and transfer to a platter lined with paper towels to absorb excess oil. Serve immediately with just about anything.

BOILED RIPE PLANTAINS
plátanos maduros sancochados

The name says it all. Remember to leave the peel on when you boil! For this recipe, use ripe yellow fruit.

4 SERVINGS

> **2 or 3 ripe plantains**

Cut off the ends of the plantains. Cut the plantains into 2-to-3-inch-thick chunks. Leave the peel on.

In a large, heavy saucepan, bring 8 to 10 cups water to a boil over high heat. Add the plantain chunks, and simmer over medium heat for about 30 minutes. Remove from heat when the plantains appear swollen and slightly outgrow their peel. Serve with peel, or peel just before serving.

BOILED GREEN PLANTAINS
plátanos verdes sancochados

This recipe is perfect with pork dishes.

4 SERVINGS

> **Juice of 1 lemon**
> **3 green plantains, peeled and cut in half crosswise**
> **Salt to taste**

In a large, heavy saucepan, bring 6 cups water to a boil over high heat. Add the lemon juice and plantains, and season with salt. Boil for 2 or 3 minutes.

Reduce heat to medium, and continue to simmer for about 30 minutes. Remove from heat when fully cooked and tender, drain, and serve immediately.

STUFFED RIPE PLANTAINS
plátanos rellenos

This can be a very festive entrée. Just accompany with a salad and a Vedado District basic broth (see page 52).

4 SERVINGS

> 4 ripe yellow plantains
> Salt and pepper to taste
> 2 cups *picadillo al guapo* (see page 281)
> 2 eggs, beaten
> 1 cup bread crumbs or cracker meal
> 1 cup vegetable oil

Cut off the ends of the plantains. Cut plantains into 2-to-3-inch-thick chunks. Leave the peel on.

In a large, heavy saucepan, bring 8 cups water to a boil over high heat. Add the plantain chunks and simmer over medium heat for about 30 minutes. Remove from heat and drain. Peel, and mash by hand or place in food processor and pulse until smooth.

Season with salt and pepper, shape the plantain into a ball about the size of a golf ball, and make an indentation in the center. Stuff with a spoonful of the *picadillo*. Reshape ball to cover filling with mashed plantain. Repeat with remaining plantain and filling. Dip the balls in the beaten eggs, roll in the bread crumbs, and set aside.

In a large, heavy skillet, heat the vegetable oil over medium-high heat to 375 degrees. Carefully add the plantain balls, and fry for about 5 minutes, turning so they brown evenly. Remove with slotted spoon and drain on paper towels. Serve immediately.

RAFTER PLANTAINS *plátanos balseros*

What can I say about the rafters, or the famous *balseros?* The *balseros* of the past decades, like the Marielitos of the 1980s, hold a very special place in Cuban American history. Imagine the unflinching courage and the amazing resilience of the Cuban immigrants who arrived, and still arrive, in this country in homemade rafts or tires, having crossed the straits to attain liberty. We are all the richer because they have been delivered from the sea. This is their special recipe.

4 SERVINGS

> **4 ripe yellow plantains**
> **Salt and pepper to taste**
> **2 cups *camarones enchilados* (see page 234), cut into smaller**
> **pieces**
> **2 eggs, beaten**
> **1 cup bread crumbs or cracker meal**
> **1 cup vegetable oil**

Cut off the ends of the plantains. Cut plantains into 2-to-3-inch-thick chunks. Leave the peel on.

In a large, heavy saucepan, bring 8 cups water to a boil over high heat. Add the plantain chunks, and simmer over medium heat for about 30 minutes. Remove from heat and drain. Peel, and mash by hand or place in food processor and pulse until smooth.

Season with salt and pepper, shape the plantain into a ball about the size of a golf ball, and make an indentation in the center. Stuff with a spoonful of *camarones enchilados.* Reshape ball to cover filling with mashed plantain. Repeat with remaining plantain and filling. Dip the balls in the beaten eggs, roll in the bread crumbs, and set aside.

In a large, heavy skillet, heat the vegetable oil over medium-high heat to 375 degrees. Carefully add the plantain balls, and fry for about 5 minutes, turning so they brown evenly. Remove with slotted spoon and drain on paper towels. Serve immediately.

MASHED GREEN PLANTAINS

plátanos verdes aplastados

This delicious dish is also a staple of Puerto Rican cookery.

4 SERVINGS

¼ pound pork cutlets cut lengthwise into thin strips
NOTE As you slice, cut off and reserve some fat from the pork
for cooking.
3 green plantains, peeled and cut into 1-inch slices
1 garlic clove, minced
Salt and pepper to taste

Heat and render the reserved pork fat in a skillet over medium heat. Add the pork strips and sauté briskly, turning occasionally, until cooked and browned, about 3 to 5 minutes. Remove the pork strips with a slotted spoon, and set aside. Also remove and reserve any pork cracklings that formed during frying.

In the same skillet, carefully place the plantain slices in a single layer. Fry the plantains for about 3 minutes on each side, until they start to turn golden. Remove the plantains, drain on paper towels, and shred into narrow strips.

Once again in the same skillet, add the garlic and sauté for about 1 minute. Put the plantains back in the skillet, then add the pork strips and any reserved cracklings. Season with salt and pepper to taste. Serve immediately as a main dish with a nice tropical fruit juice and Cuban bread (see page 78).

TEMPTING SWEET PLANTAINS
plátanos en tentación

This dish is perfect for parties and special occasions. It is a tropical jewel and looks beautiful when garnished. I love to garnish this plate with maraschino cherries and pine-apple stars. The secret is to choose very ripe plantains—so ripe that most people would throw them away. The blacker the skin, the sweeter the plantain.

4 SERVINGS

> ¼ stick (2 tablespoons) butter, plus more for the pan
> 3 very ripe plantains, peeled like bananas and cut in half
>   lengthwise
> 2 cups water
> ¼ cup white wine or dark rum
> ⅔ cup white or brown sugar, or preferably a combination
> Three cinnamon sticks
> ⅛ teaspoon ground cinnamon

Preheat oven to 350 degrees. In a buttered glass baking pan, place the plantains in a single layer.

Pour the water and the wine over the plantains, and sprinkle the sugar over the mixture. Add the cinnamon sticks, and sprinkle lightly with the cinnamon powder. Dot the butter in little pieces over the plantains.

Bake for approximately 45 minutes, covering the pan with aluminum foil for the first 30 minutes, then removing the foil for the last 15 minutes. When the plantains are browned, remove from oven, garnish to your heart's delight, and serve.

RIPE PLANTAIN ROLLS
piononos de plátano amarillo

These actually look like candy! A delicious variation on serving plantains. The filling could be ground beef, shrimp, chicken, or lobster. This makes a wonderful after-school snack for kids, and an equally wonderful *tapa* for adults with happy-hour drinks.

4 SERVINGS

> ½ cup vegetable oil
> 4 ripe plantains, peeled like bananas and cut lengthwise into
> 3 pieces
> 2 cups *picadillo al guapo* (see page 281) or shrimp *enchilados*
> (see page 234)
> 3 eggs, beaten
> 1½ cup bread crumbs or cracker meal

Heat the oil in a skillet over medium heat. (Do not overheat—if you do, the plantains will brown prematurely but remain uncooked inside.) When the oil is sizzling, place the plantain slices in it carefully to fry, a few at a time, until they are golden brown and caramelized, about 3 to 4 minutes.

Remove from heat, and let cool at room temperature for about 10 minutes. When cool enough to handle, mash them and form into cylinders (like croquettes), about 3 inches long. Make an indentation in the middle of each and fill with equal amounts of the stuffing of your choice. Reshape cylinders to cover filling with mashed plantains.

Dip the plantain cylinders in the beaten eggs, roll in the bread crumbs, and set aside.

Fry over medium heat in the skillet and oil you used before—or start with fresh vegetable oil, if you prefer. Fry for 3 or 4 minutes, then carefully lift each *pionono,* turn over, and fry on the other side, until both sides are golden brown. Serve immediately.

FRIED GREEN TOSTONES *tostones a puñetazos*

These *tostones* are *"a puñetazos"* because we punch our green plantains! With a fist, with a mallet, or with a special artisan culinary instrument called a *tostonera,* a wooden or plastic press used to make *tostones.* The process is simple. Plantain slices are fried once, so they become soft enough to lay at the bottom of the press. The press flattens out the slices. The slices are then returned to the skillet to be refried. But unless you are showing off, you really don't need a special device. The following technique is how we do it at home.

When my kids were younger, they would insist that I give them their *tostones* "to go." I would pack them inside brown paper lunch bags and take the kids to the park to play ball and eat *tostones*. Besides making a great snack, *tostones* are also perfect as a side dish to a *palomilla* steak (see page 261).

4 SERVINGS

> **4 cups vegetable oil**
> **4 green plantains, peeled and cut into 1-inch-thick slices**
> **Salt to taste**

Pour oil into a large skillet, making sure the oil comes to about $\frac{1}{2}$ inch from the bottom for deep-frying. Heat the oil over medium-high heat. (Test the temperature of the hot oil by dropping a small square of bread into it; it should turn golden brown in about 30 seconds.) Now you are ready to begin your *tostones*.

Carefully place the plantain slices in the skillet in a single layer. Do not overcrowd. Fry for about 3 or 4 minutes, or until they start taking on the desired golden color. Then transfer to a plate lined with paper towels to drain and absorb excess oil. Let cool for a few minutes to room temperature.

Now you can either use your fancy *tostonera* or do it the old-fashioned way. Place the plantain slices, one by one, between two pieces of wax paper (if you really want to be traditional, between two newspaper pages), and press down with the heel of your hand or punch down with your fist (this is where the punching comes in) until the plantains flatten out to about $\frac{1}{2}$-inch-thick slices.

Put the *tostones* back in the skillet, with the vegetable oil at just the right medium-high temperature, and fry for an additional 3 or 4 minutes. Remove, transfer to a serving platter, and season with salt. Serve immediately.

NOTE To make very tender *tostones*, expert cooks toss them in a bowl of salted water for a few seconds after the first frying step, before pressing them flat.

YELLOW TOSTONES *tostones de plátano pintón*

You can also make *tostones* with ripe yellow plantains. Because they are more delicate, you reduce the cooking time, and you do not have to press them as hard. And you don't punch these at all!

4 SERVINGS

>   **4 cups vegetable oil**
>   **4 yellow plantains, peeled and cut into 1-inch-thick slices**

Pour oil into a large skillet, making sure the oil comes to about ½ inch from the bottom for deep-frying. Heat the oil over medium-high heat. (Test the temperature of the hot oil by dropping a small square of bread into it; it should turn golden brown in about 30 seconds.) Now you are ready to begin your yellow *tostones*.

Carefully place the plantain slices in the skillet in a single layer. Do not overcrowd. Fry for about 3 or 4 minutes, or until they start taking on the desired golden color. Then transfer to a plate lined with paper towels to drain and absorb excess oil. Let cool for a few minutes to room temperature.

Place the plantain slices, one by one, between two pieces of wax paper, and press down very lightly to flatten the slices to about ¼-inch thickness.

Put the slices back in the skillet, with the vegetable oil at just the right medium-high temperature, and fry for an additional 1 or 2 minutes. Remove, transfer to a serving platter, and serve with a garlic dressing or fancy sauce of your liking.

FUFÚ *fufú de plátano pintón*

What is this crazy thing called *fufú*? Throughout my childhood in Cuba, we just thought it was the funniest thing that our grandmother was making *fufú*. Little did we know that *fufú* is to most Africans what mashed potatoes are to Americans. In Africa, *fufú* is usually made with yams or cassava. In Caribbean nations with an African population, heritage, and origin, *fufú* is made of mashed plantains and pork. They call it *mangú* in the Dominican Republic and *mofongo* in Puerto Rico. The delicate flavor and filling texture make it a great side dish. It is also a very popular stuffing for turkey or chicken.

4 SERVINGS

> ¼ **pound pork, diced**
> **NOTE** As you slice, cut off and reserve some fat from the pork for cooking.
> **2 teaspoons olive oil**
> **3 whole yellow plantains, left whole and unpeeled**

In a skillet over medium-high heat, render and heat small pieces of the reserved fat. Add the olive oil and sauté the diced pork for about 5 minutes, until tender. Remove, and drain on paper towels to absorb excess fat. Reserve any cracklings for another use.

At the same time, boil 6 cups water over high heat in a large saucepan, and add the whole unpeeled plantains (snip off both ends); cook them for about 10 minutes. Remove from heat, drain, let cool to room temperature, and peel. Mash them with a fork, or process in a food processor at very low speed. Add a bit of liquid if necessary to make softer *fufú*.

Gently fold the pork into the mashed plantains until thoroughly mixed. Transfer to a serving bowl, and keep warm and moist until ready to serve.

FRIED GREEN PLANTAIN CHIPS *mariquitas*

This is take-out and street-vendor food. These wafer-thin slices of green plantain are delicious eaten alone, or sprinkled with mojo sauce (see page 121).

4 SERVINGS

> 3 cups vegetable oil
> 3 large green plantains, peeled and cut into very thin slices, no more than 1/16 inch thick; if you can, cut lengthwise
> Salt to taste

In a large, heavy skillet, heat the oil over medium-high heat. Once the oil is hot (test the temperature by dropping a small square of bread into it; it should turn golden brown in about 30 seconds), place the thin plantain slices in the hot oil, and fry for about 2 or 3 minutes, turning occasionally, until crispy but not brown.

Remove carefully, and drain on paper towels. Salt to taste, and serve immediately on plates or in brown paper bags.

GREEN PLANTAIN FRITTERS
frituras de plátano verde

This wonderful dish should be served hot. Serve with a sweet-and-sour sauce.

4 SERVINGS

> 3 green plantains, peeled and cut in half
> 2 eggs, beaten
> 1/2 onion, peeled and chopped
> Salt and pepper to taste
> 1 teaspoon baking powder
> 1 cup cracker meal or bread crumbs
> 3 cups vegetable oil
> Lemon wedges for garnish

In a large saucepan, bring 5 cups water to a boil, add the green plantains, return to a simmer, and cook over medium-high heat until tender, for about 15 minutes. Remove from heat.

Mash the plantains by hand or in a food processor. Add the beaten eggs, onion, salt, and pepper, and continue processing or mixing until thoroughly combined. If too thick, add ½ cup ice water.

Let the mixture cool, sprinkle with baking powder, and transfer to a bowl.

Use a soup spoon to scoop balls out of the mixture; roll them in the cracker meal.

In a heavy skillet, heat the oil over medium-high heat. Once it is hot (test the temperature by dropping a small square of bread into the oil; it should turn golden brown in about 30 seconds), drop the balls into the hot oil and fry for about 2 or 3 minutes, until golden brown. Serve immediately, garnished with lemon wedges.

MANZANO BANANA FRITTERS
frituras de plátano manzano

The manzano banana is related to the common yellow Cavendish banana. It tastes like a combination of strawberries, apples, and bananas, and it is much shorter and plumper than the common banana; it is ready to eat only when it turns black, but, unlike the plantain, it does not have to be cooked to be edible. If you cannot find the manzano in your market, you definitely can make these fritters with the common yellow banana.

4 SERVINGS

> ¼ cup all-purpose flour
> 1½ teaspoons baking powder
> 2 teaspoons sugar
> ½ teaspoon salt
> 1 egg, beaten
> ½ cup milk, whole or skimmed
> 4 manzano bananas, peeled and cut into 4 slices lengthwise
> 1 cup vegetable oil
> Cinnamon or cinnamon sugar

Sift the flour with the baking powder, sugar, and salt into a mixing bowl. Add the beaten egg and milk gradually, and mix thoroughly by hand or in a food processor.

Dip the banana pieces into this mixture, and set aside.

In a heavy skillet, heat the oil over medium-high heat. (Test the

(continued on next page)

(continued from previous page)

temperature of the hot oil by dropping a small square of bread into it; it should turn golden brown in about 30 seconds.) Once the oil is hot enough, drop the banana pieces into it and fry for about 2 or 3 minutes, until golden brown. Sprinkle with cinnamon.

BARBECUED SWEET PLANTAINS
plátanos maduros a la parilla
Whether on an open grill in the backyard, on a picnic in the park, or at the beach, this is always a real treat.

4 SERVINGS

> 4 very ripe plantains, peeled (these plantains should be black)
> 4 thin strips *queso blanco,* no more than ¼ inch wide and 2 inches long
> 4 strips guava paste, no more than ¼ inch wide and 2 inches long
> NOTE You can find guava paste in the Hispanic aisle of your local supermarket; if not, use guava jelly or marmalade.

Place the peeled plantains on a hot barbecue grill and cook for about 12 minutes, turning occasionally so all sides are evenly cooked.

When the plantains are tender and golden brown, remove carefully from the grill and use a small knife to slice them in half lengthwise. Stuff the middle with the cheese and guava strips, one of each per plantain. (If using jelly or marmalade, spread evenly down the length of the plantain.) Close the plantains again. Keep sides together with toothpicks or skewers.

Return the stuffed plantains to the grill for an additional 2 or 3 minutes, or until cheese is melted and flavors are blended. Serve with any grilled meat or chicken.

MÁXIMA'S PLANTAIN SOUP
sopa de plátano Máxima

Many times, we remember our loved ones, especially our grandmothers, with recipes. The smells of the kitchen and the flavors of the foods are always intermingled with our feelings of love and nostalgia. My husband will forever link this plantain soup with his grandmother Máxima. I know he will never taste a plantain soup as good as his grandmother's. This is her recipe, handed down through the years.

4 SERVINGS

> 2 tablespoons olive oil
> 1 small onion, peeled and chopped
> 2 garlic cloves, minced
> 5 cups chicken consommé (see page 54)
> 2 green plantains, peeled and diced
> 1 bay leaf
> Salt and pepper to taste
> 2 cups fried green plantain chips (see page 152) for garnish
> 1 lemon, cut in wedges

In a large, heavy saucepan, heat the oil over medium heat, and sauté the onion and garlic. Cook until the onion is translucent and tender.

Add the consommé, and bring to a boil. Add the green plantains and the bay leaf. Season with salt and pepper. When the soup begins to boil, reduce heat, cover, and simmer over medium-low heat for about 35 minutes, until the plantains are tender and fully cooked.

Remove from heat, pour into a food-processor bowl or blender, and process to make a smooth purée. If needed, add more consommé or other liquid. Return to heat for 2 or 3 minutes. Top with green plantain chips, and add a squirt of lemon juice to each bowl as you serve.

CREAM OF PLANTAIN SOUP *crema de plátano*

4 SERVINGS

> 1 tablespoon olive oil
> 1 onion, peeled and chopped
> 2 garlic cloves, minced
> 4 green plantains, peeled and cut into 1-inch slices
> 4 cups chicken consommé (see page 54)
> 2 bay leaves
> 1 cup heavy cream or evaporated milk
> Salt and pepper to taste
> 1 cup fried green plantain chips (see page 152) for garnish

In a large saucepan, heat the oil over medium heat, and sauté the onion and garlic for 5 to 7 minutes, until the onion is translucent and tender. Add the plantain slices, and brown evenly, turning occasionally, for 3 to 5 minutes, being careful not to overbrown.

Add the chicken consommé and bay leaves, bring to a simmer, and reduce heat to medium-low. Cover, and simmer for about 20 minutes, until the plantain pieces are soft. Remove from heat when fully cooked, transfer to a food processor or blender, and process until the mixture is smooth and creamy.

Return the mixture to the saucepan and add the cream. Heat for another 7 to 8 minutes, slowly bringing soup to boiling point. Remove from heat immediately—don't let it boil. Season with salt and pepper, and transfer to bowls. Top each bowl with green plantain chips as you serve.

SWEET PLANTAINS WITH RUM-AND-COCONUT SAUCE *plátanos con ron y coco*

This dessert is sinful and delicious.

4 SERVINGS

½ stick (4 tablespoons) unsalted butter
2 very ripe plantains (black), peeled and cut into ½-inch-thick slices
1 cup sugar
2 tablespoons dark rum
½ cup coconut milk (canned is fine for this recipe)
¼ cup heavy cream

Melt butter in a skillet over medium heat. Add the plantain slices, and sauté for about 3 minutes on each side, until they turn golden brown. With a slotted spoon, transfer the slices to a plate.

Keep the butter in the skillet over moderate heat, and add sugar. Cook, stirring, for about 5 minutes, until caramelized. Meanwhile, heat the rum and coconut milk in a small saucepan over low heat until warm. Remove the skillet from the heat, and carefully whisk in the warm coconut milk mixture. Place over low heat, and continue whisking until caramel is dissolved. Add the plantains, and simmer without stirring until heated through and tender, about 5 minutes.

In another small saucepan, heat the heavy cream. Pour over plantain mixture in skillet. Gently shake, and serve immediately.

SWEET PLANTAIN OMELETTE
tortilla de plátanos maduros

This sweet combination of plantains and chorizo is the epitome of good solid Cuban food. Serve with toast made from Cuban bread (page 78) and a *cortadito* (see page 405). This is a flat omelette.

2 SERVINGS

>   2 teaspoons olive oil
>   1 onion, peeled and chopped
>   2 chorizo sausages, casings removed, chopped
>   2 very ripe plantains (black), peeled and cut into ½-inch-thick slices
>   8 eggs
>   1 teaspoon baking powder
>   Salt and pepper to taste
>   1 tablespoon butter

In a large, heavy skillet, heat the olive oil over medium heat, and sauté the onion and chorizo pieces. Add the ripe plantain slices, and continue cooking for 5 to 8 minutes, until the onion is translucent and the plantain slices and chorizo pieces are well cooked. Transfer this mixture to a colander, and drain off the oil.

Break the eggs into a bowl with the baking powder, and season with salt and pepper. Beat lightly with a fork, and stir in plantain mixture.

Melt butter in a skillet over medium heat, add the omelette mixture to the skillet, and cook over medium heat for about 5 to 7 minutes. Place a large plate over the frying pan, invert the omelette onto the plate, and slide it, uncooked side down, back into the skillet. Cook for another 5 minutes. This will ensure that the omelette is fully cooked. Serve immediately.

RICE GOES WITH EVERYTHING

el arroz va con todo

CUBANS EAT RICE with every serious meal. White rice, an inexpensive and filling carbohydrate, is a staple in our diet. The quest for the perfect white rice yields many discussions.

Rice is classified according to the length of its grains. Long-grain is the most popular rice and is used in most Cuban dishes, because it always comes out fluffy with a mild, delicate flavor if prepared correctly.

Short-grain rice (*arroz Valencia*) is used by Cubans mainly for casserole-type dishes. Short-grain rice contains more starch, which makes the grains sticky when cooked. Use short-grain Valencia rice for paella (see page 174) and *arroz con pollo,* or chicken and rice (see page 165). There are a few unwritten rules for Cuban rice dishes that we pass on to the next generation as they get ready to prepare their family meals:

- Never stir rice while cooking; leave the rice alone, and don't add anything except maybe a little lemon juice midway through cooking.
- Long-grain white rice goes with everyday meals, whereas the short-grain rice (Valencia) is used for special-occasion rice dishes.
- Don't use olive oil when cooking white rice—use vegetable oil. Olive oil is too strong and overpowers the delicate flavor of the white rice. However, be sure to use high-quality virgin olive oil in yellow rice dishes.

- When cooking yellow rice recipes, substitute beer for some of the water. It tastes great!
- I hope most of you will use an automatic rice cooker for these recipes. These cookers are foolproof, producing perfect rice every time. Always follow your rice cooker's instructions and add all the ingredients in the same order.

secrets of a Cuban cook

HOW TO RINSE RICE

Rinsing rice is recommended for many recipes. Do so in several changes of water, swirling the grains around each time, until the water runs clear. Drain rice through a sieve, colander, or strainer to get rid of as much excess water as possible.

If the label on the package says "enriched," you should not rinse it before cooking, which would cause a loss of nutrients. If you must rinse it, do it lightly and just before cooking. But really try not to; it defeats the purpose of having enriched rice.

PERFECT CUBAN WHITE RICE *arroz blanco*

If you are intent on skipping the automatic rice cooker and going the primitive and really homemade route, the following recipe presents the traditional way, *por si las moscas* (Cuban slang for "just in case").

4 SERVINGS

> 1 tablespoon vegetable oil
> 2 garlic cloves
> 1 cup long-grain white rice
> 2 cups water
> 1 teaspoon salt

In a medium-sized saucepan, heat the oil over medium heat, and sauté the garlic cloves until golden. Remove the garlic, and remove the saucepan from the heat.

Add the rice to the same saucepan, and put it back over the heat for 30 seconds. Immediately add the water and salt.

Bring to a boil in the saucepan, and right at the boiling point, lower heat, cover, and allow it to cook slowly for about 25 minutes. Fluff rice and serve.

RICE AND BEANS
arroz con frijoles

I must emphasize: There are two basic rice-and-beans recipes, white rice and red beans (*congrí*) and white rice and black beans (*cristianos y moros*). They are similar but not interchangeable. The latter is more traditionally Cuban, but *congrí* is beloved by all Cubans for producing the best leftovers.

RICE AND BLACK BEANS *moros y cristianos*

The Spanish name translates as "Moors and Christians"—a very poetic and historical name for a very hearty combination. In today's multitasking world, it is better to make the black bean soup ahead of time, and freeze and store it for later use.

4 SERVINGS

> 1 tablespoon olive oil
> 2 garlic cloves
> 2 cups enriched long-grain white rice
> 2 cups water
> 2 cups black bean soup (see page 59)
> Salt to taste
> Lemon slices for garnish

Strain the black bean soup to separate the liquid and beans.

In a large pot, heat the oil and sauté the garlic until very brown. Remove the garlic cloves, and stir in the rice.

Add the water right away, as well as the liquid from the black bean soup. Reserve the beans to add later.

Bring liquid to a boil. Right at the boiling point, lower heat, cover, and allow it to cook slowly for about 20 minutes. Add the beans from the black bean soup, and simmer over very low heat for another 10 minutes.

Fluff rice, season with salt if desired, garnish with lemon slices, and serve.

RICE AND RED BEANS *congrí*

Often compared to the Nicaraguan *gallo pinto*, this is a wonderful and colorful recipe. Serve it on special occasions, accompanied by croquettes (see pages 36–40) or *tostones* (see pages 148–150). In today's multitasking world, it is better to make the red bean stew ahead of time, and freeze and store it for later use.

4 PORTIONS

> 1 tablespoon olive oil
> 2 garlic cloves
> 2 cups enriched long-grain white rice
> 2 cups water
> 2 cups red bean stew (see page 68)
> Salt to taste
> Lemon slices for garnish

Strain the red bean stew to separate the liquid and the beans.

In a large pot, heat the oil and sauté the garlic until very brown. Remove the garlic cloves, and stir in the rice.

Add the water right away, as well as the liquid from the red bean stew. Reserve the beans to add later.

Bring to a boil. Right at the boiling point, lower heat, cover, and allow to cook slowly for about 20 minutes. Add the beans from the red bean soup, and simmer over very low heat for another 10 minutes.

Fluff rice, season with salt to taste, garnish with lemon slices, and serve.

BLACK BEAN AND RICE BAKE

arroz y frijoles negros al horno

This recipe is a winning variation on classic rice and black beans. You may want to add sour cream, or even spicy salsa.

4 SERVINGS

> 2 tablespoons olive oil
> 3 garlic cloves, minced
> 1 medium onion, chopped
> 1 small green bell pepper, seeded and chopped
> 2 cups cooked black beans
> 4 cups cooked brown rice
> 2 cups ricotta cheese
> ¼ cup milk
> 2 cups grated cheddar cheese, plus more for topping

Heat oil in skillet over medium heat. Add the garlic, onion, and green pepper, and sauté for 5 to 7 minutes, or until onion is translucent and vegetables are tender.

Stir in the beans and rice, and continue to simmer over low heat for an additional 3 minutes.

Meanwhile, in a mixing bowl, thin ricotta cheese with the milk, and blend with the cheddar cheese using an electric mixer.

Preheat oven to 350 degrees.

In a greased 5-quart baking dish, arrange a layer of the rice-and-beans mixture and top with a layer of the cheese mixture. Alternate layers, ending with a final layer of beans and rice.

Bake in oven for 30 minutes. Sprinkle with remaining cheddar cheese, return to oven, and allow to melt on top. Remove from heat, and serve immediately.

OUR LEGENDARY CHICKEN AND RICE
arroz con pollo

If you ask any Cuban American who makes the best *arroz con pollo*, they will say "My mother!" There are many variations on this dish, each country or region laying claim to a different "authentic" variety. When kids start dating, they try out each other's families' *arroz con pollo,* usually on alternate Sundays. Experiment with variations on the classic recipe. Like paella, *arroz con pollo* is (usually) made with short-grain Valencia rice. Look for it in Hispanic markets or in the Hispanic aisle of your favorite supermarket. You can also use any other variety of short-grain rice. These are all very worthy contenders for the best chicken and rice ever.

CHICKEN AND RICE CREOLE
arroz con pollo criollo a la chorrera

Cuba, 1900. Imagine this epoch—elegant Cuba at the turn of the last century! That was when this dish originated. Chicken and rice can still be found at banquets, weddings, Sunday suppers, and many of our most heartwarming occasions. It makes an excellent party or buffet dish because of its durability and flexibility, and the way it lends itself to elegant and colorful garnishing. This is a favorite recipe! Start a new family tradition. To make it *a la chorrera* means to make it runny, soupy. You can choose to make it as runny or as fluffy as you would like—manage the consistency with the amount of liquid you add to the recipe. And, yes, you can cook your rice with beer, and it tastes so good you will want to add a little beer to your rice recipes ever after.

6 SERVINGS

> 3 pounds bone-in skinless chicken breasts, thighs, and drumsticks
> 4 teaspoons vegetable oil
> ½ cup sofrito (see page 119)
> ¼ pound ham, diced
> 3 bay leaves
> Salt and pepper to taste
> ¼ teaspoon ground oregano
> 1½ cups beer
> 2 cups water
> 1 pound short-grain Valencia rice
> Saffron to taste
> ½ cup chicken stock or consommé (see page 54)
> Pitted olives, red pepper strips, asparagus spears, and/or peas for
>   garnish

Wash the chicken parts, and blot dry with paper towels. Heat the oil in a large saucepan or pot, and brown the chicken pieces. Remove, and reserve chicken pieces on a plate.

Stir the sofrito into the pan, add the diced ham, and cook, stirring, over medium heat for a few minutes. Add the bay leaves, salt, pepper, and oregano.

Add the water and 1 cup beer.

Keeping the heat on medium, add the water and rice.

Bring to a boil. Right at the boiling point, lower heat, cover, and allow to cook slowly for about 15 minutes. Add the saffron; then add the browned chicken. This is also the time to decide how much more liquid you would like to add in order to make your recipe more or less *a la chorrera*. This is where I like to add the ½ cup beer and ½ cup chicken stock. Cook over medium-low heat for another 20 minutes.

You may garnish with pitted olives, red pepper strips, asparagus spears, and/or peas for a dramatic visual effect. Serve immediately.

CREAMED CHICKEN AND RICE
arroz con pollo a la crema

The success of this dish depends on the béchamel sauce. The combination of rice and this sauce makes for a very edgy risotto-type texture. It's an elegant dish, also suitable for large dinners and parties, and you can make it ahead. You might serve it with a delicious, refreshing San Pedro mixed salad (see page 196).

4 SERVINGS

    Salt to taste
    3 pounds bone-in skinless chicken breasts
    **2 cups chicken consommé (see page 54) or celery consommé
       (see page 54)**
    3 cups béchamel sauce (see page 109)
    1½ cups cooked white rice (see page 160)
    ½ cup grated Parmesan cheese

In a medium saucepan, bring 3 cups salted water to a boil. Add the chicken breasts, and cook for about 20 minutes. Remove from the heat, drain, and let

(continued on next page)

(continued from previous page)

cool at room temperature. Shred the chicken. In a small bowl, mix the chicken broth with the shredded chicken.

Preheat the oven to 375 degrees.

In a 9-by-13-inch baking dish, spread one-third of the béchamel sauce over the bottom, and then layer evenly with the shredded-chicken mixture, another third of the béchamel sauce, the rice, and then the remaining béchamel sauce in an even layer on the top.

Sprinkle on the Parmesan cheese.

Set the baking dish in the upper third of the oven. Bake until it bubbles and the top is lightly browned, 10 to 15 minutes.

BAKED IMPERIAL CHICKEN AND RICE
arroz imperial

This is a classic recipe and real comfort food—and especially a very economical dish that can be used for large get-togethers and dressed up for parties. I know the mayonnaise sounds like a strange ingredient, but try it once.

4 SERVINGS

> Salt to taste
> 2 pounds bone-in skinless chicken breasts
> 2 cups chicken broth or consommé, celery added (see page 54)
> ¼ cup olive oil
> 1 small onion, diced
> ¼ cup seeded and diced green bell pepper
> One 15-ounce can tomato sauce
> 2 cups chopped Spanish stuffed green olives
> Saffron to taste
> 1½ cups cooked white rice (see page 160)
> Pepper to taste
> ½ cup mayonnaise
> Parmesan cheese to taste

In a medium saucepan, bring 3 cups salted water to a boil. Add the chicken breasts, and cook for about 20 minutes. Remove from the heat, drain, and when at room temperature, shred the chicken. In a small bowl, mix the chicken broth and the shredded chicken.

Heat oil in the saucepan, and sauté the onion and bell pepper for 5 to 7 minutes over medium heat. Add the tomato sauce, green olives, and saffron. Stir in the cooked rice, and simmer over very low heat for 6 to 8 minutes to marry all the flavors. Add black pepper to taste. Now you are ready to layer.

Preheat the oven to 375 degrees.

In a 9-by-13-inch baking dish, press in half of the rice mixture, and then spread the shredded-chicken mixture over it. Top with remaining rice, in as even a layer as possible. Press so rice and chicken mixtures are compacted but not blended. Spread a light layer of mayonnaise on top. Sprinkle the Parmesan cheese over the top.

Set the baking dish in the upper third of the oven. Bake until it bubbles and the top is lightly browned, 10 to 15 minutes. Serve immediately.

STUFFED RICE MERCADERES
arroz relleno Mercaderes

This is a different take on chicken and rice. Mercaderes was a very famous street in Havana, full of merchants selling silk, wool, silver, and precious metals. It was a Gypsy-like scene, and the shop owners ate on the run. This recipe originated in that colorful environment. It is especially good with tempting sweet plantains (see page 147).

8 SERVINGS

> **Salt to taste**
> **Two 2- to 3-pound chickens, quartered**
> **¼ pound (1 stick) butter**
> **1 large onion, peeled and chopped**
> **1 cup tomato sauce**
> **½ cup dry red or white wine**
> **4 cups chicken consommé (see page 54)**
> **3 cups long-grain white rice**

In a large saucepan, bring 6 cups salted water to a boil. Add the chicken pieces, and cook for about 20 minutes. Remove from the heat, drain, and when at room temperature, shred the chicken and reserve.

(continued on next page)

(continued from previous page)

Melt the butter in a skillet over low heat, and sauté onion, stirring until translucent. Add the tomato sauce, wine, and consommé.

Add the rice. Bring the mixture to a boil, lower the heat, cover, and simmer for about 20 minutes, until the rice is tender and has absorbed most of the liquid.

Preheat the oven to 375 degrees.

Place half the rice in a greased baking dish (a ring mold is best!), then spread on the shredded chicken, and top with a layer of the remaining rice.

Set the baking dish in the upper third of the oven. Bake until it bubbles and the top is lightly browned, for about 10 minutes. Serve immediately.

RICE WITH TENDER CORN *arroz con maíz tierno*

What a great dish! It is so nourishing and filling. You may use split peas instead of corn for a more earthy flavor. This rice dish goes great with any baked fish recipe (such as those on pages 223–228). Or you may serve it as an entrée, with a salad and some plantains, cooked in whatever way you prefer for a great vegetarian dinner.

4 SERVINGS

¼ cup olive oil
2 garlic cloves, minced
1 medium onion, peeled and chopped
1 green bell pepper, seeded and chopped
¼ cup tomato purée
2 cups enriched long-grain white rice
3 cups water
2 cups fresh or frozen corn kernels
Lemon slices for garnish

In a large saucepan, heat the oil over high heat and add the garlic, onion, pepper, and tomato purée.

Lower the heat to medium, and add the rice and water.

Bring to a boil. Right at the boiling point, lower heat, cover, and allow it to cook slowly for about 20 minutes. Add the corn, and simmer for another 10 minutes

Fluff rice, garnish with lemon slices, and serve.

OKRA RICE *arroz con quimbombó*

Okra was a crop imported to Cuba from Africa as part of the slave culture. Our Spanish, African, and Creole influences are why Cuban cooking has so much in common with New Orleans cooking. Okra has a unique capacity to absorb strong flavors and become meltingly tender, which you and yours will experience firsthand with this dish.

6 SERVINGS

> ½ **pound fresh okra**
> **Juice of 3 lemons**
> ½ **cup vegetable oil**
> **1 large onion, peeled and chopped**
> **1 medium green bell pepper, seeded and chopped**
> **1 garlic clove, minced**
> **1 cup tomato sauce**
> ½ **cup dry white wine**
> ¼ **pound cooked ham, cubed**
> **1 small chorizo sausage, peeled and cut into** ½**-inch rounds**
> 2½ **cups chicken consommé (see page 54)**
> **Salt and pepper to taste**
> **2 cups short-grain Valencia rice**

Slice the fresh okra into ½-inch rounds, and soak in 2 cups cold water with the lemon juice for 30 minutes or more. Drain, blot the pods with paper towels, and set them aside to dry completely.

Heat the oil over medium heat in a pan. Sauté the onion, green pepper, and garlic for a few minutes.

Stir in the tomato sauce and the wine, and cook for a few minutes longer. As the sauce simmers, stir in the reserved okra slices. Stir in the ham and chorizo, and cook slowly for another 5 minutes.

Add the chicken consommé, salt, and pepper, and stir lightly.

Now add the rice, stirring lightly. Bring the mixture to a boil, lower the

(continued on next page)

(continued from previous page)

heat, cover, and simmer for about 20 minutes, until the rice is tender and has absorbed most of the liquid.

SAFFRON RICE AND VEGETABLES
arroz amarillo con vegetales

This lively rice dish abounds with contrasts in flavor and color and texture. You can add in other favorite vegetables (adjusting amounts as necessary). It can be made a day or two in advance of an occasion. Accompany with a tomato *sol* salad (see page 199) and you have a lovely and nutritious meal for your family table.

4 SERVINGS

> 2 teaspoons olive oil
> 1 garlic clove, minced
> 2 medium onions, peeled and chopped
> 3 tomatoes, peeled and chopped
> ½ cup sliced fresh carrots
> ½ cup sliced green beans
> ½ cup corn kernels
> 3 cups water
> 1 cup chicken consommé (see page 54)
> 1 pound long-grain white rice
> 1 pinch saffron

In a large saucepan, heat the olive oil and stir in the garlic, onions, and tomatoes.

Immediately stir in the other vegetables, and sauté for a few minutes.

Add the water, consommé, salt, pepper, and finally the rice, stirring lightly. Bring the mixture to a boil, lower the heat, stir in the saffron, cover, and simmer for about 20 minutes, until the rice is tender and has absorbed most of the liquid. Serve immediately.

FRIED RICE ZANJA *arroz frito Calle Zanja*

Chinese Cubans abound on the island and are an integral part of Cuban society. All over Havana, there were small Chinatowns, neighborhoods that housed Cuban Chinese businesses, family homes, and most of all restaurants that boasted the best Chinese food with just a touch of Cuban flavor. Even today, in most of Miami's Chinese restaurants, you will find fried rice featured with fried plantains. For a party, you can also serve this fried rice inside a pineapple to really impress your guests. Cut the pineapple in half lengthwise. Scoop out all the fruit, dice, and add to the fried rice as well. Serve the rice inside the pineapple "bowl."

4 SERVINGS

> 3 tablespoons vegetable oil
> 2 garlic cloves, minced
> 1 small onion, peeled and chopped
> 3 cups cooked long-grain white rice (see page 160)
> 1 chorizo sausage, peeled and chopped
> 1 cup small shrimp, cooked
> 1 cup smoked-pork strips (see page 172)
> Ground ginger to taste
> Soy sauce to taste
> 2 scrambled eggs, cooked

Heat oil in a shallow frying pan, and sauté garlic and onion. When the onion starts to become translucent, add the cooked rice, and stir continuously over high heat for about 5 minutes.

Add the chorizo, shrimp, and smoked pork, and continue cooking and stirring. Add the ginger and soy sauce, and continue cooking and stirring quickly. Lower heat, cover, and cook for 7 or 8 minutes.

Add the scrambled eggs, and stir the rice thoroughly, seasoning with more soy sauce as needed. Serve immediately.

secrets of a Cuban cook

HOW TO SMOKE PORK CUBAN STYLE

Preheat oven to 200 degrees; place a tray underneath the rack to catch drippings. To smoke 1 pound of pork, season first with the following mojo: minced garlic, orange juice, and salt and pepper to taste. Marinate the meat for at least 4 hours. Place your meat directly on the rack in the upper third of your oven. Bake for about 1 hour. Every 15 minutes, baste the meat with the mojo.

Once your meat is almost cooked, add a tablespoon of honey, and brush all over the top of the meat, making sure you cover the entire area. Continue cooking for another hour. Raise the temperature in the oven to 375 degrees during the last 15 minutes. Of course, you can buy the meat already smoked, but this homemade version is delicious.

ASPARAGUS FRIED RICE   *arroz frito con espárragos*

4 SERVINGS

> 4 fresh asparagus stalks, sliced
> 4 teaspoons olive oil
> 2 garlic cloves, minced
> 4 cups cooked white rice (see page 160)
> 3 tablespoons soy sauce

In a large skillet over medium heat sauté sliced asparagus spears in hot oil with the garlic. When tender, remove asparagus with slotted spoon and set aside. Leave skillet over heat.

Stir rice into the hot oil, and cook, stirring constantly, for 3 or 4 minutes. Add soy sauce, and continue cooking until completely heated through. Add the asparagus again at the end, and sauté to reheat. Serve immediately.

RICE WITH CALAMARI RÍO CRISTAL
arroz con calamares Río Cristal

Río Cristal is a water-themed restaurant on the famous highway Rancho Boyero in Havana, near Havana International Airport. This restaurant and its surrounding gardens, waterfalls, and ecological park are still a tourist site today. In the early 1960s, Río Cristal was the ultimate destination for families. And I have named this dish after the great memories of our family trip there, where I first enjoyed this wonderful rice.

For this recipe, buy only a Spanish or Italian brand of *calamares en su tinta* (squid stewed in its own black ink). For a wonderful garnish, you can also deep-fry calamari rings, and top your dish with alternating calamari rings and lemon slices.

4 SERVINGS

> Two 4-ounce cans chopped squid rings stewed in black ink
>   (*calamares en su tinta*)
> 2 garlic cloves, minced
> 1 medium onion, peeled and chopped
> 1 green bell pepper, seeded and chopped
> ½ cup dry white wine
> 1 pound enriched long-grain white rice
> 3 cups water
> Salt and pepper to taste
> Lemon slices for garnish

In a large saucepan over medium heat, stir the squid rings in their own ink. Add the garlic, onion, and green pepper, and sauté until soft.

Add the wine, cover, and simmer for 10 minutes. Then add the rice, water, salt, and pepper, stirring lightly.

Bring the mixture to a boil, lower the heat, cover, and simmer for about 30 minutes, until the rice is tender and has absorbed most of the liquid. Garnish with lemon slices. Serve immediately.

PAELLA CUBAN STYLE *paella a la cubana*

Of course we are all aware that the traditional paella originated in Spain, and no Cuban would ever dare challenge a Spaniard on the merits of a true paella. Yet we have our own version. This paella is lighter in color and has more tropical seafood, such as lobster and crab, instead of cold-water shellfish. Don't be stiff or formal about your paella. Just respect your own taste buds as you choose the seafood combination you want to include. As long as it is all fresh, you will have a successful paella. In Miami, there are paella chefs who take their craft into your home for a perfect festive occasion, using giant paella skillets and cooking as you party.

8 SERVINGS

1 cup vegetable oil

2 large onions, peeled and chopped

4 garlic cloves, minced

2 green bell peppers, seeded and chopped

One 2-pound chicken, cut into 8 pieces

1 pound steamed oysters or clams

1 pound meat from steamed or boiled crabs cut into bite-sized pieces

1 pound meat from steamed or boiled lobsters cut into bite-sized pieces (reserve shells for garnish)

½ pound ham, cut into julienne strips

½ pound pork, cut into bite-sized pieces

½ pound grouper or snapper, cut into bite-sized pieces

1 cup tomato sauce

1 cup roasted sweet red peppers, cut into julienne strips, plus more for garnish

1 teaspoon paprika

2 bay leaves

1 teaspoon white vinegar

4 cups dry white wine

4 cups chicken consommé (see page 54)

Salt and pepper to taste

2 pounds short-grain Valencia rice

Peas for garnish

Heat the vegetable oil in a very large, heavy pot. Add the onions, garlic, and green peppers, and sauté for 5 to 7 minutes over medium heat. Add the chicken pieces, oysters or clams, crabmeat, lobster meat, ham, pork, and fish.

Continue cooking over low heat, stirring until most of the meat is light golden. Now add the tomato sauce, roasted peppers, paprika, bay leaves, vinegar, and wine.

Add the consommé, salt, pepper, and finally the rice, stirring lightly. Bring the mixture to a boil, lower the heat, cover, and simmer for about 35 minutes, until the rice is tender and has absorbed most of the liquid.

Garnish, garnish, garnish! Use the leftover shells from your seafood, and incorporate peas and roasted red pepper strips in a geometric design.

NOTE If you prefer, instead of boiling, you may transfer the paella to a baking dish and bake at 300 degrees for about 30 minutes.

PASTAS
CUBAN STYLE

pastas italianas a la cubana

CUBAN COOKING has its own unique pasta repertoire, and all these recipes abound with flavorful ingredients. Cuban pasta recipes tend to call for well-cooked pasta; none of them ever require pasta to be al dente. The average cooking time for pasta is at least 7 to 10 minutes (or, if you are my husband, 30!) Many of the dishes are even baked after the pasta is cooked; casseroles are perennial favorites. These recipes also use less tomato sauce than traditional Italian pastas and contain more cheese.

CUBAN SPAGHETTI *espaguetis a la cubana*

This is Cuban comfort food at its best, and it is also very easy to prepare. The dish can be accompanied by a simple green salad and a piece of Cuban bread. The recipe uses a small amount of tomato sauce, so the marriage of flavors of the capers and the chorizo is delicious. Spaghetti with a twist!

4 SERVINGS

¼ cup vegetable oil
1 onion, peeled and chopped
1 green bell pepper, seeded and chopped
2 garlic cloves, minced
½ pound ground beef
¼ pound ground pork
¼ pound ground sweet ham
¼ pound chorizo sausage, peeled, chopped
¾ cup capers
Salt and pepper to taste
¼ cup chopped pimiento-stuffed green olives
½ cup tomato sauce
¼ cup dry white wine
1 pound spaghetti, cooked and drained
2 cups shredded *queso blanco* or cheddar cheese
1 cup pitted and chopped Spanish green olives

Heat the oil in a large skillet over medium heat. Add the onion, green pepper, and garlic, and sauté for a few minutes, until the onion becomes translucent and the pepper tender.

Add the beef, pork, ham, and sausage, and sauté, stirring constantly, until all the ingredients mix and the meats have browned. Stir in the capers, season with salt and pepper, and add the green olives, stirring constantly. Add the tomato sauce and wine, lower heat, and simmer, covered, for about 25 minutes.

When the mixture is thoroughly cooked, remove from heat and set aside, ready to assemble.

Preheat oven to 350 degrees

In a large baking pan, spread half of the meat mixture; add a layer of half

(continued on next page)

(continued from previous page)

the spaghetti and a layer of 1 cup shredded cheese. Repeat layers of meat and pasta, and top off with the Spanish olives and the remaining cheese.

Bake in oven for about 50 minutes, or until top begins to turn golden brown and bubbles.

CANNELLONI AU GRATIN *canelones al gratín*

This is a great combination of ham stuffing with béchamel sauce. Cannelloni are large round pasta tubes usually stuffed and baked in a sauce.

4 SERVINGS

8 cannelloni
Salt and pepper to taste
1 teaspoon olive oil
½ pound ground cooked ham (smoked or sweet)
4 cups béchamel sauce (see page 109)
2 cups grated Parmesan cheese
2 tablespoons bread crumbs or cracker meal
Butter, for topping

In a large saucepan over medium-high heat, bring 10 cups water to a boil. Stir in the cannelloni, and add the salt, pepper, and olive oil. Cook for about 12 minutes, until tender. When done, remove from heat and drain immediately.

Preheat oven to 375 degrees.

Fill the cannelloni with the ground ham, and place in a greased baking dish. Cover with the béchamel sauce, and top off with the Parmesan cheese and bread crumbs. Sprinkle a few dollops of butter on top, and bake for about 20 minutes, or until it is bubbling and the top is browned—do not overcook. Serve immediately.

CUBAN MACARONI AND CHEESE
macarrones gratinados

Here is the Cuban take on this comfort food. The sweetness or smokiness of the ham gives the dish a delicious flavor.

4 SERVINGS

> **1 pound rigatoni, penne, or any short tubular pasta**
> **Salt and pepper to taste**
> **1 teaspoon butter**
> **4 cups béchamel sauce (see page 109)**
> **½ pound ground cooked ham (smoked or sweet)**
> **2 cups shredded Parmesan cheese**
> **2 tablespoon bread crumbs or cracker meal**

In a large saucepan over medium-high heat, bring 8 cups water to a boil. Stir in the rigatoni, and add the salt, pepper, and butter. Cook for 7 to 10 minutes, until tender. When done, remove from heat and drain immediately.

Whisk the béchamel sauce together with the ham in a mixing bowl, and set aside.

Preheat oven to 350 degrees.

In a large baking pan, spread half of the ham mixture; add a layer of half the penne pasta and a layer of 1 cup shredded cheese; repeat layers of meat and pasta, and top off with cheese and bread crumbs.

Bake in oven for about 40 minutes, or until top begins to turn golden brown and bubbles.

NOTE This pasta is also good without the ham; you can also substitute ½ teaspoon olive oil for the butter.

MAC AND CHICKEN AND CHORIZO
macarrones con pollo y chorizo

The combination of ham, chicken, and chorizo makes this a hearty dish. It's great for picnics; serve with a simple green salad and a tall glass of sangria (see page 21). A real crowd-pleaser!

4 SERVINGS

> 1 pound penne, rigatoni, or other tube pasta
> Salt and pepper to taste
> ½ teaspoon olive oil
> ¼ cup vegetable oil
> 1 onion, peeled and chopped
> 1 green bell pepper, seeded and chopped
> 2 garlic cloves, minced
> ½ pound ground cooked ham (smoked or sweet)
> ½ pound shredded cooked chicken
> ¼ pound chorizo sausage, peeled, chopped
> ¾ cup capers
> ¼ cup chopped pimiento-stuffed green olives
> ½ cup tomato sauce
> ¼ cup dry white wine
> 1 cup pitted and chopped Spanish green olives
> 2 cups shredded *queso blanco* or cheddar cheese

In a large saucepan over medium-high heat, bring 8 cups water to a boil. Stir in the penne, and add the salt, pepper, and olive oil. Cook for about 7 to 10 minutes, until tender. When done, remove from heat and drain immediately. Set aside.

Heat the vegetable oil in a large skillet over medium heat. Add the onion, green pepper, and garlic, and sauté for a few minutes, until the onion becomes translucent and the pepper tender.

Add the ground ham, chicken, and chorizo sausage, and sauté, stirring constantly, until all the ingredients mix and the meats brown. Stir in the capers, season with salt and pepper, and add the green olives, stirring constantly. Add the tomato sauce and wine, lower heat, and simmer, covered, for about 25 minutes.

When the mixture is thoroughly cooked, remove from heat and set aside, ready to assemble.

Preheat oven to 350 degrees.

In a large baking pan, spread half of the meat mixture; add a layer of half the penne, and a layer of 1 cup shredded cheese; repeat layers of meat and pasta, and top off with Spanish olives and cheese.

Bake in the oven for about 50 minutes, or until top begins to turn golden brown and bubbles.

FETTUCCINE MILANESE *tallarines a la milanesa*
4 SERVINGS

> **1 pound fettuccine**
> **Salt and pepper to taste**
> **½ teaspoon olive oil**
> **1 cup cream of tomato soup (see page 65) or canned condensed
>   tomato soup**
> **1 cup shredded American cheese**
> **½ cup bread crumbs or cracker meal**
> **1 teaspoon butter, melted**

In a large saucepan over medium-high heat, bring 8 cups water to a boil. Stir in the fettuccine, and add the salt, pepper, and olive oil. Cook for 7 to 10 minutes, until tender. When done, remove from heat and drain immediately. Set aside.

Preheat oven to 350 degrees.

In a large baking pan, spread half of the tomato soup, add a layer of half the fettuccine and a layer of ½ cup shredded cheese; repeat layers of soup and pasta, and top off with cheese and bread crumbs. Drizzle with butter.

Bake in the oven for about 50 minutes, or until top begins to turn golden brown and bubbles.

PASTA PAELLA *paella de pasta*

This version of paella is excellent for pasta lovers. The combination of meats and sea-food goes wonderfully with the fettuccine. Accompany this dish with white wine, or even a bubbly champagne cocktail (see pages 23–24).

6 SERVINGS

> 1 pound fettuccine
> Salt and pepper to taste
> ½ teaspoon olive oil
> 2 tablespoons vegetable oil
> 1 medium onion, peeled and chopped
> 2 garlic cloves, minced
> 1 green bell pepper, seeded and chopped
> ½ cup diced cooked chicken
> 1 cup bite-sized pieces of steamed or boiled crabmeat
> 1 cup bite-sized pieces of steamed or boiled lobster meat (reserve
>   shells for garnish)
> ½ cup julienne strips of ham
> ½ cup bite-sized pieces of grouper or snapper
> 1 cup tomato sauce
> 1 cup roasted sweet red peppers, cut into julienne strips
> Pinch of paprika
> 1 bay leaf
> 1 teaspoon white vinegar
> 1 cup chicken consommé (see page 54)
> 1 cup grated Parmesan cheese
> 2 tablespoons bread crumbs or cracker meal
> 1 teaspoon butter, melted

In a large saucepan over medium-high heat, bring 8 cups water to a boil. Stir in the fettuccine, and add the salt, pepper, and olive oil. Cook for 7 to 10 minutes, until tender. When done, remove from heat and drain immediately. Set aside.

Heat the vegetable oil in a very large, heavy pot; add the onion, garlic, and green pepper, and continue cooking over medium heat for 5 to 7 minutes. Add the chicken, crabmeat, lobster meat, ham, and fish. Continue cooking over low heat, stirring until the meat is light golden. Now add the tomato sauce, roasted peppers, salt and pepper to taste, paprika, bay leaf, vinegar, and chicken consommé. Cook for 12 to 15 minutes, or until thoroughly cooked and tender. Add the cooked fettuccine, and mix thoroughly.

Preheat oven to 350 degrees.

Transfer mixture to a large baking pan, and top off with cheese and bread crumbs. Drizzle with butter.

Bake in oven for about 50 minutes, or until top begins to turn golden brown and bubbles.

MAC, SHRIMP, AND CHORIZO

macarrones con camarones y chorizo

This is another hearty meal. The combination of shrimp with chorizo makes the dish very flavorful. It is great for kids and buffet-style entertaining.

4 SERVINGS

> 1 pound penne, rigatoni, or other tube pasta
> Salt and pepper to taste
> 1/2 teaspoon olive oil
> 1/4 cup vegetable oil
> 1 onion, peeled and chopped
> 1 green bell pepper, seeded and chopped
> 2 garlic cloves, minced
> 1/2 pound small or medium shrimp, shelled, deveined, and cooked
> 1/4 pound chorizo sausage, peeled and chopped
> 3/4 cup capers
> 1/4 cup chopped pimiento-stuffed green olives
> 1/2 cup tomato sauce
> 1/4 cup dry white wine
> 2 cups shredded *queso blanco* or cheddar cheese
> 1 cup pitted and chopped Spanish green olives

In a large saucepan over medium-high heat, bring 8 cups water to a boil. Stir in the penne, and add the salt, pepper, and olive oil. Cook for about 7 to 10 minutes, until tender. When done, remove from heat and drain immediately. Set aside.

(continued on next page)

(continued from previous page)

Heat the vegetable oil in a large skillet over medium heat. Add the onion, green pepper, and garlic, and sauté for a few minutes, until the onion becomes translucent and the pepper tender.

Add the shrimp and chorizo sausage, and sauté, stirring constantly, until all the ingredients mix and the meat browns. Stir in the capers, season with salt and pepper, and add the green olives, stirring constantly. Add the tomato sauce and wine, lower heat, and simmer, covered, for about 12 minutes.

When the mixture is thoroughly cooked, remove from heat and set aside, ready to assemble.

Preheat oven to 350 degrees.

In a large baking pan, spread half of the shrimp mixture; add a layer of half the penne and a layer of 1 cup shredded cheese; repeat layers, and top off with Spanish olives.

Bake in the oven for about 50 minutes, or until top begins to turn golden brown and bubbles.

SPAGHETTI WITH OIL AND GARLIC
espaguetis con aceite y ajo

This dish is very easy to prepare. The garlic-and-olive-oil combination gives it a lot of flavor. Accompany it with a piece of Cuban bread (see page 78) and a green salad.

4 SERVINGS

> 1 pound spaghetti
> Salt and pepper to taste
> ½ teaspoon plus ¼ cup olive oil
> 8 garlic cloves, minced
> 1 cup chicken consommé (see page 54)
> 1 cup chopped fresh parsley
> ½ cup grated Parmesan cheese

In a large saucepan over medium-high heat, bring 8 cups water to a boil. Stir in the spaghetti, and add the salt, pepper, and ½ teaspoon olive oil. Cook for 7 to 10 minutes, until tender. When done, remove from heat and drain immediately. Set aside in the saucepan.

Heat the ¼ cup oil in a small skillet over medium heat. Add the garlic, and sauté for 1 or 2 minutes, stirring occasionally, until golden brown.

Add the chicken consommé and fresh parsley to the pasta, and simmer until broth is absorbed. Spread the heated olive oil and garlic over the pasta. Toss thoroughly with Parmesan cheese. Serve.

PASTA WITH CHORIZO AND PEPPERS
pasta con chorizo y aíies

Chorizo and peppers, a great combination, make this dish very flavorful.

4 SERVINGS

> 1 pound penne, rigatoni, or other tube pasta
> Salt and pepper to taste
> ½ teaspoon olive oil
> ¼ cup vegetable oil
> 1 onion, peeled and chopped
> 3 green bell peppers, seeded and cut into julienne strips
> 2 garlic cloves, minced
> ½ pound chorizo, peeled, cut into ¼-inch slices
> ¾ cup capers
> ¼ cup chopped pimiento-stuffed green olives
> ½ cup tomato sauce
> ¼ cup dry white wine
> 1 cup shredded *queso blanco* or cheddar cheese

In a large saucepan over medium-high heat, bring 8 cups water to a boil. Stir in the penne, and add salt, pepper, and olive oil. Cook for about 7 to 10 minutes, until tender. When done, remove from heat and drain immediately. Set aside in a mixing bowl.

Heat the vegetable oil in a large skillet over medium heat. Add the onion, peppers, and garlic, and sauté for a few minutes, until the onion becomes translucent and the peppers are tender.

Add the chorizo sausage, and sauté, stirring constantly, until all the ingredients mix and the meat browns. Stir in the capers, season with salt and

(continued on next page)

(continued from previous page)

pepper, and add the olives, stirring constantly. Add the tomato sauce and wine, lower heat, and simmer, covered, for about 25 minutes.

When the mixture is thoroughly cooked and piping hot, remove from heat and pour over pasta. Toss thoroughly with cheese. Serve immediately.

THIN NOODLES IN AVOCADO SAUCE
fideos en salsa de aguacate
4 SERVINGS

> 1 pound vermicelli, thin spaghetti, or *fideos*
> Salt and pepper to taste
> ½ teaspoon olive oil
> 1 recipe (2 cups) avocado sauce (see page 108), egg whites and
>   Spanish olives reserved
> ½ cup grated Parmesan cheese

In a large saucepan over medium-high heat, bring 8 cups water to a boil. Stir in the vermicelli and add the salt, pepper, and olive oil. Cook for about 3 to 5 minutes, until tender. When done, remove from heat and drain immediately. Set aside in a mixing bowl.

Prepare the avocado sauce according to the recipe, but reserve egg whites and chopped Spanish olives for garnish.

Pour the sauce over pasta. Toss well with Parmesan cheese. Garnish with chopped olives and egg whites.

PASTA WITH AURORA SAUCE
pasta con salsa aurora

4 SERVINGS

> 1 pound penne or rigatoni
> Salt and pepper to taste
> ½ teaspoon olive oil
> 1½ cups béchamel sauce (see page 109)
> ½ cup tomato sauce
> ½ cup grated Parmesan cheese

In a large saucepan over medium-high heat, bring 8 cups water to a boil. Stir in the penne, and add the salt, pepper, and olive oil. Cook for about 10 minutes, until tender. When done, remove from heat and drain immediately. Set aside in a mixing bowl.

Whisk together the béchamel sauce and the tomato sauce in a bowl until thoroughly combined.

Transfer sauce to a medium saucepan, and simmer over low heat for about 5 minutes, whisking and stirring occasionally.

When the aurora sauce is piping hot, remove from heat and pour over pasta. Toss thoroughly with Parmesan cheese. Garnish as you like, and serve in a large pasta bowl to pass around the table.

PASTA WITH CUBAN SALSA *pasta con salsa cubana*

4 SERVINGS

> 1 pound penne or rigatoni
> Salt and pepper to taste
> ½ teaspoon olive oil
> 1 recipe (2 cups) Cuban salsa (see page 112)
> ½ cup grated Parmesan cheese

In a large saucepan over medium-high heat, bring 8 cups water to a boil. Stir in the penne, and add the salt, pepper, and olive oil. Cook for about

(continued on next page)

(continued from previous page)

10 minutes, until tender. When done, remove from heat and drain immediately.

Place in a large bowl, pour salsa over the pasta, and toss thoroughly with Parmesan cheese. Serve immediately.

PASTA WITH CITRUS VINAIGRETTE
pasta con vinagreta de cítricos

A very light and refreshing dish. Accompanied by a tall glass of sangria (see page 21), this dish is especially good for lazy summer afternoons—besides acting as a cooling agent, it is also very healthful. It is an impressive entrée.

4 SERVINGS

> 1 pound penne or rigatoni
> Salt and pepper to taste
> ½ teaspoon olive oil
> 1½ cups citrus vinaigrette (see page 107)
> NOTE Always make a fresh batch of dressing for this dish.
> ½ cup grated or shaved Parmesan cheese

In a large saucepan over medium-high heat, bring 8 cups water to a boil. Stir in the penne, and add the salt, pepper, and olive oil. Cook for about 10 minutes, until tender. When done, remove from heat and drain immediately. Set aside in a mixing bowl.

Pour thoroughly mixed vinaigrette over pasta. Toss well with Parmesan cheese.

COLD GUAVA AND PASTA   *guayaba fría y pasta*

Cubans love guava in any dish, and this is a refreshing and very cooling dish. Grown-ups will especially love this sweet fruit recipe and will appreciate the flavor that comes through loud and clear.

4 SERVINGS

> 1 pound penne or rigatoni
> Salt and pepper to taste
> ½ teaspoon olive oil
> 1½ cups guava-mint vinaigrette (see page 108), at room
>   temperature
> NOTE Always make a fresh batch of dressing for this dish.
> ½ cup grated or shaved Parmesan cheese

In a large saucepan over medium-high heat, bring 8 cups water to a boil. Stir in the penne, and add the salt, pepper, and olive oil. Cook for about 7 to 10 minutes, until tender. When done, remove from heat and drain immediately. Set aside in a mixing bowl.

Pour the thoroughly mixed guava-mint vinaigrette over pasta. Toss well with Parmesan cheese, and chill in refrigerator for about 25 minutes. Serve cold.

PASTA WITH GREEN PARSLEY SAUCE
pasta con salsa verde

Parsley is a staple in Italian cooking, but Cubans have adopted the fragrant herb, and in this recipe the flavor of the parsley enhances the pasta. Long pastas like spaghetti or fettuccine are just as good in this recipe as penne and rigatoni.

4 SERVINGS

> 1 pound penne or rigatoni
> Salt and pepper to taste
> ½ teaspoon olive oil
> 1 cup green parsley sauce (see page 117)
> ½ cup grated or shaved Parmesan cheese

In a large saucepan over medium-high heat, bring 8 cups water to a boil. Stir in the penne, and add the salt, pepper, and olive oil. Cook for about 10 minutes, until tender. When done, remove from heat and drain immediately. Set aside in a mixing bowl.

Heat the green parsley sauce in a medium saucepan over medium heat. When thoroughly heated, pour over pasta. Toss well with Parmesan cheese.

CUBAN SALADS

ensaladas cubanas

THESE DAYS, salads can be main courses. They are also great for marrying colors, ingredients, and flavors that we would not ordinarily mix. The dressing can range from a very traditional olive oil and white vinegar to guava-infused vinaigrettes and other unusual combinations. Our hearty salads are also wonderful accompaniments to soups, including broths and cream soups. Forget the tired old lettuce-and-tomato dinner salad, and experiment! Always use the freshest vegetables and explore different dressings. The trick is to not drown the salad in dressing. Don't pour in the dressing too far in advance—and toss, toss, toss. You will find many recipes for fresh new dressings on pages 106–109.

AVOCADO AND PINEAPPLE SALAD

ensalada de aguacate y piña

The sweet taste of the avocado and the tangy taste of the pineapple are a perfect match, and thrilling on the palate. The avocado is remarkably high in protein, rich in fiber and carbohydrates, endowed with essential vitamins and minerals, and easily digested. Just remember to cut the avocado right before using, since it gets dark very easily once opened. When buying avocados, look for unblemished fruit, free of bruises; if you shake it and you hear the pit loose inside, you will know that it is ready to eat.

This colorful and elegant salad can serve as a side dish for a simple *palomilla* steak (see page 261).

4 SERVINGS

> 2 large, ripe avocados (soft to the touch)
> 1 medium pineapple
> Salt to taste
> ½ cup dressing of your choice (see pages 106–109)

Peel and cut the avocados in half lengthwise, remove the pits, and cut flesh into ½-inch cubes.

Peel the pineapple, and cut fruit into ½-inch cubes (see page 31).

Mix both fruits in a salad bowl, and add the salt and dressing to taste. Garnish as you like, cover, refrigerate, and serve very cold.

AVOCADO MANGO SALAD

ensalada de aguacate y mango

You can make your fruit salads more inventive by cutting the fruits into varied shapes. Round, oval, or star-shaped pieces make for a very appealing dish.

4 SERVINGS

> 2 cups peeled and diced mango (see page 21)
> 1 cup peeled and diced avocado
> 2 tablespoons minced cilantro
> Juice of 1 lime
> Salt and pepper to taste
> 1 teaspoon olive oil

(continued on next page)

(continued from previous page)

Not more than 10 minutes before serving, combine the mango, avocado, cilantro, and lime juice in a mixing bowl, and toss to mix. Season with salt and pepper to taste, and dribble olive oil on top. Serve immediately.

CHICKPEA AND BLACK BEAN SALAD
ensalada de garbanzos y frijoles negros
4 SERVINGS

> 1 cup black beans, cooked
> 1 cup canned whole chickpeas (garbanzo beans)
> One 8.5-ounce can whole-kernel corn
> 1 onion, peeled and chopped
> 1 small green bell pepper, seeded and chopped
> 1 celery stalk, chopped
> Salt and pepper to taste
> 1 tomato, diced
> ½ cup basic Cuban dressing (see page 106)

In a mixing bowl, combine the black beans, chickpeas, corn, onion, green pepper, and celery. Season with salt and pepper.

Add the diced tomato, and toss with the basic Cuban dressing. Chill, covered, in refrigerator for about 1 hour. Remove from refrigerator when well chilled, and serve.

ORANGE ONION SALAD
ensalada de naranja y cebolla

4 SERVINGS

> 5 oranges, peeled and cut in crosswise slices
> 3 tablespoons white vinegar
> 2 tablespoons olive oil
> 1 teaspoon dried parsley flakes
> 1 teaspoon dried oregano
> 1 medium red onion, peeled and thinly sliced
> 1 cup pitted and sliced Spanish green olives
> Salt and pepper to taste
> ½ cup citrus vinaigrette (see page 107)

Combine the oranges, vinegar, oil, parsley, oregano, and onion in a mixing bowl, and toss with the olives. Season with salt and pepper and toss well with the citrus vinaigrette. Refrigerate, covered, for about 2 hours.

Remove from refrigerator when well chilled and serve.

CUBAN CABBAGE SALAD *ensalada de col cocida*

Cabbage is rich in vitamins and very versatile. This recipe comes from Galicia (in the north of Spain), the birthplace of most Spaniards who ended up immigrating to the sunny beaches of Cuba.

4 SERVINGS

> 1 medium cabbage
> 2 teaspoons olive oil
> 1 teaspoon white vinegar
> Salt and pepper to taste
> ½ cup dressing of your choice (see pages 106–109)

Discard any wilted or discolored leaves from the cabbage. Cut the head into small wedges, and wash well. Place 2 cups water and cabbage in large saucepan, bring to a boil, and cook for 10 minutes over medium heat, until cabbage is tender.

(continued on next page)

(continued from previous page)

Drain, and in a mixing bowl season cabbage with olive oil, vinegar, and salt and pepper to taste. Pour the dressing over it and toss. Serve immediately, hot, or serve later, at room temperature, or even refrigerate and serve cold.

VARADERO LOBSTER SALAD
ensalada de langosta Varadero

Varadero, without the slightest doubt, was (and still is) Cuba's top beach resort and the subject of many good-time stories. In the 1950s most *habaneros* used to escape the city to sunbathe, fish, relax, drink, and eat in Varadero. They were joined by hordes of American tourists. The hotels were modern, their nightclub shows extravagant. Varadero was the setting of grand parties and lavish buffets. Fresh lobster, grilled or in salads, was always the best choice on the menu.

4 PORTIONS

> **4 uncooked lobster tails, split down the back and deveined (see
>   page 195)**
> **½ cup pickled sweet cocktail onions (canned or jarred)**
> **2 teaspoons sweet relish**
> **1 cup regular mayonnaise or green mayonnaise (see page 118)**
> **4 lettuce leaves**
> **Lemon slices and parsley for garnish**

In a large saucepan, boil lobster tails for 10 minutes. Remove from heat, drain the lobster tails, remove meat from shells, and cool to room temperature. (Please remember, lobster becomes becomes dry and tough when overcooked.)

Cut the lobster meat into chunks, removing any remaining bits of shell. In a mixing bowl, combine lobster chunks with the cocktail onions, relish, and mayonnaise. Toss lightly, cover, and refrigerate until ready to serve.

Arrange the lettuce leaves in a shallow serving bowl. Spoon the cold lobster salad into the center of the bowl, and garnish with lemon slices and parsley.

secrets of a Cuban cook

HOW TO DEVEIN LOBSTER

It is very important to devein the lobster tail. Place the tail securely on a cutting surface and hold it firmly with one hand. Using a knife, split the tail in half lengthwise through the shell. You can then remove the vein from the tail.

LIGHT CUBAN SALAD *ensalada ligera*

This is a light meal by itself. Add a scoop of canned or cooked salmon or tuna for variety and more protein. Experiment by adding a fresh vegetable or tossing with a different dressing. This is a great make-ahead dish. Serve at parties, or for a lazy Sunday brunch with a cool drink.

4 SERVINGS

> 3 potatoes, peeled and diced
> 1 small onion, peeled and chopped
> ½ cup chopped celery
> 1 cup basic Cuban dressing (see page 106)
> 4 lettuce leaves
> 4 tomatoes, chopped, for garnish
> 3 hard-boiled eggs (see page 201), sliced, for garnish

In a large casserole, boil 3 cups water and drop in the potatoes; cook for 20 minutes, until potatoes are tender. Remove from heat and drain. Cool to room temperature.

In a mixing bowl, combine potatoes, onion, and celery. Add the dressing, and toss lightly. Cover, and refrigerate until ready to serve.

Arrange the lettuce leaves in a shallow serving bowl. Spoon the cold salad into the center of the bowl, and garnish with the chopped tomatoes and hard-boiled eggs.

SAN PEDRO MIXED SALAD
ensalada mixta San Pedro

6 SERVINGS

> 2 small white cabbages
> 1 medium cucumber, diced
> 2 tomatoes, diced
> 2 bunches watercress, chopped
> One 8-ounce can sliced beets
> 1 small avocado, peeled and diced
> 2 cups basic vinaigrette (see page 107)

Shred cabbage by leaving long, loose heads whole and cutting across the leaves.

In a large mixing bowl, combine cabbage, cucumber, tomatoes, watercress, beets, and avocado.

Add the dressing, and toss. Serve immediately.

NOTE You can add steamed carrots to this salad for another pop of color.

CREAMED POTATO SALAD
ensalada de papas a la crema

This salad is ideal with most fish dishes. You can also pipe low-fat sour cream on top of this dish for an easy, attractive garnish. Pipe it in a pretty pattern. Piping is not just for cake decorating but looks great on salads and even soups.

4 SERVINGS

> 2 pounds potatoes, peeled and diced
> 1 teaspoon salt
> 1 small onion, peeled and chopped
> 1 small green bell pepper, seeded and chopped
> 2 cups cream cheese, softened
> ½ cup mayonnaise
> Lettuce leaves for garnish

Put the potatoes in a large saucepan and cover with 8 cups cold salted water. Bring to a boil, and simmer until cooked by not mushy. Remove from heat and drain.

Place the potatoes in a large mixing bowl, and add the chopped onion and green pepper. Cover, and refrigerate for 1 hour.

In a food processor or blender, mix the softened cream cheese and the mayonnaise, and add to the refrigerated potato mixture. Toss, and refrigerate for another hour.

Garnish with lettuce leaves on a serving platter, and serve immediately.

CUBAN CHICKEN SALAD
ensalada de pollo a la cubana

This delicious salad reminds me of birthday parties where both kids and mothers enjoyed it, accompanied by guava pastries (see variation on page 387) and croquettes (see pages 36–40). Today, I serve this chicken salad as an entrée with chicken or ham croquettes.

10 SERVINGS

> Two 2- to 3-pound chickens, quartered
> 1½ cups (3 sticks) butter
> 1 teaspoon salt, plus more to taste
> 2 pounds potatoes, peeled and diced
> 1 large apple, peeled, cored, and diced
> 2 hard-boiled eggs (see page 201), chopped
> ½ cup chopped celery
> ½ cup pitted and chopped Spanish green olives
> 2 cups mayonnaise
> One 8-ounce can or jar asparagus for garnish, liquid reserved
>   (optional)
> 1 cup roasted sweet red peppers, cut into julienne strips,
>   for garnish, liquid reserved (optional)
> 1 cup sweet green peas (petits pois; canned are okay) for garnish

Preheat oven to 325 degrees.

Arrange the chicken in a single layer in a large, shallow baking pan, and

(continued on next page)

(continued from previous page)

spread the butter on top. Bake in oven for 1 hour. Baste with butter often, to avoid drying out.

Meanwhile, put the potatoes in a large saucepan, and cover with 6 cups cold salted water. Bring to a boil, and simmer for 20 minutes. Remove from heat and drain.

When chicken is fully baked, allow to cool to room temperature, and shred into bite-sized pieces, making sure to remove all bones. If you like, you can leave some bits of skin for extra flavor.

Combine the chicken and potatoes in a large bowl, and add the rest of the ingredients except garnishes. For extra-moist chicken salad, add the liquid from the asparagus and from the roasted sweet pepper.

Toss well, and refrigerate, covered, for at least 4 hours. Taste, and correct seasoning before garnishing.

For a gathering or for a special family meal, arrange the salad on a bed of lettuce on a large serving platter, and garnish with the peas, asparagus, and roasted peppers in a pleasing design.

NOTE If you like, you can add a peeled and chopped onion and/or a seeded and chopped green bell pepper. If kids are included in the party or meal, skip these ingredients.

TOMATO SOL SALAD *ensalada de tomate sol*

The word *sol* means "sun" in Spanish. This salad is perfect for those hot, sunny summer days, to help you refresh and rejoice.

4 SERVINGS

> 3 small potatoes, peeled and diced
> 1 teaspoon salt, plus more to taste
> 1 small onion, peeled and chopped
> ½ cup diced celery
> Oil and vinegar to taste
> Pepper to taste
> 4 lettuce leaves
> 4 tomatoes, quartered
> 3 hard-boiled eggs (see page 201), halved

Put the potatoes in a large saucepan, and cover with 4 cups cold salted water. Bring to boil, and simmer for 20 minutes. Remove from heat and drain.

In a mixing bowl, combine the potatoes with the onion and celery. Toss with the oil and vinegar, and add salt and pepper.

Arrange on a bed of lettuce on a serving platter, garnished with the tomatoes and hard-boiled eggs. Serve at room temperature, and provide your guests with extra oil and vinegar or any of our great Cuban dressings (see pages 106–109).

HOLY FRIJOLES SALAD

Aaron Freedman is a special man—friendly, courteous, and always happy about life. It turns out he is quite a chef and caterer, too. He started his business, Sidewalk Salads, selling his salad creations on the sidewalks of downtown Miami. His business evolved into a full catering operation, and today he is proud to cater the best parties in Miami. He later joined a friend and competing chef who sold crêpes, also on the sidewalks of downtown Miami. Together they opened up their own restaurant, Sidewalk Crêpes and Salads. This is one of Aaron's Cuban salads—a great side dish, and a play on the classic rice-and-beans recipe. It is best served at room temperature or cold, so it can easily be made in advance.

10 SERVINGS

(continued on next page)

(continued from previous page)

FOR DRESSING

Salt and pepper to taste

1/4 cup lemon juice

1/4 cup white vinegar

5 garlic cloves

1 cup mayonnaise

3 bunches cilantro, chopped

3 cups vegetable oil

FOR SALAD

2 pounds orzo, cooked, drained, and rinsed

Two 15-ounce cans black beans, drained and rinsed with
cold water

1 cup corn kernels, frozen or canned, drained

4 tomatoes, diced

1 teaspoon ground cumin

1/4 cup chopped fresh cilantro

1–2 cups Green Goddess dressing (see above)

Prepare dressing: Combine the salt, pepper, lemon juice, vinegar, garlic cloves, mayonnaise, and cilantro in a food processor. Process for 1 minute, shut off the motor, scrape down the sides of the bowl, and process for another 20 seconds.

Gradually add the oil in a slow, steady stream. Whisk to blend, and serve or store.

Prepare salad: In a large mixing bowl, combine the orzo, black beans, corn, and tomatoes. Season with cumin, and add the cilantro.

Pour the Green Goddess dressing over the salad and toss gently. Refrigerate, covered, for at least 1 or 2 hours.

CUBAN
EGG RECIPES
platos rápidos con huevos

EGGS ARE not usually part of a Cuban breakfast. Cubans don't like to mess with their daily ritual of toasted Cuban bread and *café con leche* (see page 406). Even croquettes are a more common breakfast dish for us than eggs. But eggs make elegant dishes, and omelettes are always welcome on top of a *palomilla* steak (see pages 261–263), a special combination called *palomilla a caballo* (*palomilla* steak on horseback). To enjoy these and other egg dishes at lunch, brunch, or even dinner, try pairing with tropical juices or milkshakes and a light garden salad. Use fresh eggs. When making omelettes or *pistos,* to achieve a soft, fluffy texture, do not overbeat. The possibilities for egg dishes are endless!

PERFECT HARD-BOILED EGGS
huevos duros perfectos Hilda Ortiz

My sister-in-law, Hilda Ortiz, is a super-detail-oriented person who happens to make perfect hard-boiled eggs. Her method helps keep the eggs from cracking while they cook. She used to put a hard-boiled egg in her daughter's lunch box every day for extra nutrition. I imagine she will now do the same in her granddaughter's lunch bag, when *she* starts school. Hilda always told me that, even if they do not eat the rest of their lunch, she can be sure the kids are well fed if they have one of her hard-boiled eggs every day. People used to be scared of eating eggs because of the high cholesterol in the egg yolk, but now research has shown that eggs also raise the good cholesterol that

(continued on next page)

(continued from previous page)

bodies need. So, after all, my sister-in-law, the great Cuban mom and grandmom, was absolutely right. We love to have her hard-boiled eggs at all family brunches.

3 SERVINGS

6 eggs

Place the eggs in a single layer in a saucepan and cover with at least 2 inches of cold water.

Over high heat, bring the eggs to a boil. As soon as the water starts to boil, remove the pan from the heat for a few seconds while you reduce the heat to low. Return the pan to the heat, and let simmer for about 3 minutes.

Remove the pan from the heat, and cover. Let the pan sit for about 10 minutes.

Remove the eggs from the pan with a slotted spoon, and place them in a bowl of ice water. Once they have cooled, drain the eggs and store in a covered container in the refrigerator. Use them that very same day, or keep for a couple of days for any other use or recipe. Crack and peel at will!

CUBAN CREAMED EGGS *huevos a la crema*

Cuban bread (see page 78) and a great salad are all you need to make this a wonderful dinner or lunch for loved ones or guests.

4 SERVINGS

5 slices enriched white or whole-wheat bread, cubed
2 cups whole or skim milk
8 eggs
¼ cup shredded cheddar cheese
2 teaspoons butter
1 teaspoon fresh chopped parsley
Salt and pepper to taste
Zest of 1 lemon, grated (see page 345)

Over medium heat, simmer the bread cubes in a large skillet with 1 cup of the milk for about 10 minutes, until you get a purée.

Lower the heat, beat six of the eggs, and pour in all at once. Add the cheese. As the bottom of the omelette begins to set, lift it with a fork to allow the uncooked egg to run underneath.

Once the egg mixture is done to your liking (don't worry if your omelette is not too neat and tidy), remove from the heat, let cool slightly, and cut into squares.

In another saucepan, melt the butter, add the parsley, and season with the salt and pepper. Sprinkle with lemon zest. Beat the remaining two eggs and add them and the remaining cup of milk to the butter mixture, and simmer slowly for 15 minutes. Stir occasionally.

Pour on top of the squares of the original omelette. Serve immediately.

GUAJIRA EGGS *huevos a la guajira*

Guajira (female) or *guajiro* (male) is Cuban slang for a woman or man from the countryside. But it means so much more! It is also a genre of music (much like American country-and-western sound) and it represents simplicity, humility, and Creole, or traditional, flavor. The so-called *guajiras* were among the prettiest of Cuban women, along with the *mulatas* (those who were racially mixed). All tastes and sounds that are *guajiro* are traditional and true to their roots. This wonderful, versatile dish is ideally enjoyed outdoors—at a picnic, or simply in your backyard—with some Cuban guitar music playing in the background. It's a great party dish!

4 SERVINGS

> 8 hard-boiled eggs (see page 201), chilled
> ¼ pound cooked sweet ham, minced
> 1 teaspoon yellow or Dijon mustard
> 1 cup mayonnaise
> Salt and pepper to taste
> Lettuce leaves for garnish
> 2 parsley sprigs for garnish

Peel the hard-boiled eggs. Cut in half lengthwise. Remove the yolks, smash them in a separate bowl, then add the ham, mustard, and mayonnaise. Season with salt and pepper. This will be your filling.

Fill each egg white with a spoonful of the filling, using a spoon or a pastry

(continued on next page)

(continued from previous page)

bag. The pastry bag gives you more precision, and you can make wonderful designs, but the spoon method works great and saves time.

Arrange on a bed of lettuce on a serving platter, and garnish with the parsley sprigs.

NOTE For a more country or *guajira* flavor, substitute minced cooked bacon pieces for the ham.

EGGS MÁLAGA STYLE *huevos a la malagueña*

Long live Mother Spain. Cubans know that somewhere in their ancestry were some Spaniards, and many of those ancestors came from Málaga, the heart of the sunny Costa del Sol and Andalusia, in the southern part of Spain. This is the land of matadors, flamenco dancers, and Gypsies—or *gitanos,* as we call them. We serve this dish to our soul mates and lovers in the morning.

4 SERVINGS

> **2 teaspoons butter**
> **¼ pound sweet or Serrano ham, diced**
> **NOTE** Serrano ham, a specialty ham that is cured in many parts of Spain, resembles its more famous Italian counterpart, prosciutto.
> **¼ pound shrimp, cooked, peeled, and deveined**
> **1 cup sweet green peas (petits pois; canned are okay)**
> **4 asparagus tips**
> **4 eggs**

Preheat oven to 325 degrees.

Lightly butter four individual (6-inch diameter) ovenproof round soufflé dishes or ramekins.

Place a spoonful of diced ham in each dish first. Layer with two or three shrimp, and then with a spoonful of peas. Next layer with an asparagus tip, and top by cracking an egg into each ramekin.

Bake in oven about 15 minutes, until the eggs are cooked to your liking. Serve immediately.

BAKED POPEYE EGGS *huevos al Popeye*

When I was growing up, all my aunts and uncles and other extended family members bemoaned the fact that I was "too *flaca*"—too skinny. They would always suggest to my mom that she make me "*huevos al Popeye,*" which was simply fresh spinach and eggs. I grew to love this dish growing up, and confess I fed it to my kids whenever I was able to see their rib cages!

4 SERVINGS

> **1 package fresh spinach, washed, or, if you must, frozen or canned**
> **2 teaspoons butter**
> **1 cup grated Parmesan cheese**
> **4 eggs, beaten**

Preheat oven to 350 degrees.

Butter a 10-inch square baking pan, and place the spinach in the bottom of the pan. Put dollops of butter on top, and sprinkle evenly with ½ cup of the grated Parmesan cheese.

Bake in oven for 10 minutes.

Once the cheese is melted over the spinach, remove pan from the oven. Pour the beaten eggs over the spinach mixture, and sprinkle with the remaining ½ cup of Parmesan cheese.

Bake again, still at 350 degrees, for another 12 minutes, or until eggs are cooked to your liking. Serve immediately.

CUBAN EGGS BENEDICT *huevos benedictinos*

This Cuban version of eggs Benedict has a few twists, including using a convenient and inexpensive deviled ham spread. If you have homemade ham salad, you can of course substitute it. Enjoy this one on a late Sunday morning, reading the paper and drinking a *café bon bon* (see page 407).

6 SERVINGS

(continued on next page)

(continued from previous page)

6 slices bran or whole-wheat bread
One small can deviled ham spread, or 1 cup homemade
   ham-salad spread
6 soft-boiled eggs (see page 210)
1 cup béchamel sauce (see page 109)
¼ cup chopped parsley

Preheat oven to 375 degrees.

Toast the slices of bread in toaster or oven, and cut into ½-inch-wide strips.

Spread the bread strips with the deviled ham paste, and place in a rectangular or round 9-inch baking pan. Bake in oven for 3 minutes.

Remove from the oven, and top with the soft-boiled eggs.

Top each egg with the béchamel sauce, and garnish by sprinkling on the chopped parsley. If you desire, you may return dish to oven for 1 more minute. Serve immediately.

EGGS AND MUSHROOMS *huevos con champiñones*

This is a great recipe for vegetarians or those who want a lighter meal at breakfast or lunch—or anytime. Try it with orange-carrot juice (see page 31). Serve with a salad or toasted Cuban bread (see page 78).

4 SERVINGS

4 teaspoons butter
2 cups sliced fresh mushrooms
8 eggs, beaten
Salt and pepper to taste

In a skillet, heat the butter and sauté the mushrooms for about 5 minutes, until golden. Remove from heat.

Place the mushrooms in a square or round 9-inch baking pan, and pour in the beaten eggs. Season to your liking with salt and pepper.

Bake in oven for about 12 minutes, until the eggs are cooked to your liking. Serve immediately.

EGGS AND ASPARAGUS *huevos con espárragos*

You may use canned artichoke hearts instead of asparagus for this recipe.

4 SERVINGS

> 1 stick (½ cup) butter
> 4 cups fresh or canned asparagus spears cut to 4 inches
> 8 eggs
> Salt and pepper to taste

Preheat oven to 350 degrees.

Use a little of the butter to grease a 9-inch baking pan. Add the asparagus pieces, and top with bits of butter.

Carefully crack the eggs (as if you were going to fry them in a pan) right on top of the asparagus, and season with salt and pepper.

Bake in the oven for about 15 minutes, or until the eggs are done to your liking. Serve immediately.

ONIONED EGGS *huevos encebollados*

The Spanish name for this recipe is very hard to translate literally. It is really eggs on a bed of onions, and the aroma and taste are intoxicating and can permeate your entire kitchen. Rave reviews are sure to follow.

4 SERVINGS

> 4 teaspoons butter
> 2 large onions, chopped
> 8 eggs
> Salt and pepper to taste
> ¼ pound sweet ham, diced
> 1 teaspoon chopped fresh parsley

Melt half the butter in a skillet over low heat, and add the chopped onions. Cook, stirring, over medium-high heat for 5 minutes, until golden. Be careful not to overcook.

Preheat oven to 350 degrees.

Lightly butter four individual (6-inch diameter) ovenproof round soufflé

(continued on next page)

(continued from previous page)

dishes or ramekins. Spoon the onion mixture evenly into each dish. Carefully crack two eggs into each dish as if you were going to fry the eggs in a pan. Season with salt and pepper.

Top with the ham, and sprinkle with chopped parsley. Add the remaining butter in dollops over each portion.

Bake in oven for about 15 minutes, or until eggs are done to your liking. Serve immediately.

BAKED SLICED EGGS *huevos en ruedas*

Start your day with this energizing and warming dish.

4 SERVINGS

> 8 hard-boiled eggs (see page 201), chilled
> 4 teaspoons olive oil, plus more for greasing pan
> 1 medium onion, peeled and chopped
> ¼ cup cracker meal or bread crumbs
> Salt and pepper to taste
> ¼ cup Cheddar cheese, shredded

Crack and peel eggs, and slice crosswise carefully and evenly. Set aside for later.

Preheat oven to 350 degrees.

In a skillet, heat 2 teaspoons of the olive oil and sauté the onion for about 5 minutes, until translucent. Do not brown or overcook.

Place the egg slices in a greased 9-inch baking pan, sprinkle with the remaining olive oil, and layer with the onion and cracker meal. Season with salt and pepper. Top with the shredded cheese.

Bake in oven for 10 minutes. Serve immediately.

HAVANA EGGS *huevos habaneros*

I know that if you like ethnic cooking you probably love making the famous Mexican *huevos rancheros.* Here is a Cuban version. Cuban cooking is not spicy at all, and hot sauce is hardly ever used—a big difference between Cuban and Mexican recipes. This dish is perfect for those lazy Sunday mornings when we wake up too late for a proper breakfast and too early for lunch. Enjoy a mojito (see page 14) before, and slices of *timba* (guava and *queso blanco;* see page 340) after, as dessert.

4 SERVINGS

> **8 hard-boiled eggs (see page 201), chilled**
> **1½ cups sofrito (see page 119)**
> **2 teaspoons butter, plus more for greasing pan**

Preheat oven to 350 degrees.

Peel the hard-boiled eggs. Cut in half lengthwise. Place in a greased 9-inch round or square baking pan. Dot with the butter.

Pour the sofrito on top of the eggs.

Bake in oven for 15 minutes, until the dish is warmed through. Serve immediately.

SOFT-BOILED EGGS *huevos pasados por agua*

The Spanish name for this recipe literally translates as "eggs passed through water," which describes just how we would like our soft-boiled eggs to come out each and every time. They're perfect for adding nutritional value to your favorite grilled steak. I love them with my *picadillo* (see pages 280–281). My mother-in-law, Gardenia, would have these eggs with half a loaf of Cuban bread (see page 78) as an early dinner.

NOTE   This little formula leads to the best soft-boiled eggs.

> Small eggs: boil about 2 minutes.
> Medium eggs: boil about 3 minutes.
> Large eggs: boil about 4 minutes.

4 SERVINGS

> **4 eggs**
> **1 teaspoon butter**
> **Salt and pepper to taste**

Place eggs in a saucepan with 4 cups cold water and cook over medium heat. When the water begins to boil, use the above table to time how long your eggs should boil. When done, remove from heat.

Remove the eggs from the pan with a slotted spoon, and place them in small cups. Crack the top of each egg, top with a drop of butter, and season with salt and pepper to taste. Serve immediately.

STUFFED EGGS *huevos rellenos*

Easy, fun, and tasty! Play with different ingredients in the stuffing. I love adding chopped pitted black olives with just a bit of mayonnaise.

4 SERVINGS

> **4 hard-boiled eggs (see page 201)**
> **¼ cup chopped fresh parsley**
> **4 teaspoons butter**
> **Salt and pepper to taste**
> **2 teaspoons ketchup**
> **Lettuce leaves for garnish**
> **Parsley sprigs for garnish**

Peel the hard-boiled eggs. Cut in half lengthwise. Remove the yolks, and smash them in a separate bowl. Add to them the chopped parsley and butter. Season with salt and pepper. This will be your filling.

Cook this filling over very low heat for a couple of minutes, to marry all the flavors. Add the ketchup, and remove from heat. Cool to room temperature.

Fill each egg white with a spoonful of the filling, and refrigerate.

Arrange on a bed of lettuce on a serving platter, and garnish with the parsley sprigs.

VICTORIAN EGGS *huevos victorianos*

If you like anchovies, this is a great recipe for you. My father, Manolo, used to substitute chopped canned sardines for the anchovies.

4 SERVINGS

> 8 hard-boiled eggs (see page 201)
> 1 tablespoon olive oil
> Two 2-ounce tins anchovies, chopped
> 1 cup chopped and pitted Spanish green olives
> ¼ cup chopped fresh parsley
> Salt and pepper to taste

Preheat oven to 350 degrees.

Peel the hard-boiled eggs. Cut in half lengthwise. Grease a 9-inch square or round baking pan with the olive oil and place the eggs inside.

Layer with the chopped anchovies and olives, and sprinkle with the chopped parsley. Season with salt and pepper.

Bake in the oven for 10 minutes, until the dish is heated through. Serve immediately.

EGGS YUMURÍ *huevos Yumurí*

The Yumurí Valley, in the province of Matanzas, is one of the most beautiful and signifi-
cant landscapes in Cuba. This dish honors its greenery and the beautiful river that runs
right into it. With this, you must have a *guarapo* (see page 32) or one of the delicious
tropical juices so native to the island as a refreshing drink.

4 SERVINGS

> 1 tablespoon olive oil
> 4 cups fresh or canned asparagus spears cut to 4 inches
> 2 cups Vedado District basic broth (see page 52)
> ¼ cup chopped fresh parsley
> 8 hard-boiled eggs (see page 201), chopped
> Salt and pepper to taste

In a skillet, heat the olive oil and sauté the asparagus pieces for about
5 minutes. Do not brown or overcook.

Add the broth and the parsley. Simmer uncovered for another 7 minutes,
until the broth is reduced.

Add the chopped hard-boiled eggs, and stir. Season with salt and pepper
to taste. Serve immediately.

NITZA VILLAPOL'S CUBAN SCRAMBLED EGGS *revoltillo cubano de Nitza Villapol*

This was the one dish that Nitza Villapol, a very famous Cuban TV chef, recommended
to all newlywed brides. She would always point to this as a very delicious and simple
way to a Cuban man's heart! Nitza Villapol was the Julia Child of Cuba. Her television
show in the 1950s gave rise to her great popularity, and to Cuban cooking as an art. Her
book *Cocina al Minuto* was a perennial wedding gift. As time went on, even Nitza had
to adapt her recipes to the scarcity of ingredients in revolutionary Cuba. Her recipes
for croquettes omitted the béchamel sauce and called for evaporated milk, and many
of her meat dishes began calling for the use of Spam. As the revolution wore on, eggs
were probably the only food not scarce in Cuba, so Nitza had a great repertoire of egg
recipes. It is said by many journalists that Nitza Villapol died a very bitter chef, because
she never received the worldwide recognition that she desired. If only she knew how
many mothers tell their Cuban American daughters, "This recipe comes directly from
Nitza Villapol."

These tender, creamy scrambled eggs are perfect for breakfast, but you can also add herbs, cooked diced vegetables, or a little grated cheese for lunch or dinner. I love to surprise my family and fold peeled cooked shrimp into scrambled eggs. Be sure to accompany with a tropical mango *batido* (see page 28).

4 SERVINGS

> **8 eggs**
> **½ cup milk or cream**
> **Salt and pepper to taste**
> **4 teaspoons butter**

Break the eggs into a bowl, and add the milk and the salt and pepper. Beat the eggs with a fork until they are well blended.

Melt the butter in a skillet over moderately low heat (make sure that it covers the bottom of the skillet generously), and pour in the beaten eggs.

Cook over low heat, stirring and scraping and turning the eggs over, for about 5 minutes, or until they are softly set and still moist.

NOTE The eggs will continue to cook after being removed from the heat, so undercook them slightly even if you prefer your eggs firmer.

CUBAN TORTILLAS
tortillas

The Cuban tortilla is nothing like the Mexican tortilla, which is a flatbread made from corn or wheat. In Cuban cooking, a tortilla is a flat, round Spanish-style omelette. The Spanish tortilla (not to be confused with the Spanish omelette served in diners in the States) is the most popular, and it is a wonderful *tapa* appetizer. My family's favorite tortilla/omelette is the sweet plantain omelette (see page 158).

Another one often found in restaurants is *tortilla de chorizo*—chorizo omelette. You can create your own variations, following the same precedures.

SPANISH OMELETTE *tortilla a la española*

A classic entrée that you can make at home! Cuban cooks do not fold or roll omelettes. We love our flat omelettes as much as Italians love their frittatas. A flat omelette is thicker than a folded omelette, and is usually cut into wedges; it can be served hot, warm, or even cold.

4 SERVINGS

> 8 eggs
> 1 teaspoon baking powder
> Salt and pepper to taste
> 1 cup sweet green peas (petits pois; canned are okay)
> 2 teaspoons butter or olive oil

Break the eggs into a bowl with the baking powder, and season with salt and pepper. Beat lightly with a fork, and add the sweet green peas.

In a skillet over medium-low heat, melt the butter. Tilt and rotate the skillet to coat the bottom and the sides as well.

When the butter is sizzling, pour in the egg mixture, and once again tilt and rotate the skillet, to spread the eggs in an even layer over the bottom. Reduce the heat, and cook for 5 minutes. When the base of the omelette starts to set, use a spatula to lift the cooked base and tilt the skillet so the uncooked egg mixture runs underneath, onto the pan bottom. Continue cooking the same way for another 5 minutes. Place a large plate over the frying pan, invert the omelette onto the plate, and slide it, uncooked side down, back into the skillet. Return to heat and cook for about 5 minutes. This will ensure a moist, creamy, but fully cooked omelette. Serve immediately, or just save for a later time in the day.

EGG SOUFFLÉ OMELETTE *tortilla de huevo suflé*

Cubans have always admired French culture. Today many exiles have found refuge in Paris, where they roam the streets and cafés in haute-couture *guayaberas*. Enjoy this recipe with some croissants with cream cheese and guava jelly (found in the Hispanic aisle of your supermarket). Follow it up with *café bon bon* (see page 407).

4 SERVINGS

> **8 eggs**
> **1 tablespoon sugar**
> **1 teaspoon flour**
> **Juice of 1 lemon**
> **Salt and pepper to taste**
> **1 teaspoon baking powder**
> **1 cup béchamel sauce (see page 109), warmed**

Separate the eggs. To the yolks add the sugar, flour, lemon juice, salt, and pepper. Beat until thick.

Beat or whisk the egg whites until they hold stiff peaks, add the baking powder, and continue mixing. Fold the egg whites into the yolk mixture as lightly as possible.

Pour into a skillet, and cook over medium heat for about 15 minutes, until golden. You may transfer the skillet to a 350-degree oven for about 5 minutes for an extra-golden color.

Pour the béchamel sauce over the omelette just before serving.

PISTOS

I love our Cuban *pisto*. There is something magical about mixing great vegetables, meats, and seafood together. It is an excellent entrée, one that can be enjoyed by the entire family. The secret to a great *pisto* is the freshness of the ingredients. So, if you are eco-minded and have a vegetable patch, a *pisto* is the best showcase for your crops. Enjoy with a glass of wine and a green salad, and *dale* (our own word for *voilà*)!

PISTO
4 SERVINGS

> ½ pound potatoes, peeled and cut into julienne strips
> ½ cup extra-virgin olive oil
> 8 eggs
> 1 teaspoon baking powder
> ¼ cup sofrito (see page 119)
> ¼ pound cooked Virginia ham, diced
> ½ cup sweet green peas (petits pois; canned are okay)
> Salt and pepper to taste

In a large skillet over medium heat, fry the potatoes in about half of the olive oil until golden. Remove potatoes with a slotted spoon and lay on paper towels to absorb excess oil.

Break the eggs into a mixing bowl, and add the baking powder, sofrito, ham, sweet green peas, and, finally, the potatoes. Mix lightly and season with salt and pepper.

Heat the remaining olive oil in a skillet over medium heat, and pour in the egg mixture. Cook for 10 to 15 minutes, stirring and tossing constantly, so mixture will not stick. Serve immediately.

RAQUEL'S PISTO MANCHEGO
pisto manchego de Raquel

Straight from Castilla–La Mancha, Spain, this easy recipe lends itself to substitutions and variations. Don't be put off by the number of ingredients and steps. Create your own *pisto,* and give it your own name. This one is uniquely mine!

6 SERVINGS

> ½ pound potatoes, peeled and cut into julienne strips
> ¼ pound pork tenderloin, cubed
> ¼ pound cooked Virginia ham, diced
> ½ cup vegetable oil
> 1 large onion, peeled and chopped
> 3 garlic cloves, minced
> 1 green bell pepper, seeded and chopped

½ cup tomato sauce

¼ cup dry white wine

½ pound shrimp, boiled, peeled, and deveined

10 eggs, beaten

Salt and pepper to taste

One 8-ounce can asparagus tips, drained

½ cup sweet green peas (petits pois; canned are okay)

6 slices bread (French or Cuban, preferably), toasted

1 cup roasted sweet red peppers, cut into julienne strips

In a medium skillet over medium heat, fry the potatoes, pork tenderloin cubes, and diced ham in about half the vegetable oil. Set aside.

In another skillet over medium heat, sauté the onion, garlic, and green pepper in the remaining oil for about 5 minutes. Add the tomato sauce and wine. Cook for another 4 or 5 minutes, stirring once in a while. Add the cooked potatoes, pork, and ham, and continue stirring for 1 or 2 minutes. Then add the shrimp and the eggs, and season with salt and pepper.

Lower the heat, and let the mixture cook, stirring constantly, till the eggs have set. Now add half the asparagus tips and peas. Continue cooking and stirring until eggs are done to your liking. Don't let them dry or become stiff!

Serve immediately over toasted bread, and garnish with the remaining asparagus tips and peas, and with the roasted peppers.

MIXED PISTO *pisto mixto*

4 SERVINGS

> ¼ pound potatoes, peeled and cut into julienne strips
> 1 tablespoon olive oil
> Salt to taste
> ¼ pound beef tenderloin, cubed
> 8 eggs
> ½ pound shrimp, boiled, peeled, and deveined
> Salt and pepper to taste
> 2 teaspoons butter
> 1 cup sofrito (see page 119)

In a large skillet over medium heat, fry the potatoes in olive oil until golden. Remove potatoes with a slotted spoon and lay on paper towels to absorb excess oil.

Boil 2 cups salted water in a saucepan, and boil the beef for 7 minutes. Drain and set aside.

Break the eggs into a mixing bowl, and add the boiled shrimp, beef cubes, and fried potatoes. Mix lightly, and season with salt and pepper.

Melt the butter in a skillet over medium heat, and pour in the egg mixture. Add the sofrito, and cook for 10 to 15 minutes, stirring and tossing constantly, so mixture will not stick, till eggs are done to your liking. Serve immediately.

FISH PISTO *pisto de pescado*

It is common knowledge that the Cuban sea is in excellent condition. The high degree of conservation of its coral formations yields an exciting variety of underwater life. This *pisto* makes use of the best tropical fish and other seafood. Choose a white fish like tilapia or even cod for this recipe.

4 SERVINGS

> **Salt to taste**
> **½ pound skinless, boneless white fish fillets, cut into pieces**
> **½ pound fresh shrimp, peeled and deveined**
> **½ pound clams, scrubbed, shucked, and coarsely chopped**
> **2 teaspoons butter**
> **10 eggs, beaten**
> **1 teaspoon baking powder**
> **¼ cup milk**
> **½ cup sofrito (see page 119)**

Boil 4 cups salted water in a large saucepan. Add the fish, shrimp, and clams, and cook gently for about 6 minutes. Drain and set aside.

Melt the butter in a skillet over medium heat, and pour in the beaten eggs. Cook for about 1 minute, and add the boiled fish, shrimp, and clams and the baking powder. Add the milk and the sofrito, stirring constantly. Simmer for another 10 minutes. Serve immediately, and enjoy the catch of the sea.

TROPICAL
CATCH OF THE DAY
con el sabor del Mar Caribe

ERNEST HEMINGWAY immortalized the thrill of deep-sea fishing off the island of Cuba. His *Old Man and the Sea* captures the wonderful flavors of the yellowtail grouper, red snapper, and multicolored mahi mahi. But the varieties of Caribbean fish are endless. Some other favorites are kingfish, swordfish, bass, trout, and of course cod. Among the shellfish, Cuban recipes call for crabmeat, lobster, blue crab, and shrimp. Most fish are seasonal, so learn what you can substitute, and follow a very simple, crucial rule: Make sure it's fresh. That's all!

In our family, we all fish, snorkel, and dive. We are in glory when it is lobster season in the Florida Keys. We love to cook fish at home, Cuban style, and we love to go to our favorite fish market in Miami and eat the freshest catch there on the spot. My husband, Rogelio, an avid angler, took me to La Camaronera—a restaurant and market owned by the García brothers, who own a fleet of fishing vessels—for our first date. We still frequent it and stand in line to eat standing up (there are no chairs) the freshest fish that you can imagine. The best way to store fish at home is on ice, just as the markets do. Bring your fish home, rinse under cold water, and store in a plastic bag on a bed of ice until you are ready to cook—that very same day. Don't delay, and do enjoy.

JERKED CODFISH *aporreado de bacalao*

Salt cod, or *bacalao*, goes back to the days when it was used to provision the wooden ships that crossed the Atlantic to the New World. Once cheap and plentiful, it is now considered a delicacy and is often sold in gourmet markets, in small quantities, already soaked. It is much more fun and definitely cheaper when found in its original kite shape, whether in your regular supermarket or in your neighborhood bodega. The taste is pungent and salty. Salt cod needs to be soaked in several changes of water for about 24 hours, because it rehydrates to about three times its volume. The finished product should be a bit chewy, so don't oversoak.

4 SERVINGS

> **1 pound salt cod**
> **3 tablespoons olive oil**
> **1 medium onion, peeled and chopped**
> **2 garlic cloves, minced**
> **1 medium green bell pepper, seeded and cut into julienne strips**
> **1 cup tomato sauce**
> **Salt and pepper to taste**
> **2 bay leaves**
> **¼ cup dry white wine**
> **1 cup roasted sweet red peppers, cut into julienne strips**
> **6 eggs, beaten**

Soak the codfish in a large bowl of water for 24 hours in the refrigerator, changing the water every few hours.

Drain the cod, and put it in a large saucepan with another 3 cups water. Bring to a boil over high heat, and right at the boiling point, lower heat, cover, and allow to simmer slowly for 15 to 20 minutes, until it flakes easily.

When the fish begins to soften, remove from heat and drain. When it has cooled to room temperature, shred into bite-sized pieces, making sure you remove and discard any bones.

In a large skillet, heat olive oil over medium heat, and sauté the onion, garlic, and green pepper for 5 to 7 minutes. Add the tomato sauce, salt, pepper, bay leaves, wine, and half the roasted red peppers with all their liquid, and simmer for a few more minutes. Add the cod, and cook over low heat for about 20 minutes, stirring constantly.

(continued on next page)

(*continued from previous page*)

When the cod is nice and soft and fragrant, pour in the beaten eggs, and stir until well mixed. Cook for an additional 2 minutes. Remove from heat, and garnish with the remaining red peppers. Accompany with bread, and serve immediately.

CODFISH VIZCAYA STYLE *bacalao a la Vizcaína*

This was the twentieth-century Spanish poet Federico García Lorca's favorite dish. García Lorca used to hang out at La Zaragozana, a restaurant founded in 1830 in Havana. Folks claim he used to spend half his time reciting poetry in the kitchen, entertaining the chefs as they cooked him this wonderful Spanish dish.

4 SERVINGS

> 1 pound salt cod
> 1 teaspoon all-purpose flour
> 1 tablespoon olive oil
> 1 onion, peeled and chopped
> 2 garlic cloves, minced
> 1 green bell pepper, seeded and chopped
> 1 cup tomato sauce
> Salt and pepper to taste
> 1 parsley sprig, chopped
> ¼ cup dry white wine
> One 12-ounce jar roasted sweet red peppers, mashed or
>   puréed in their liquid
> 4 hard-boiled eggs (see page 201), sliced, for garnish
> 4 slices Cuban bread (see page 78) for garnish

Soak the codfish in a large bowl of water for 24 hours in the refrigerator, changing the water every few hours.

Drain the cod, and put it in a large saucepan with another 3 cups water. Bring to a boil over medium heat, and right at the boiling point, lower heat, cover, and allow to simmer slowly for about 10 minutes.

When the fish begins to soften, remove from heat and drain. When it has cooled to room temperature, tear into bite-sized pieces, making sure you remove and discard any bones. Lightly dredge the pieces in flour, and shake off any excess.

In a large skillet, heat olive oil over medium heat and sauté the onion, garlic, and green pepper for 2 to 3 minutes. Add the lightly floured salt-cod pieces, tomato sauce, salt, pepper, parsley, wine, and red peppers, and simmer for about 20 minutes.

Remove from heat. Transfer to a serving platter and garnish with sliced eggs and bread. Serve immediately.

CAYO LARGO STUFFED GROUPER
pargo relleno Cayo Largo
6 SERVINGS

FOR FISH

>One 8- to 10-pound grouper or red snapper
>4 garlic cloves, minced
>Salt and pepper to taste
>Juice of 2 lemons
>2 medium onions, peeled and thinly sliced
>2 medium green bell peppers, seeded and cut into julienne strips
>4 medium potatoes, peeled and thinly sliced

FOR STUFFING

>2 pounds shrimp, cooked and peeled
>1 pound lobster meat, cooked
>½ pound sweet ham, diced
>½ stick (4 tablespoons) butter, plus more for greasing the pan
>1 large onion, peeled and chopped
>2 teaspoons lemon juice
>¼ cup dry white wine
>1 teaspoon Worcestershire sauce
>2 teaspoons all-purpose flour

(continued on next page)

(continued from previous page)

Clean, scale, gut, and trim fish. Open the cavity lengthwise, and remove and discard bones.

Season and marinate fish on the outside and inside the cavity with garlic, salt, pepper, and lemon juice (see page 105). Cover the outside of the whole fish with onion slices and green pepper strips. Allow to marinate, refrigerated, for at least 3 hours.

Meanwhile, get the stuffing ready: Grind the shrimp, lobster, and ham in a food processor or blender, and reserve this mixture. Melt 2 tablespoons of the butter in a skillet over medium heat. Add the onion and the shrimp, lobster, and ham mixture. Sauté for about 8 minutes. Add the lemon juice, wine, Worcestershire sauce, and flour, stirring frequently. Remove from heat, and let cool to room temperature.

Preheat oven to 375 degrees.

Stuff the cavity of the fish, and close with skewers, toothpicks, or string.

Place your stuffed fish in a greased baking pan on a layer of sliced potatoes. Cover with the same onion and pepper slices used to marinate, and bake in oven for about 1½ hours. Cover with aluminum foil for the first 45 minutes. Melt the remaining butter and baste the fish often with it. To determine whether fish is properly cooked, make a small slit in the thickest

secrets of a Cuban cook

HOW TO CLEAN, SCALE, GUT, AND TRIM FISH

There is nothing more magical than cooking and eating your own catch. But be ready to do some prep work. First scrape off the scales with a dull knife. Then spread the abdominal cavity with your fingers and drag the entrails out (gutting your fish). Follow this by rinsing the cavity out with a good stream of water, and wash the skin while you are at it. Last, if the fish is to be cooked whole, leave the fins, tail, and head, but trim them in order to keep the shape intact in the oven. When cleaning fish, always use a clean surface or the kitchen sink. One great way to carry out this chore is to take it outside, to your backyard if possible—less mess and more fun! And for those of you who don't want to get your hands dirty, remember, the fish market will always do it for you.

part. Lift skin with a knife or fork and look into the opening. The flesh should still be a bit translucent, but you should be able to separate it into flakes. Basic rule: If you can separate the flakes, your fish is cooked. Remember that fish continues to cook even after you remove it from heat. Do not overcook—the fish will become dry. Serve immediately.

BAKED CUBAN FISH *pescado asado a la cubana*

This is so simple and so good.

6 SERVINGS

> One 8- to 10-pound fish, preferably snapper or grouper
> Juice of 1 lemon
> 1 medium onion, peeled and chopped
> 3 garlic cloves, minced
> 1 teaspoon dried oregano
> 2 bay leaves
> 1 teaspoon paprika
> Salt and pepper to taste
> 2 teaspoons white vinegar
> ¼ cup olive oil
> 1 red pepper, seeded and cut into julienne strips

Clean, scale, gut, and trim fish. Open the cavity lengthwise, and remove and discard bones (see page 224).

Season and marinate fish on the outside and inside the cavity with the rest of the ingredients except the red pepper (see page 105). Allow to marinate, refrigerated, for at least 3 hours.

Preheat oven to 325 degrees.

Bake in oven for at least 1 hour, basting frequently with the marinade liquid. Turn over twice, so it cooks and browns on both sides. Test for doneness. Basic rule: If you can separate the flesh into flakes, your fish is cooked. Remember that fish continues to cook even after you remove it from heat.

Garnish with the red pepper and serve immediately.

secrets of a Cuban cook

DEBONING FISH

Removing the small bones from a fish fillet is more easily done before the fish is cooked. Run your fingers against the grain of the flesh so that the bones protrude. Grab hold of each bone with a pair of needle-nose pliers, or even tweezers, and pull. Repeat and run your hand against the grain to feel for any remaining bones.

Removing the bones from a whole fish is easier after the fish is cooked. Use a small boning knife with a curved, thin blade. Set the fish on its side and insert the knife into the spine side, making a shallow slit down the spine from the tail to the head. Gently fold the skin back and lift the fillet off the bones. Then lift off the spine and discard the bones.

GRILLED FISH *pescado asado a la parrilla*

This recipe is great for an outdoor grill as well as for an indoor broiler. It's a tasty, light way to prepare fish.

6 SERVINGS

> One 8- to 10-pound fish, preferably snapper or grouper
> Juice of 1 lemon
> ¼ cup olive oil
> 1 parsley sprig, chopped
> Salt and pepper to taste
> ½ cup cracker meal

Clean, scale, gut, and trim fish (see page 224). Open the cavity lengthwise, and remove and discard bones.

Season and marinate fish on the outside and inside the cavity with lemon juice, olive oil, parsley, salt, and pepper (see page 105).

Sprinkle the entire outside of fish with cracker meal, and wrap in greased aluminum foil. Foods baked in aluminum foil retain their maximum moisture and flavor.

Place in outdoor grill or indoor broiler for about 25 minutes. Test for doneness by opening the packet a bit and following the basic rule: If you can separate the flesh into flakes, your fish is cooked. Remember that fish continues to cook even after you remove it from heat.

Transfer to a serving platter, and open the foil packet at the table. Serve immediately.

FISH COCO LOCO *pescado coco loco*

Use grouper, mahi mahi, or snapper. If you are lucky enough to find fresh wahoo, it is also a wonderful fish for this recipe.

4 SERVINGS

> **One 5- to 7-pound fish**
> **1 coconut**
> **6 slices bread (preferably Cuban bread)**
> **1 ripe plantain, peeled and mashed**
> **1 cup raisins**
> **½ cup pine nuts, toasted**
> **¼ cup dry white wine**
> **1 onion, peeled and finely chopped**
> **½ cup tomato sauce**
> **2 teaspoons sugar**
> **1 bay leaf**
> **1 parsley sprig, finely chopped**
> **Salt and pepper to taste**

Preheat the oven to 375 degrees.

Clean, scale, gut, and trim fish (see page 224). Open the cavity lengthwise, and remove and discard bones (see page 226). Set aside, covered.

Crack the coconut (see page 356), and pour coconut juice into a bowl. Soak the bread in the coconut juice, and transfer to a large saucepan. Add the mashed plantain, raisins, pine nuts, wine, onion, tomato sauce, sugar, bay leaf, and parsley. Season to taste with salt and pepper, and cook over low heat for about 20 minutes, stirring constantly. Drain and reserve any excess liquid. Reserve this mixture for stuffing the fish.

Meanwhile, pry the meat out of the coconut shells in chunks with a sturdy knife. Grate the meat with a shredder, or grate the coconut-meat chunks in a

(continued on next page)

(continued from previous page)

food processor. Reserve some shreds for garnish. For the rest, add a cup of water as you shred or grate. The coconut should have a creamy texture. Add to stuffing mixture.

Stuff the fish. Secure with skewers, toothpicks, or string, and transfer to a baking dish. Cover with reserved liquid, and bake in oven for about 1 hour. Test for doneness following the basic rule: If you can separate the flesh into flakes, your fish is cooked. Remember that fish continues to cook even after you remove it from heat. Transfer to a serving platter, garnish with coconut flakes, and serve immediately.

FISH WITH AVOCADO *pescado con aguacate*
4 SERVINGS

> 1 tablespoon olive oil
> 1 large onion, peeled and chopped
> 4 skinless snapper fillets (about 2½ pounds total)
> 2 cups avocado sauce (see page 108)

In a large skillet, heat the olive oil over medium heat and sauté the onion until translucent, 3 or 4 minutes.

Add the fillets, and sauté each side for about 3 minutes. When both onion and fish fillets are golden, remove from heat.

Serve with avocado sauce on top of or on the side of the snapper fillets.

LIEUTENANT REY'S FISH IN CREAM
pescado en crema Teniente Rey

Lieutenant Rey was Félix del Rey, the first lieutenant on the island of Cuba in 1781. Lore has it that he loved his fresh catch prepared this traditional way, because, after all, he was British.

4 SERVINGS

4 skinless snapper fillets (about 2½ pounds total)
1 pound clams, scrubbed, shucked, and coarsely chopped
½ pound small shrimp, peeled and deveined
Salt and pepper to taste
2 cups béchamel sauce (see page 109)
2 tablespoons cracker meal or bread crumbs

Bring 2 cups water to a simmer in a saucepan. Poach the fish fillets in this over medium-low heat until tender and flaky, no more than 5 to 7 minutes. Bring another 2 cups water to a boil in another saucepan, and simmer the clams and shrimp together over medium heat for about 10 minutes.

Preheat oven to 350 degrees.

When both fish and shellfish are tender and fully cooked, remove from heat, drain, and place in a glass baking pan. Season with salt and pepper, and spoon the béchamel sauce over everything. Sprinkle with the cracker meal or bread crumbs, and bake for about 12 minutes. When lightly browned on top, remove from heat and serve immediately.

PRETTY FISH FILLETS IN MILK
pescaditos en leche

This fish dish has a great aroma.

4 SERVINGS

4 skinless snapper fillets (about 2½ pounds total)
1 cup milk, whole or skim
Salt and pepper to taste
1 bay leaf
¼ stick (2 tablepoons) butter for greasing pan
4 egg whites
1 lemon, sliced, for garnish
1 cup pitted Spanish green olives for garnish

(continued on next page)

(continued from previous page)

Place the fish fillets in a saucepan, and cover with milk. Add the salt, pepper, and bay leaf, and poach over very low heat for about 10 minutes. Make sure that you don't overcook, and that the fillets retain their shape. Transfer to a baking pan greased with butter.

Preheat oven to 350 degrees.

Whisk the egg whites until they hold stiff peaks, and spoon them over the fish fillets.

Bake in the oven for about 15 minutes. Remove from oven, and garnish with lemon slices and olives. Serve immediately.

LA CORUÑA FISH IN PARSLEY SAUCE
pescado en salsa verde a la coruñesa

My father grew up in a coastal town in the north of Spain named La Coruña, which is still famous for this recipe. Serve the colorful dish with simple boiled potatoes. The taste of the sauce is strong but much subtler than that of Italian pesto.

4 SERVINGS

> 1 recipe green parsley sauce (see page 117)
> 2 tablespoons olive oil
> 4 skinless fish fillets (grouper, snapper, wahoo, or mahi mahi;
>   about 2½ pounds total)

Heat the olive oil in a large skillet over medium heat. Add the fish fillets. Cook the fish for 1 minute per side—do not overcook. Pour the parsley sauce over the fish fillets, cover, and simmer for about 15 minutes over low heat. Transfer to a serving platter, garnish as you like, and serve immediately.

ROGELIO'S FISH IN TOMATO SAUCE
pescado en tomate Rogelín

My husband, Rogelio, is an angler at heart. He loves to come home and cook what he catches. This is his special recipe. It is wonderful that he brings home the fish already cleaned, gutted, and in fillets!

4 SERVINGS

¼ stick (2 tablespoons) butter, for greasing pan
4 skinless white fish fillets (any fresh fish; about 2½ pounds total)
Salt and pepper to taste
1 cup tomato sauce
3 tablespoons dry white wine
1 teaspoon dried oregano
1 lemon, cut in half

Arrange the fish fillets in a greased shallow baking pan. Season with salt and pepper.

Preheat oven to 375 degrees.

In a mixing bowl, combine the tomato sauce, wine, and oregano. Pour over the fish fillets.

Bake in oven for 15 to 20 minutes. Test for doneness following the basic rule: If you can separate the flesh into flakes, your fish is cooked.

Transfer to a serving platter, and squeeze juice of one half of the lemon over the fish. Cut the other half into wedges and use as garnish. Serve immediately.

CUBAN SWORDFISH CEVICHE
pescado en escabeche

Ceviches have become very trendy. Chefs everywhere are experimenting with exotic combinations. The basic ingredient of ceviche is raw fish cut into bite-sized pieces and marinated in lime, salt, and other seasonings, and that has been true since the Incas.Ceviche is an old tradition in South America, on the premise that the lime marinade "cooks" the fish. Cuban cuisine gives it another twist in this *escabeche*. The fish is actually lightly floured and cooked for a few minutes before being marinated. (This makes for a safer dish, because marinades do not kill bacteria and parasites as well as heat does.) As always for ceviches as well as *escabeches,* it is important to start with the freshest, cleanest fish available. For this traditional dish, you can use virtually any white fish, including flounder, halibut, and cod. My mom used to make a huge batch of *escabeche* every month. It's a favorite dish all year round. The ceviche will keep for 2 days after its 3-day marination.

10 SERVINGS

(continued on next page)

(continued from previous page)

1½ cups all-purpose flour

3–4 pounds ½-inch-thich skinless fish fillets or steaks

1½ cups olive oil

Juice of 2 lemons

2 medium onions, peeled and cut into thin rings

2 green bell peppers, seeded and cut into julienne strips

1 cup Spanish green olives, pitted

½ cup capers

2 garlic cloves, minced

½ cup white vinegar

Salt and pepper to taste

Flour the fish fillets lightly. Heat ¼ cup of the oil in a large skillet over medium heat, and sauté the fish, turning frequently, for 3 or 4 minutes. Do not overcook. Remove the fish from the skillet, and drain on paper towels. Transfer to a wide, shallow bowl.

In a mixing bowl, combine the remaining olive oil, the lemon juice, onions, peppers, olives, capers, garlic, and vinegar. Season with salt and pepper, and pour over the fish. Cover tightly with plastic wrap or aluminum foil, and refrigerate for 3 days, basting occasionally. Serve at will!

CUBAN FISH HASH *picadillo de pescado a la cubana*

What a healthy way to enjoy hash!

4 SERVINGS

4 skinless fish fillets (grouper, snapper, or any other fresh fish; about 2½ pounds total)

1 small onion, peeled and chopped

1 parsley sprig, chopped

1 hard-boiled egg (see page 201), chopped

3 slices white bread

1 cup milk

Salt and pepper to taste

¼ teaspoon grated nutmeg
¼ cup vegetable oil
Juice of 2 lemons

Bring 3 cups water to a simmer in a saucepan, and poach the fish fillets over medium-low heat until tender and flaky, no more than 5 to 7 minutes. Remove from heat, and drain.

Transfer fish to a mixing bowl, and mash with a fork. Add the onion, parsley, and chopped hard-boiled egg, and mash together to mix.

In a separate bowl, soak the bread in the milk. Add to the fish mixture. Season with salt, pepper, and nutmeg. Mash the mixture again, and form it into 1-inch balls.

In a skillet, fry the fish balls in vegetable oil until they are golden, approximately 5 minutes. Remove, and drain on paper towels. Serve on a platter and top with lemon juice.

SHELLFISH CUBAN STYLE
mariscos a la cubana

Cuban cooking celebrates a wide variety of shellfish. Prevalent on our island and in our culture are the Creole recipes for shrimp, lobster, and crabs. Other popular shellfish include the blue crabs called *jaibas,* oysters, clams, and other mollusks. All these shellfish can be done *enchilado* style, which among Cubans refers not to a tortilla dish (as in Mexican cooking) but to a seafood stew flavored with sofrito (see page 119). These *enchilados* have to be accompanied by fluffy white rice (see page 160) and fried ripe plantains (see page 142). What a feast!

SHRIMP ENCHILADOS *camarones enchilados*

4 SERVINGS

> 4 tablespoons olive oil
> 4 garlic cloves, minced
> 1 medium onion, peeled and chopped
> 1 green bell pepper, seeded and chopped
> 2 pounds shrimp, shelled and deveined
> One 4-ounce jar whole sweet pimientos, drained,
>   cut into julienne strips
> 1 parsley sprig, finely chopped
> 1 cup tomato sauce
> ¼ cup dry white wine
> 1 bay leaf
> Salt and pepper to taste
> 1 teaspoon sugar

Heat the olive oil in a skillet over medium heat, and sauté the garlic, onion, and green pepper for about 5 minutes on high. Stir in the shrimp, red pepper, and parsley, and lower the heat. Sauté for 2 minutes more.

Stir in the tomato sauce, wine, and bay leaf. Cover, and simmer for about 15 minutes, stirring once in a while. Watch the shrimp for doneness, and don't overcook—they can become tough. Remove from heat, and remove the bay leaf. Season with salt and pepper, and add sugar.

Transfer to a serving platter, and garnish as you like. Serve on top of a mound of white rice, and enjoy with family and friends.

EL PATIO LOBSTER ENCHILADA
langosta enchilada El Patio

El Patio is a very famous and old restaurant in Havana. It was once an estate owned by Cuban nobility. *El marques de Aguas Claras* (in English, the marquis of Clear Waters) never imagined that his beautiful house overlooking the ocean would become the most romantic restaurant in Cuba. Enchilada and Creole recipes became the signature dishes of this great establishment.

This is one recipe where substitution just won't be the same—you must use Florida lobsters (see Resources, page 417).

secrets of a Cuban cook

COOKING LOBSTER AND OTHER SHELLFISH

When cooking lobster and other shellfish, if you keep them in the shell your recipe will be tastier. As a rule, lobster tails are cooked in the shell. So that the meat can be easily removed when served, crush shells slightly.

This Creole lobster dish is prepared exactly the same way as *camarones enchilados* (preceding recipe). The same goes for *cangrejos enchilados* (crab Creole) and *mariscos enchilados* (Creole shellfish; recipes follow). It is the most traditional and delicious way to cook our shellfish. Mix and match and you will find your perfect combination.

4 SERVINGS

> **4 or 5 Florida lobster tails (3 pounds total)**
> ½ **cup olive oil**
> **1 medium onion, peeled and chopped**
> **1 green bell pepper, seeded and chopped**
> **3 garlic cloves, minced**
> **1 parsley sprig, chopped**
> **1 cup roasted sweet red peppers, cut into julienne strips,**
>   **in their liquid**
> **1 cup tomato sauce**
> ¼ **cup ketchup**
> **1 teaspoon white vinegar**
> ½ **cup dry white wine**
> **Salt and pepper to taste**
> **1 teaspoon sugar**
> **1 bay leaf**
> **1 teaspoon Worcestershire sauce**
> **1 teaspoon Tabasco sauce (optional)**
> **4 cups cooked white rice (see page 160)**

With a sharp chef's knife, cut through the lobster tails (shells on) crosswise at each joint, to make 2-inch pieces. Use a toothpick to push out the reddish vein that runs down the back of each section of the tails.

(continued on next page)

(continued from previous page)

Heat the oil in a large, heavy skillet, and sauté the lobster pieces until the shells turn red, about 5 minutes.

Add the onion, pepper, garlic, and parsley, and continue cooking over medium heat, stirring, for about 3 more minutes, or until the onion becomes translucent.

Stir in the red peppers in their liquid as well as the tomato sauce, ketchup, vinegar, and wine. Season with salt and pepper, and add the sugar, bay leaf, Worcestershire sauce, and Tabasco sauce (if desired). Cover, bring to a simmer, reduce the heat to low, and cook gently for about 20 minutes, until the lobster meat is firm and opaque, stirring constantly. Once again, do not overcook. Remove from heat, discard the bay leaf, and serve over a mound of fluffy white rice.

secrets of a Cuban cook

CHOOSING LOBSTER

There are two types of lobsters available: clawed and spiny (or rock) lobsters. Florida lobsters are spiny; they are what we use in Cuban recipes. Most of the meat will be found in the tails. You are more likely to find spiny, rock, or Florida lobster in the Caribbean islands, anywhere in Florida, and on the West Coast of the United States or Canada. Frozen spiny lobster tails are available in most supermarkets. The meat in these will tend to be firm and stringy, good to eat, and not too expensive. You can also find Florida spiny lobster readily available online (see Resources, page 417).

CRAB CREOLE *cangrejos enchilados*

4 SERVINGS

> 4 or 5 soft-shell crabs
> ½ cup olive oil
> 1 medium onion, peeled and chopped
> 1 green pepper, seeded and chopped
> 3 garlic cloves, minced
> 1 parsley sprig, chopped
> 1 cup roasted sweet red peppers, cut into julienne strips
> 1 cup tomato sauce
> ¼ cup ketchup
> 1 teaspoon white vinegar
> ½ cup dry white wine
> Salt and pepper to taste
> 1 teaspoon sugar
> 1 bay leaf
> 1 teaspoon Worcestershire sauce
> 1 teaspoon Tabasco sauce (optional)
> 4 cups cooked white rice (see page 160)

Clean crabs, and wash well. Remove claws and shell, and pound claws slightly. Cut crabmeat into 1-inch pieces, and cut claws in half.

Heat the oil in a large, heavy skillet, and sauté the crab pieces with the claws until the shells turn red, about 5 minutes.

Add the onion, green pepper, garlic, and parsley, and continue cooking over medium heat, stirring, for about 3 more minutes, or until the onion becomes translucent.

Stir in the sweet red peppers as well as the tomato sauce, ketchup, vinegar, and wine. Season with salt and pepper, and add the sugar, bay leaf, Worcestershire sauce, and Tabasco sauce (if desired). Cover, bring to a simmer, and reduce the heat to low. Cook gently for about 15 minutes, until the crabmeat is firm and opaque, stirring constantly. Once again, do not overcook. Remove from heat, discard the bay leaf, and serve over a mound of fluffy white rice.

CREOLE SHELLFISH *mariscos enchilados*

4 SERVINGS

2 lobster tails
2 soft-shell crabs
½ cup olive oil
½ pound shrimp, peeled and deveined
1 medium onion, peeled and chopped
1 green bell pepper, seeded and chopped
3 garlic cloves, minced
1 parsley sprig, chopped
One 4-ounce jar whole sweet pimientos, drained, cut into
    julienne strips
1 cup tomato sauce
¼ cup ketchup
1 teaspoon white vinegar
½ cup dry white wine
Salt and pepper to taste
1 teaspoon sugar
1 bay leaf
1 teaspoon Worcestershire sauce
1 teaspoon Tabasco sauce (optional)
4 cups cooked white rice (see page 160)

With a sharp chef's knife, cut through the lobster tails (shells on) crosswise at each joint, to make 2-inch pieces. Use a toothpick to push out the reddish vein that runs down the back of each section of the tails.

Clean crabs, and wash well. Remove claws and shell, and pound claws slightly. Cut crabmeat into 1-inch pieces, and cut claws in half.

Heat the oil in a large, heavy skillet, and sauté the lobster and crab pieces and shells until the shells turn red, about 5 minutes. Stir in the shrimp, and sauté for a couple more minutes.

Add the onion, green pepper, garlic, and parsley, and continue cooking over medium heat, stirring, for about 3 more minutes, or until the onion becomes translucent.

Stir in the red peppers as well as the tomato sauce, ketchup, vinegar, and wine. Season with salt and pepper, and add the sugar, bay leaf, Worcestershire sauce, and Tabasco sauce (if desired). Cover, bring to a simmer, and reduce the heat to low. Cook gently for about 10 to 15 minutes, stirring constantly, until the shrimp is cooked but tender and the lobster and crabmeat are firm and opaque. Be careful not to overcook. Remove from heat, discard the bay leaf, and serve over a mound of fluffy white rice.

SHRIMP CAMAGÜEY *camarones al estilo Camagüey*

Camagüey, a province in Cuba, is famous for many historic cities, railroads, and its seafood. This recipe was born in that beautiful landscape. Serve this over white rice (see page 160) or pasta.

4 SERVINGS

> 5 teaspoons olive oil
> 2 pounds shrimp, shelled and deveined
> 1 cup sofrito (see page 119)
> 1 cup green peas
> One 4-ounce jar whole sweet pimientos, drained, cut into
>   julienne strips
> 1 parsley sprig, chopped
> 1 cup fish stock (see page 55)
> 1 tablespoon all-purpose flour
> Salt and pepper to taste

Heat the olive oil in a skillet over medium heat, and sauté the shrimp for about 5 minutes. Stir in the sofrito, and add the green peas, red peppers, and parsley.

Add the fish stock, bring to a simmer, and then reduce heat to low. Cook gently for 15 minutes, stirring occasionally. Add the flour toward the end, to make the sauce thicker. Season with salt and pepper.

Garnish as you like, and serve immediately.

SHRIMP IN WHITE SAUCE
camarones en salsa blanca
4 SERVINGS

> ¼ stick (2 tablespoons) butter
> 2 pounds shrimp, peeled and deveined
> Salt and pepper to taste
> Juice of 1 lemon
> 2 cups white sauce (see page 110)
> ½ cup shaved Parmesan cheese

Preheat oven to 350 degrees. Grease a baking pan with butter.

Arrange shrimp in the pan, and bake in oven for 10 minutes, until shrimp are opaque.

Remove from oven, season with salt and pepper, and sprinkle lemon juice over them. Cover shrimp with the white sauce, and top with the Parmesan cheese.

Return to oven for 3 to 5 minutes, until the cheese bubbles and the top is lightly browned. Serve immediately.

CORNMEAL AND CRABS 1830
harina con cangrejos 1830

This ancient recipe is the ultimate comfort food. *Harina* can mean cornmeal or corn flour, either yellow or white, fine-ground or coarse, precooked. It is found in the Hispanic aisle of your supermarket. But you can substitute polenta, or even grits! You can also substitute crabmeat or Alaskan king crab or even stone crab claws for the crabs, but the flavor of the shells is intense and provides the ultimate experience. Here is the traditional way of preparing this mouth-watering delight.

4 SERVINGS

4 or 5 soft-shell crabs
½ cup olive oil
2 medium onions, peeled and chopped
2 garlic cloves, minced
1 green bell pepper, seeded and chopped
1 cup tomato sauce
1 teaspoon white vinegar
12 cups water
2 cups precooked cornmeal (yellow or white), coarse if possible
Salt and pepper to taste

Clean crabs, and wash well. Remove claws and shell, and pound claws slightly. Cut crabmeat into 1-inch pieces, and cut claws in half. For extra flavor, cook the crab claw shells as well.

Heat the oil in a large, heavy saucepan and sauté the crab pieces until the shells turn red, about 5 minutes.

Add the onions, garlic, and green pepper, and continue cooking over medium heat for about 3 more minutes, or until the onions become translucent. Add the tomato sauce and vinegar, and cook, stirring constantly for a few more minutes.

Add the water and cornmeal, and reduce the heat to low, covering the pan. Cook for 1 hour, until the mixture is thick and creamy. Stir occasionally to prevent lumps. Season with salt and pepper to taste, and serve in bowls.

EL JARDÍN STUFFED CRABS
cangrejos rellenos El Jardín

This recipe comes from El Jardín, which has always been one of the most beautiful and best restaurants in the Vedado District. The dish is complicated but worth the effort.

4 SERVINGS

> 4 or 5 soft-shell crabs
> 1 cup milk
> 6 slices white bread, diced
> ½ cup sofrito (see page 119)
> ½ cup dry white wine
> 2 teaspoons butter, melted
> Salt and pepper to taste
> 1 tablespoon capers, mashed
> 3 hard-boiled eggs (see page 201), chopped
> Lettuce leaves for serving

Bring 3 cups water to a boil in a large saucepan, and add the crabs. Continue boiling for about 10 minutes. Remove from heat, and carefully pick the meat from the shells without breaking the shells.

Prepare the stuffing by soaking the crabmeat in the milk with the diced bread. Add the sofrito to this mixture, and then add the wine, butter, salt, pepper, capers, and eggs. Cook this mixture in a saucepan over very low heat for 5 to 7 minutes in order to merge all the flavors. Remove from heat, and let cool to room temperature.

Preheat oven to 450 degrees.

Stuff the shells with the crabmeat mixture, and bake in oven for about 5 minutes. Watch carefully. Remove from oven, transfer to a bed of lettuce leaves on a serving platter, and serve immediately.

OASIS GRILLED LOBSTER
langosta a la parrilla Oasis

When I was a child, El Oasis Hotel on Varadero Beach seemed to me timeless. Its dream beach of fine white sand was my playground on lazy summer days. The hotel still stands today. It was there that I first tasted the sweet flavor of grilled lobster. This simple recipe brings back memories, but, more important, it brings many compliments from family and friends.

Lobster dries out easily and becomes tough when overcooked, so be careful.

4 SERVINGS

> ½ stick (4 tablespoons) butter (preferably sweet cream)
> 1 parsley sprig, finely chopped
> 1 garlic clove, minced
> Juice of 1 lemon
> Salt and pepper to taste
> 4 lobster tails, uncooked, deveined (see page 195), split down
>   the back

Preheat the broiler, and set the broiler tray about 3 inches from the heat.

Melt the butter in a saucepan over medium heat. Add the parsley and garlic, and continue cooking for about 1 minute. Remove the pan from the heat, and add the lemon juice, salt, and pepper.

Arrange the lobster tails in a baking pan, cut side up, and spoon the butter mixture on top of shells.

Broil for about 4 minutes, until the top is slightly browned and the butter mixture is bubbling. Once again, be careful not to overcook, and rotate pan when necessary to brown evenly.

To eat, pull lobster meat out with fork (and wear a lobster bib!).

CHICKEN
THE CUBAN WAY
pollo a la cubana

WE CUBANS love our tropical chicken recipes. In addition to our many wonderful variations on *arroz con pollo* (see pages 163–168), we enjoy chicken in appetizers such as croquettes (see page 38) and *empanadas* (see pages 40 and 43), and as main dishes: as fricassee, in pot pies, in casseroles, and more. Chicken can make a hearty family meal, or an elegant party dish.

BOHÍO CHICKEN FRICASSEE

fricasé de pollo bohío

Nothing could be more typical of Cuban cooking than a chicken fricassee, and nothing is more typical of Cuba itself than a *bohío,* the traditional home of a Cuban farmer. Cuban artists always add a *bohío* to their landscape paintings. It is just a Cuban thing! And so is this recipe.

4 SERVINGS

> **One 3- to 4-pound chicken, cut into 8 pieces**
> **3 garlic cloves, minced**
> **Juice of 1 sour orange (see page 120)**
> **¼ cup olive oil**
> **1 medium onion, peeled and chopped**
> **1 medium green bell pepper, seeded and chopped**
> **1 parsley sprig, chopped**
> **1 cup tomato sauce**
> **2 cups chicken consommé (see page 54)**
> **1 cup diced cooked ham**
> **½ cup capers**
> **Salt and pepper to taste**
> **1 cup dry white wine**
> **½ pound potatoes, peeled and diced**
> **4 cups cooked white rice (see page 160)**

In a mixing bowl, combine the chicken pieces, garlic, and sour-orange juice. Toss, and marinate for at least 2 hours, covered, in the refrigerator.

Heat the oil in a large, heavy saucepan, and add the chicken pieces with their marinade. Sauté over medium heat until the chicken is browned on both sides, 6 or 7 minutes per side. Add the onion, green pepper, and parsley, and continue cooking for about 2 more minutes.

Stir in the tomato sauce, chicken consommé, ham, and capers. Season with salt and pepper, and stir in the wine. Add the potatoes.

Cover, bring to a simmer, and reduce the heat. Continue simmering until the chicken is cooked and the potatoes are tender, about 45 minutes. Stir occasionally, and correct the seasoning if necessary. When done, serve immediately over a bed of white rice.

CUBAN CHICKEN POT PIE *pastel de pollo*

This recipe is not for the novice cook. If you have a food processor, this is the perfect time to use it.

4 TO 6 SERVINGS

FOR THE PIE CRUST

> 3 cups all-purpose flour
>
> 2 teaspoons baking powder
>
> 2 teaspoons sugar
>
> Salt to taste
>
> ½ stick (4 tablespoons) butter or 5 teaspoons vegetable shortening
>
> 1 tablespoon white vinegar
>
> 2 egg yolks, plus (optional) 1 beaten egg for glazing crust
>
> 2 tablespoons water
>
> Flour for dusting

FOR THE FILLING

> 2 tablespoons olive or vegetable oil
>
> 1 large onion, peeled and chopped
>
> 1 garlic clove, minced
>
> 1 cup mixed vegetables such as carrots, green beans, celery, winter squash, diced
>
> 4 skinless, boneless chicken breasts, diced
>
> 1 cup chicken consommé (see page 54)
>
> ¼ cup dry white wine
>
> Salt and pepper to taste

Prepare the pie crust: Put the flour, baking powder, sugar, and salt in the food-processor bowl, and pulse for a few seconds to mix.

Put half of the butter in the food-processor bowl with the dry ingredients, and pulse for a few more seconds to mix.

Cut in the remaining half of the butter with the processor, making sure to leave visible chunks and not to overmix.

In a measuring cup, mix egg yolks and vinegar together, and chill for 3 or 4 minutes.

Put flour-and-shortening mixture from processor in a large mixing bowl, and sprinkle over it about 5 teaspoons of the egg-and-vinegar mixture, a little at a time, mixing gently with a fork. Add a few teaspoons of water, but make sure you do not end up with a wet dough.

Place the dough in plastic wrap or a plastic bag, and chill in the refrigerator for a few more minutes.

Prepare the filling: Heat oil in a large skillet over medium heat, and sauté the onion, garlic, vegetables, and diced chicken pieces until they brown slightly.

Add the chicken consommé and wine and season with salt and pepper. Bring the mixture to a boil. Reduce the heat, cover, and gently simmer until the chicken is tender. Remove from heat, and cool to room temperature.

NOTE You can also freeze the dough for up to 1 month and use at a later date.

TO ASSEMBLE PIE

Lightly flour a work surface and rolling pin. Roll prepared refrigerated dough, and separate into two equal parts. Roll one part out, and place into the bottom of a 9-inch round aluminum or glass pie plate. Roll out the second part of the dough and reserve.

Preheat oven to 350 degrees.

Pour the chicken filling into the bottom crust, stirring gently (so as not to damage the crust) until well distributed.

Place the second part of the rolled dough on top of the pie as the top crust, and mash the edges with a fork to seal them. Then, with a knife, make slits in the top crust to allow the pie to breathe.

Place pie on top rack in oven and bake for 1 hour, or until top crust is lightly browned. Cut into the crust to see if the filling is done all the way through. If not, lower temperature and bake for an additional 15 to 20 minutes.

NOTE For a beautiful golden pie crust, glaze with beaten egg before you bake.

secrets of a Cuban cook

HOW TO CUT IN SHORTENING BY HAND

Make sure the shortening is chilled but not too cold. You should be able to mold it with your fingers.

Mix the dry ingredients, including flour, according to your recipe.

Cut the shortening into large chunks.

Add the shortening all at once to the dry ingredients.

Mix the shortening with your hands so that each piece gets coated with dry ingredients. (You can also use a food processor to cut in shortening.)

Scoop up some of the coated pieces and loose flour. Rub the shortening pieces through your fingers, breaking them into smaller pieces.

Continue doing this until the mixture is loose, crumbly, but still coarse. Different-sized pieces of shortening, plus a small amount of loose flour, create the ideal texture,

Continue with your recipe.

MIDNIGHT CHICKEN PIE *pastel de medianoche*

This is another complex but wonderful dish. A delicious and nutritious snack at any time, worth the effort.

4 TO 6 SERVINGS

FOR THE PIE CRUST

> 3 cups all-purpose flour
> 2 teaspoons baking powder
> 2 teaspoons sugar
> Salt to taste
> ½ stick (4 tablespoons) butter or 5 teaspoons vegetable shortening
> 2 egg yolks, plus (optional) 1 beaten egg to glaze crust
> 1 tablespoon white vinegar
> 2 tablespoons water
> Flour for dusting

FOR THE FILLING

>   1 tablespoon mustard
>   ½ pound cooked sweet ham, sliced
>   ½ pound cooked pork, sliced
>   ½ pound cooked chicken breast, sliced
>   ½ pound Swiss cheese, sliced
>   ½ cup sliced sweet pickle

Prepare the pie crust: Put the flour, baking powder, sugar, and salt in the food-processor bowl, and pulse for a few seconds to mix.

Put half of the butter in the food-processor bowl with the dry ingredients, and pulse for a few more seconds to mix.

Cut in the remaining half of the butter very briefly with the processor, making sure to leave visible chunks and not to overmix.

In a measuring cup, mix egg yolk and vinegar together, and chill for 3 or 4 minutes.

Put flour-and-shortening mixture from processor in a large mixing bowl, and sprinkle over it about 5 teaspoons of the egg-and-vinegar mixture, a little at a time, mixing gently with a fork. Add a few teaspoons of water, but make sure you do not end up with a wet dough.

Place the dough in plastic wrap or a plastic bag, and chill in the refrigerator for a few more minutes.

NOTE You can also freeze the dough for up to 1 month and use at a later date.

TO ASSEMBLE PIE

Lightly flour a work surface and rolling pin. Roll prepared refrigerated dough, and separate into two equal parts. Roll one part out, and place into the bottom of a 9-inch round aluminum or glass pie plate. Roll out the second part of the dough and reserve.

Preheat oven to 350 degrees.

Spread mustard over the bottom crust evenly but gently, so as not to damage the crust. Next layer with the slices of ham, pork, chicken breast, Swiss cheese, and pickle.

(continued on next page)

(continued from previous page)

Place the second part of the rolled dough on top of the pie as the top crust, and mash the edges with a fork to seal them. Then, with a knife, make slits in the top crust to allow the pie to breathe.

Place pie on top rack in oven and bake for 1 hour, or until top crust is lightly browned. Cut into the crust to see if the filling is done all the way through. If not, lower temperature and bake for an additional 15 to 20 minutes.

NOTE For a beautiful golden pie crust, glaze with beaten egg before you bake.

COMPLETE CUBAN CHICKEN CASSEROLE
pollo a la completa

Cubans and Miamians alike tend to go into a restaurant and ask for the daily special, or *una completa,* literally "one complete." It is usually whatever the Cuban cook has put together for that day, offered at a very reasonable price. This dates back to the 1950s in Havana, where hordes of retail and factory workers would crowd the cafeterias during lunchtime and would have to wolf down a meal in a few minutes. Today you will find workers lining the sidewalks of downtown Miami or Hialeah (in the working-class factory city), clamoring for the complete meal of the day. This recipe is the true definition of *una completa.* If you are counting calories, serve over a bed of lettuce; if not, over a mound of white rice (see page 160) or yellow rice.

4 SERVINGS

One 2½- to 3-pound chicken, quartered
3 garlic cloves, minced
Juice of 1 sour orange (see page 120)
Salt and pepper to taste
2 teaspoons butter
½ pound ham, diced
1 medium onion, peeled and chopped
6 tomatoes, diced
One 12-ounce jar roasted sweet red peppers, cut into julienne
    strips, drained

1 parsley sprig, chopped

2 teaspoons oregano

½ cup capers

½ cup chopped and pitted Spanish green olives

½ cup sliced toasted almonds

2 cups chicken consommé (see page 54)

3 fried ripe plantains (see page 142)

In a mixing bowl, combine the chicken pieces, garlic, and sour-orange juice. Season with salt and pepper. Toss, and marinate for at least 2 hours, covered, in the refrigerator.

Heat the butter in a large, heavy saucepan, and add the chicken pieces with their marinade. Sauté over medium heat until the chicken is browned on both sides, 1 or 2 minutes per side. Add the ham, onion, tomatoes, red peppers, and parsley, and continue cooking for about 2 more minutes.

Stir in the oregano, capers, olives, and toasted almonds. Add the chicken consommé and simmer over low heat for about 40 minutes, or until the chicken is tender and the flavors are completely merged.

When the chicken is almost done, add the fried plantains and stir gently. Serve immediately as a one-dish meal.

secrets of a Cuban cook

Since we are using a whole chicken, this is the time to go over the rules for cleaning and preparing a chicken for cooking. Remember to wash your hands with soap and hot water, before and after, and please be sure that your utensils are also clean. Remove the giblets from the body cavity. The chicken itself should be thoroughly cleaned and rinsed, inside and out, under a cold running tap and patted dry with paper towels.

CHICKEN DEMIDOFF *pollo Demidoff*

Why would a chicken dish named after a Russian prince who was a patron of the arts be considered part of our Cuban cuisine? After much research, I have yet to find out. But this elaborate dish has an explosion of flavors that will thrill any palate.

4 SERVINGS

½ stick (4 tablespoons) butter

One 2- to 3-pound chicken, cut into 8 pieces

1 parsley sprig, chopped

½ pound carrots, peeled and diced

4 celery stalks, diced

1 large onion, peeled and chopped

3 garlic cloves, minced

Salt and pepper to taste

1 cup chicken consommé (see page 54)

½ cup dry white wine

5 ripe tomatoes, seeded and peeled

4 cups cooked white rice (see page 160)

¼ pound cooked ham, diced

1 cup cleaned and sliced mushrooms

1 tablespoon all-purpose flour

In a large saucepan over medium heat, melt the butter and sauté the chicken pieces until golden. Add the parsley, carrots, celery, onion, and garlic. Continue cooking, stirring often, for about 5 minutes, until the chicken is browned on both sides. Season with salt and pepper.

Add the chicken broth and wine, reduce the heat, and simmer for about 30 minutes. Add the tomatoes, and cook for an additional 10 minutes to integrate the flavors.

Transfer only the chicken pieces to the center of a serving platter and encircle with the ham and mushrooms. Surround with mounds of white rice.

Continue to simmer the sauce, and add flour to thicken. Bring just to the boiling point, and pour over chicken on serving platter or serve on the side.

CHICKEN IN A POT *pollo en cazuela*

This dish is perfect to make ahead for the work week—just refrigerate and store! Accompany with a loaf of homemade Cuban bread (see page 78) and a light Cuban salad (see page 195).

4 SERVINGS

> 1 teaspoon ground cumin
> 3 garlic cloves, minced
> Salt and pepper to taste
> One 2½-pound chicken
> Juice of 1 sour orange (see page 120)
> 1 medium onion, peeled and chopped
> ½ stick (4 tablespoons) butter or 5 teaspoons shortening
> 1 teaspoon ground oregano
> ½ cup dry white wine
> 1 or 2 cups chicken consommé (see page 54)

Mix the cumin, garlic, salt, and pepper, and rub the mixture over the chicken, both outside and inside the cavity. Add the sour-orange juice and onion. Cover with aluminum foil, and refrigerate for 2 hours.

In a large and deep casserole, melt the butter over medium heat and add the whole chicken. Next add the oregano and wine. Finally pour in the chicken consommé (adding 2 cups of consommé will make the chicken more tender).

Bring just to the boiling point. Reduce heat, and simmer over low heat for about 35 minutes, adding liquid if necessary, until it is tender and cooked through.

Transfer to a serving platter, and enjoy.

CREOLE FRIED CHICKEN *pollo frito cubanito*

This is very aromatic and delicious. Use the freshest ingredients, and garnish with lemon slices.

4 SERVINGS

> 3 garlic cloves, minced
> 1 teaspoon ground cumin
> 1 tablespoon ground oregano
> Juice of 1 sour orange (see page 120)
> ½ cup vegetable oil
> One 2½- to 3-pound chicken, cut into 8 pieces
> ½ cup all-purpose flour

In a bowl, mix the garlic, cumin, oregano, and sour-orange juice, and pour over chicken pieces. Cover with aluminum foil, and refrigerate for 2 hours.

Heat the vegetable oil in a skillet over medium heat.

Meanwhile, lightly coat the moist marinated chicken with flour, and when the oil is very hot in the skillet, add the chicken pieces, skin side down. Do not crowd them or they will not brown evenly; make in batches if necessary. Fry until golden brown all over, turning the pieces often; continue frying until all the chicken pieces are thoroughly cooked, about 15 minutes. Remove pieces with a slotted spoon, and drain on paper towels.

NOTE Remove breast pieces before drumsticks or thighs, since dark meat takes longer to cook than white meat.

DRUNK CHICKEN *pollo borracho*

This is a great recipe for a party. The name comes from the abundance of wine in the dish.

4 SERVINGS

> One 2- to 3-pound chicken, cut into 8 pieces
> 1 cup all-purpose flour
> ½ stick (4 tablespoons) butter
> Salt and pepper to taste
> 1 teaspoon garlic powder
> 1½ pounds pearl or boiling onions, peeled
> NOTE Marble-sized pearl onions are perfect for this recipe, because they offer a milder, one-bite alternative to regular onions. You may also use boiling onions, which are just a bit larger. Sold in mesh bags, they should look dry but uncracked. Always store in a cool, dry place.
> 1½ cups dry white wine

Lightly coat the chicken with flour.

In a large saucepan over medium heat, melt the butter and sauté the chicken pieces for 3 to 5 minutes, until golden on all sides. Season with salt, pepper, and garlic powder.

When the chicken pieces turn a golden color, add the onions, sauté for 2 or 3 minutes, and immediately add the wine.

Reduce the heat, cover, and simmer for about 40 minutes, until chicken is tender and done and onions are translucent and soft. Transfer to a serving bowl, and serve immediately.

MEDITERRANEAN CHICKEN *pollo mediterraneo*

This recipe is light and airy. Serve with white rice boiled in onion broth. You will get rave reviews for a very elegant meal.

4 SERVINGS

> ¾ cup sofrito (see page 119)
> One 2- to 3-pound chicken, cut into quarters
> ½ cup dry white wine
> One 7-ounce jar roasted sweet red peppers, drained, cut into
>   julienne strips
> 1 tablespoon butter
> 4 eggs

In a deep skillet over low heat, simmer the sofrito for 5 minutes, and then add the chicken pieces. Cook over low heat for about 15 minutes. Do not add water or liquid; just let the chicken cook in the sofrito.

Now add the wine and the red peppers, and continue cooking for another 7 or 8 minutes. When the chicken is cooked and tender, remove from the pan with a slotted spoon and reserve. Continue simmering the sauce over very low heat.

In another skillet, melt the butter over medium heat and fry the eggs to your family's liking.

Arrange chicken in the center of a serving platter, and the fried eggs in a circle around the chicken pieces. Serve the sauce on the side, or pour on top of the chicken pieces and eggs on the platter.

STUFFED CHICKEN *pollo relleno*

What makes this recipe authentically Cuban is the stuffing. No bread stuffing here, but a combination of ground pork and Serrano ham (if that is unavailable, use prosciutto).

6 SERVINGS

> **One 3- to 4-pound chicken**
> **Salt and pepper to taste**
> **¼ stick (2 tablespoons) butter**
> **½ cup dry white wine**

Preheat oven to 375 degrees.

Stuff the cavity with either one of the stuffing choices described below. I recommend that you truss the chicken with kitchen twine or skewers to prevent the stuffing from falling out. Season with salt and pepper.

Place in a large buttered baking pan, and pour the wine on top of the bird to prevent drying out. Bake in the oven for about 1½ hours.

Remove from oven, untruss the chicken, and allow to rest for at least 15 minutes before serving. (You can make a simple sauce or gravy with the juices left in pan.) Carve and serve.

INGREDIENTS FOR STUFFING NO. 1

> **½ pound cooked ground or crumbled pork**
> **½ pound ground Serrano ham or prosciutto**
> **2 medium onions, peeled and chopped**
> **¼ cup tomato sauce**
> **1 sweet red pepper, seeded and chopped**
> **4 slices white bread, cubed**
> **1 cup milk, whole or skim**
> **¼ cup slivered almonds**
> **¼ cup raisins**
> **¼ cup pitted Spanish green olives**
> **½ cup dry white wine**

In a food processor, combine all the ingredients, and pulse to chop and mix. (Leave chunky—do not overprocess.)

(continued on next page)

(continued from previous page)

INGREDIENTS FOR STUFFING NO. 2

    ½ pound chorizo sausage, peeled, chopped

    2 medium onions, peeled and chopped

    1 green bell pepper, seeded and chopped

    4 slices Cuban bread (see page 78)

    1 cup milk, whole or skim

    ¼ cup raisins

    ¼ cup pitted olives

    ½ cup dry white wine

In a skillet, sauté the chopped chorizo over medium heat. Add the chopped onions and green pepper, and cook until tender and lightly colored, about 5 minutes. Transfer this mixture to the food processor, and add the bread, milk, raisins, olives, and wine. Pulse to chop and mix. (Leave chunky—do not overprocess.)

BEEF

carne de res

THE MOST commonly used cuts in preparing beef for Cuban recipes are:

Club steak—*riñonada*
Cube steak—*palomilla*
Delmonico—*centro de lomo*
Eye round—*boliche*
Flank brisket—*falda*
Rib—*costilla*
Round steak—*cañada*
Rump—*palomilla*
Saratoga—*bola*
Sirloin—*bola de lomo*
Sirloin steak—*riñonada, palomilla, filete*
Skirt steak—*churrasco*
Standing ribs—*costillas de lomo*
T-bone steak—*costilla riñonada*

GUANABACOA MEATBALLS
albóndigas de Guanabacoa

Guanabacoa is a township in the eastern tip of Havana, famous for its colonial archi-
tecture. In the 1950s, it was also famous for its lunch counters, which served up the best
meatballs on the island. Here is the recipe. Serve these over rice or pasta.

4 SERVINGS (8 MEATBALLS)

FOR THE MEATBALLS

> 1½ cups vegetable oil
> 1 small onion, chopped
> 1 garlic clove, minced
> 1 small green bell pepper, seeded and chopped
> 1½ pounds ground sirloin
> 2 eggs, beaten
> ½ cup milk, whole or skim
> 1 cup cracker meal or bread crumbs
> 1 teaspoon mustard
> Salt and pepper to taste
> ½ cup all-purpose flour

FOR THE SAUCE

> ¼ cup olive oil
> 2 garlic cloves, minced
> 1 small onion, peeled and chopped
> 2 cups tomato sauce
> ⅓ cup ketchup
> 1 teaspoon sugar
> ½ cup dry wine
> 1 bay leaf
> Salt and pepper to taste

Prepare the meatballs: Heat ¼ cup of the vegetable oil in a skillet over
medium heat. Add the onion, garlic, and green pepper. When onion is
translucent and pepper is tender, remove with a slotted spoon and reserve.
Cool to room temperature.

In a large mixing bowl, combine ground sirloin with the cooked onion,
garlic, and green pepper, and mix in the beaten eggs. Add the milk, cracker

meal, and mustard, and season with salt and pepper. Combine all the ingredients gradually and slowly, and form into medium-sized balls.

Roll the balls in flour, and set aside.

In a large skillet, heat the remaining oil over medium heat. Place the meatballs in the skillet, and fry slowly for 3 to 5 minutes on high heat, turning them often so they will cook evenly. When the meatballs are fully cooked and browned evenly, remove one by one and drain on paper towels. Reserve.

Prepare the sauce: In a large skillet, heat olive oil over medium heat. Add the garlic and onion, and continue cooking until the onion is translucent. Mix in the tomato sauce, ketchup, sugar, wine, and bay leaf. Season with salt and pepper. Stir well, cover, and continue cooking over low heat for about 25 minutes, until the sauce has thickened to your liking.

When the sauce is ready, add the meatballs and reheat gently, so they retain their shape and flavor. Remove from heat after 3 to 5 minutes, and serve immediately.

NOTE You can also make a larger number of meatballs, and freeze some for later use. They will be good for four to six weeks.

PAN-BROILED PALOMILLA STEAK
bistec palomilla a la parrilla

This is the most traditional of all Cuban steak recipes. Usually you serve it with grilled onions on top, and with white rice and fried ripe plantains (see pages 160 and 142). But long ago, when exiles started pouring into Miami in the 1960s, there was a tiny restaurant in the Little Havana section of our city called Lila's. This restaurant was famous for its *palomilla* steak, served with a huge mound of shoestring French fries on top. This was where we all hung out, adults and kids alike, talking about what it was like in Cuba and what it was going to be like when we went back. The conversations went on for hours among our parents at different tables, while us kids spent the time eating through the fries to get to the steak. The restaurant is gone today, and so are most of that first generation. The kids are now the grown-ups, but ask any Cuban immigrant in Miami why he remembers Lila's Restaurant, on Calle Ocho, and you will inevitably get the answer: *la palomillla con las papitas,* the pan-broiled steak with the shoestring fries. In honor of Lila's, and in honor of those early days, I always pair this steak with a mound of French fries thinly cut.

4 SERVINGS

(continued on next page)

(continued from previous page)

> 4 boneless sirloin or top-round steaks (2 pounds total)
> Juice of 1 lime or sour orange (see page 120)
> 3 garlic cloves, minced
> Salt and pepper to taste
> 4 teaspoons olive oil
> 1 onion, peeled and chopped
> 1 lemon, cut in 4 wedges, for garnish
> ½ cup chopped parsley for garnish

Pound the steaks with meat mallet until thin (about ¼ inch is the perfect thickness).

In a bowl, cover the steaks with the lime or sour-orange juice and garlic. Add the salt and pepper, and refrigerate, covered, for about 2 hours. This marinade will further tenderize the thin steaks.

Remove the steaks from the refrigerator, and reserve ¼ cup of the marinade.

Heat oil in a large skillet over medium-high heat, and drop steaks, one at a time, into the hot oil. Cook each side for 1 or 2 minutes, and set aside until all the steaks are cooked.

Once the steaks are pan-fried, sauté the onion in the same oil and the reserved marinade until the onion is tender and the juices are reduced.

Transfer steaks to serving platter, and place the onion and juices on top of each steak, with a wedge of lemon and chopped parsley.

BREADED PALOMILLA STEAK *bistec empanizado*

Bread your thinly sliced *palomilla* steak ahead of time and refrigerate, or even freeze for a make-ahead meal (it will keep for up to 30 days). If you frequent a Hispanic bodega, they will bread it for you!

4 SERVINGS

> **4 boneless sirloin or top-round steaks (2 pounds total)**
> **Juice of 1 lemon or sour orange (see page 120)**
> **3 garlic cloves, minced**
> **Salt and pepper to taste**
> **Onion powder to taste**
> **3 eggs**
> **1 cup cracker meal or bread crumbs**
> **½ cup all-purpose flour**
> **¼ cup vegetable oil**
> **1 lemon, cut in 4 wedges, for garnish**

Pound the steaks with meat mallet until thin (about ¼ inch is the perfect thickness).

In a bowl, cover the steaks with the lemon or sour-orange juice and garlic. Add the salt and pepper and onion powder, and refrigerate, covered, for about 2 hours. This marinade will further tenderize the thin steaks.

Remove the steaks from the refrigerator, and pat dry with paper towels.

In a shallow bowl, beat the eggs. In another shallow bowl, combine the cracker meal and flour. One at a time, dip the marinated steaks in the eggs, and turn them to coat all over. Then dip in the flour-and-cracker-meal mixture and shake off any excess.

In a skillet, heat the oil over medium heat and fry each steak individually for about 2 minutes on each side, until the crust is golden brown. Transfer to a serving platter, and serve with a wedge of lemon.

CUBAN AMERICAN HAMBURGERS
bistec hamburguesa

This recipe is from my mother, who used to vacation in Miami in the late 1950s. My mother and my aunt were English teachers in an American school in Cuba and always took back to Havana their favorite classic American recipes. My grandmother and the rest of the family would ultimately add new ingredients. The game was, we all had to speak English at the table when my mom had cooked American hamburgers. This game served us well when we arrived in Miami later on.

4 SERVINGS (4 BURGERS)

> 1½ pounds ground sirloin
> 1 egg, beaten
> Salt and pepper to taste
> 1 garlic clove, minced
> 1 teaspoon onion powder
> 2 teaspoons milk, whole or skim
> 1 teaspoon dry white wine
> ½ cup cracker meal or fine bread crumbs
> 2 strips bacon, each cut in half

In a bowl, mix the ground beef with the egg, salt, pepper, garlic, onion powder, milk, wine, and cracker meal. Mix everything thoroughly with your hands, and form and flatten the beef into four patties about ½ inch thick and about 5 inches in diameter.

Heat the bacon strips in a skillet over medium heat until crisp. Drain with a slotted spoon, and reserve the bacon fat for frying the hamburger patties. Lower the heat to medium, and place the patties in the skillet one by one. Fry each for 5 to 7 minutes, turning often so they brown and cook evenly.

Remove the patties from heat once they are fully cooked, drain on paper towels, transfer to a serving platter, and top with the bacon strips. Serve on buns, sliced bread, or, if you are calorie-conscious, on a bed of lettuce. Serve with French fries or cassava fries (see page 49).

CHEF INFANTE'S SKIRT STEAK STUFFED WITH CHOPPED SPINACH *churrasco a la Infante*

Chef Jorge Infante is one of my favorite customers at our bookstore in downtown Miami. He is Cuban with an American twist. Whenever he comes in for a book, I don't even give him a chance to say what he's looking for. I bombard him with cooking questions, asking him for recipes—and he takes the abuse with relish. He went to culinary school in New York City, but, more important, his eyes light up and actually twinkle when he talks about food. This is the *churrasco* he prepares at home. Serve it with jasmine rice, fried ripe plantains (see page 142), and *chimichurri* sauce (see page 111).

4 SERVINGS

> 4 skirt steaks (*churrascos*; 2½ pounds total)
> 2½ cups chopped spinach, cooked as you like (I prefer to
>   stir-fry it)
> 1½ cups grated Parmesan cheese
> 1½ cups pine nuts, toasted
> Salt and pepper to taste

With a sharp knife, butterfly the steak: Split down the center, not quite cutting through, then open the two halves flat to resemble a butterfly.

Preheat oven to 400 degrees.

Spread cooked spinach evenly with a spatula on the butterflied steak. Sprinkle the Parmesan cheese on, and add a top layer of the toasted pine nuts. Roll and tie. (It doesn't have to be perfect; it just has to hold together while baking.)

Bake in oven for 8 to 10 minutes for medium, or until done as you like. Serve immediately.

BEEF POT ROAST *boliche asado en cazuela*

The *boliche* originally comes from the western part of Cuba. The meat is cooked very slowly, making it ideal for a crockpot or pressure cooker, and can be stuffed with ham, bacon, or chorizo, and sometimes with hard-boiled eggs. The variations are many, but one thing is consistent: It is the perfect Sunday supper.

6 SERVINGS

> 4 pounds eye round (*boliche*)
> Juice of 1 sour orange (see page 120)
> Salt and pepper to taste
> 3 garlic cloves, finely minced, or garlic powder to taste, plus (optional) garlic slices
> 2 teaspoons dried oregano
> ½ pound sweet ham, bacon, or chorizo sausage, chopped
> Chopped-up prunes (optional)
> ½ cup vegetable oil
> 1 large onion, peeled and chopped
> 2 bay leaves
> ½ cup dry white wine or red wine, or more as needed
> 1 cup Vedado District basic broth (see page 52)

Marinate the eye round with the sour-orange juice, salt, pepper, garlic, and oregano. Refrigerate, covered, for about 2 hours. Even better, for the tastiest *boliche* ever, leave overnight.

When you are ready to cook, remove the eye round from refrigerator, reserve the marinade, and place the meat on a cutting board. Make a slit lengthwise down the center of the meat in order to create a pocket. Stuff with the ham, sausage, or bacon. You can also cut smaller slits and insert garlic slices or chopped-up prunes.

Heat the vegetable oil in a large, heavy casserole or Dutch oven over medium-high heat. Add the eye round, and brown on all sides. You are not cooking it at this time, just browning it, so the whole process should only take about 5 minutes. Turn the meat using two spatulas or spoons, since piercing with a fork would let the juices escape.

Remove the meat, and set aside. In the same casserole, sauté the onion for about 3 minutes, or until translucent, and add the bay leaves, reserved marinade, wine, and broth. Then return the meat to the pot, and simmer over medium-low heat, covered, for 75 to 90 minutes, making sure you lift the lid from time to time to let the steam escape. If you like, you may leave the lid slightly ajar for the entire cooking time.

When the meat is tender and fully cooked, remove it from the pot and slice evenly. Taste the cooking juices, correct seasoning, and if sauce is too thick dilute with a little more wine.

Transfer *boliche* slices to a serving platter, and top with sauce. Serve immediately, and accompany with yellow rice or white rice (see page 160) and fried ripe plantains (see page 142) or *tostones* (see pages 148–150).

HAVANA BEEF FILLET IN CAPER SAUCE
filete alcaparrado

Many Havana dishes, especially chicken and meat recipes, make frequent use of an *alca-parrado,* a sauce that mixes olives, raisins, and capers to provide a great sweet-and-sour flavor. Serve with rice with tender corn (see page 168) or with mashed *malanga* (see page 134), and a tomato salad.

4 SERVINGS

FOR THE BEEF

> One 3-pound beef rump-roast fillet
> ½ cup diced ham
> 1 carrot, grated
> Salt and pepper to taste
> 2 teaspoons butter
> Juice of 1 lemon

FOR THE ALCAPARRADO SAUCE

> 1 onion, peeled and chopped
> ½ stick (4 tablespoons) butter
> 4 teaspoons all-purpose flour
> 1 cup Vedado District basic broth (see page 52)
> ½ cup dry red wine
> ¼ cup capers, drained
> ¼ cup raisins
> ¼ cup pitted and chopped Spanish green olives

(continued on next page)

(continued from previous page)

Prepare the beef: Use a sharp knife to trim skin, rind, and fat from the surface of the meat. Cut away any tough connective tissues. Make a slit lengthwise down the center of the meat in order to create a pocket. Stuff with the ham and grated carrot. Season with salt and pepper.

Heat the butter in a large, heavy casserole or Dutch oven over medium-high heat. Add the meat, and brown on all sides. You are not cooking it at this time, just browning it, so the whole process should only take about 5 minutes. Turn the meat using two spatulas or spoons, since piercing with a fork would let the juices escape.

Once the meat is browned, add the lemon juice and the following sauce.

Prepare the sauce: In a separate saucepan, sauté the onion in butter over medium heat. Add the flour slowly, and cook gently. Add the broth and wine, stirring constantly. Add the capers, raisins, and olives.

Pour the sauce over the browned meat. Lower heat, and simmer for about 45 minutes, until tender and fully cooked. Remove from heat, and slice evenly. Transfer slices to a serving platter, and spoon sauce over them. Garnish as you like, and serve immediately, accompanied by additional sauce.

secrets of a Cuban cook

FLAMBÉING

When you flambé, you are topping the food with a liquor—usually brandy, but you may also use sherry or 80-proof liquors—and lighting a fire. The liquor must be warmed to about 130 degrees yet still remain well under the boiling point. Always remove the pan from the heat source before adding liquor, to avoid danger. Also, keep a lid nearby, in case you need to smother the flames. The alcohol vapor generally burns off by itself in seconds.

FLAMBÉED BEEF FILLET WITH
CHICKEN LIVERS *filete flambeado con hígados de pollo*

Such an unusual dish. It's lots of work, but it will bring you lots of compliments. This French method of igniting foods came to Cuba with the many French and Haitian immigrants who lived on the island, and was often practiced in the most elegant restaurants of Havana.

6 SERVINGS

> One 3-pound bottom-round or rump roast
> 1 cup diced ham
> Salt and pepper to taste
> ½ stick (4 tablespoons) butter
> ½ cup peeled and chopped carrot
> 2 green peppers, seeded and chopped
> 2 cups small pasta
> 1 pound chicken livers, halved, trimmed, and patted dry
> ½ cup white wine
> ¼ cup sherry
> ¼ cup Cuban salsa (see page 112)
> 1 tablespoon Vedado District basic broth (see page 52)

Preheat oven to 325 degrees.

Use a sharp knife to trim skin, rind, and fat from the surface of the meat. Cut away any tough connective tissues. Make a slit lenghthwise down the center of the meat in order to create a pocket. Stuff with the ham. Season with salt and pepper.

Place meat in a baking pan with 1 tablespoon of the butter, surrounded by the carrot and peppers. Bake for about 1½ hours. Remove from oven when meat is tender and fully cooked.

Meanwhile, in a separate saucepan, boil the pasta in 6 to 8 cups water for 10 minutes, until soft, then drain and add 1 tablespoon of the butter to the cooked pasta.

In a skillet, sauté the chicken livers with the remaining 2 tablespoons of the butter.

Mix the wine and sherry, and pour into another skillet, one with rounded, deep sides and a long handle. Heat the liquids slowly, over very low heat.

(continued on next page)

(continued from previous page)

Ignite them with a long match or a barbecue lighter. Stir in the Cuban salsa and broth slowly. Season with salt and pepper, and cook until the flames die out. Please be careful; when a flame is involved, extra attention is required.

You are now ready to put this dish together: Transfer the beef to a serving platter, and arrange the livers on top, and the pasta surrounding the meats. Spoon sauce over the entire dish, and serve immediately. Accompany with a very light green salad.

CUBAN BEEF AND POTATO STEW
carne con papas

If your loved one is a meat-and-potatoes kind of person, then this simple dish is the recipe for you to make on that very special occasion. An excellent accompaniment is an avocado and pineapple salad (see page 191), and don't forget the *plátanos maduros fritos* (see page 142), and of course the ever-present white rice (see page 160).

6 SERVINGS

½ cup vegetable oil
2 pounds round steak, cubed
1 teaspoon salt
1 teaspoon paprika
½ teaspoon pepper
1 bay leaf
1 onion, peeled and chopped
2 garlic cloves, finely chopped
1 green bell pepper, seeded and cut into quarters
1 cup tomato sauce
1 cup dry red wine or sherry, plus more as needed
1 cup water, plus more as needed
2 pounds potatoes, peeled and cut into uneven chunks
1 handful of capers

In a large saucepan, heat the oil over medium heat and brown the meat on all sides for 5 to 7 minutes.

Add the salt, paprika, pepper, bay leaf, chopped onion, garlic, and green pepper.

As the browned meat simmers in the pot, pour in the tomato sauce, wine, and water.

Simmer over low heat, and when the meat is almost done, add the potato chunks and capers.

Continue to cook over low heat until the meat is tender and flakes apart and the potatoes are fully cooked.

HINT As you watch your stew brew, add a little more wine and water to make it more tender.

MEATLOAF *pulpeta*

American meatloaf and Cuban meatloaf are actually light-years apart. The first differ-ence is that Cuban meatloaf, or *pulpeta,* is not actually baked in a pan, but seared and gently cooked in a sauce. Accompany this meatloaf with a loaf of Cuban bread (see page 78) and avocado and pineapple salad (see page 191).

6 SERVINGS

> 1½ pounds lean ground sirloin
> ½ pound ground pork
> ¼ pound sweet ham, chopped, or 1 small can deviled ham
> ½ cup cracker meal or bread crumbs
> 2 eggs, beaten (divided)
> Salt and pepper to taste
> ½ teaspoon dried oregano
> 1 carrot, grated
> 2 hard-boiled eggs (see page 201)
> 4 teaspoons olive oil
> 2 garlic cloves, minced
> 1 medium onion, peeled and chopped
> 1 green bell pepper, seeded and chopped
> ½ cup tomato sauce
> ½ cup capers
> ½ cup dry red wine
> 1 cup Vedado District basic broth (see page 52) or other beef broth

Wash your hands and roll up your sleeves. There is no better way. In a large bowl, combine the sirloin, pork, and ham. To this mixture add half of the cracker meal, one of the beaten eggs, salt, pepper, oregano, and grated carrot. Work it and knead it together until all the ingredients are thoroughly combined and the texture is moist. Shape into an oblong or rectangular loaf (approximately 9 by 5 inches).

Create a well in the center of the loaf, and push the hard-boiled eggs into the loaf so that they end up right in the center. Fold the meat mixture over them to enclose them entirely, and shape the meat carefully back into its original oblong shape. Dip the loaf in the other beaten egg, and sprinkle with the remaining cracker meal to coat lightly. Refrigerate, covered, in a pan for at least 1 hour.

Heat oil in a large, heavy pot over medium-high heat. Add the loaf, and brown on all sides. Turn the loaf carefully, using two spatulas or spoons, since piercing with a fork could break up the shape. You are not cooking it at this time, just browning it, so the whole process should only take about 3 to 5 minutes.

Remove loaf from the pot, and resume heating the oil over medium-high heat. Sauté the garlic, onion, and green pepper until the onion is translucent and the pepper is tender. Add the tomato sauce, capers, and wine. Simmer for about 5 minutes, and then gently place the browned meatloaf back in the pot with the tomato mixture. Reduce heat to medium-low, cover and cook for about 60 minutes, letting the sauce simmer slowly. Spoon sauce occasionally over the loaf, and add broth for desired consistency. When fully cooked, transfer to a serving platter and slice. Serve immediately, and reserve leftovers for another wonderful meal.

CUBAN OXTAIL STEW *rabo encendido*

What a name! What a recipe! *Rabo encendido* is literally "flaming tail." Oxtails are the tails of beef cattle and are generally sold cut into lengths of 3 inches, resembling miniature osso bucco (cut veal shanks). Oxtails are pure protein and have a rich gelatin content, making them a perfect soup base. You can find frozen oxtails, which have been cleaned and disjointed. If you buy fresh, be sure to specify to your butcher to cut and disjoint them. Otherwise, to disjoint oxtails, cut into sections at the joints with a butcher knife carefully, without splintering any bones.

Serve this over a mound of white rice (see page 160) or yellow (saffron) rice.

4 SERVINGS

(continued on next page)

(continued from previous page)

2 pounds oxtails, disjointed
¼ cup olive oil
½ cup dry red wine
Salt and pepper to taste
⅓ cup vegetable oil
4 garlic cloves, minced
1 large onion, peeled and chopped
1 green bell pepper, seeded and chopped
1 sweet red pepper, seeded and chopped
1 carrot, peeled and diced
2 cups tomato sauce
2 cups Vedado District basic broth (see page 52)
5 small potatoes, peeled and diced
1 cup almonds, toasted and chopped
½ cup capers
2 bay leaves
Pinch cornstarch (optional)

Marinate the oxtails in a mixture of olive oil, wine, salt, and pepper in the refrigerator for at least 8 hours or overnight. Drain and discard marinade.

Heat the vegetable oil in a large, heavy casserole or Dutch oven over medium-high heat. Add the oxtails, and brown on all sides. Turn the meat carefully, using two spatulas or spoons, since piercing with a fork would let the juices escape. You are not cooking it at this time, just browning it, so the whole process should only take about 5 minutes. Remove the meat and set aside.

To the same casserole, add the garlic, onion, chopped peppers, and carrot, and sauté until the onion is translucent and vegetables are tender. Return the oxtails to the casserole. Add the tomato sauce and the broth, bring to a simmer, and reduce heat. Now add the potatoes, almonds, capers, and bay leaves, and continue cooking over low heat for about 2 hours.

The oxtails will be very soft and tender and will break apart with a fork. Add liquid if necessary while cooking; or, if you need to thicken, you can add a pinch of cornstarch mixed with water. Taste, and correct seasoning if necessary. Turn the stew out into a serving dish, and serve immediately.

INNARDS

The French, Italians, and Asians love to cook organ meats. So do Cubans. The most renowned chefs love to cook—and to eat—innards. Put aside any preconceived notions and enjoy some of these economical, nutritious, and exotic recipes.

LIVER ITALIAN STYLE *hígado a la italiana*

Don't let the name fool you! This dish is served as a staple item in every authentic Cuban restaurant in Miami. My recipe, however, came from my mom, and I always found it to be more tender than any restaurant's.

4 SERVINGS

> 1 pound beef liver, thinly sliced and cut into ½-inch-wide strips
> 1 onion, peeled and thinly sliced
> 1 green bell pepper, seeded and cut into julienne strips
> 1 sweet red pepper, seeded and cut into julienne strips
> 1 bay leaf
> ⅓ cup white vinegar
> ½ cup dry white wine
> Salt and pepper to taste
> 1 garlic clove, minced
> 1 tablespoon all-purpose flour
> 4 tablespoons olive oil
> 4 cups cooked white rice (see page 160)

Place the liver pieces in a large mixing bowl or casserole, and cover them with the onion, peppers, and bay leaf. In a smaller mixing bowl, combine the vinegar, wine, salt, pepper, garlic, and flour. Mix well, and pour over the liver pieces. Cover the casserole, and refrigerate for at least 2 hours.

Heat the olive oil in a large skillet over medium-high heat. Add the liver and the rest of the marinated ingredients, and sauté, stirring constantly, for about 10 minutes, until the liver and vegetables are well cooked but still tender. Add more liquid if needed, and correct seasoning. Remove from the heat, and serve immediately over—what else?—a mound of fluffy white rice.

BATTER-DIPPED CALF BRAINS *sesos rebozados*

I know it might sound pretty gross or downright dangerous—especially if you are paranoid about mad-cow disease—but many cultures cook cow and calf brains in some form. Mexicans love brains in authentic homemade tacos, and we Cubans batter-dip and fry brains. It is an acquired taste, but with a squirt of lemon it's a dish for the culinary adventurer. Serve these with French fries and tomato salad.

4 SERVINGS (8 PIECES)

> 1 pound (8 pieces) calf or cow brain meat, soaked overnight in
>   water
> 1 teaspoon vinegar
> ½ cup all-purpose flour
> 1 parsley sprig, chopped
> ¼ cup seasoned bread crumbs
> 1 egg, beaten
> ½ cup vegetable oil
> Salt and pepper to taste
> 1 lemon cut into wedges for garnish

After soaking the brains overnight in water in the refrigerator, carefully trim the membranes. Place the brains and vinegar in 2 cups boiling water in a saucepan over medium-high heat. Continue boiling slowly for about 15 minutes. Remove with a slotted spoon, and place in a bowl of ice water.

In a bowl, mix the flour, parsley, and bread crumbs. First dip the brain pieces in the beaten egg, and then coat in the flour mixture.

Heat the oil in a skillet over medium-high heat, add the breaded brain pieces a few at a time, and fry for 3 to 5 minutes, until golden brown and cooked through. Remove from the skillet and keep hot while you fry the remaining pieces. Pat with paper towels to remove excess grease, and transfer to a serving platter. Season with salt and pepper, squeeze lemon over pieces, and garnish with lemon wedges.

BEEF TONGUE WITH MUSHROOMS
lengua con champiñones

Accompany this with saffron rice and a watercress salad.

4 SERVINGS

> 1 beef tongue
> ¼ stick (2 tablespoons) butter
> Salt to taste
> 1 onion, peeled and chopped
> 1 celery stalk, chopped
> 4 strips bacon
> 1 bay leaf
> 8 tomatoes, peeled and chopped
> 1 cup dry red wine
> 1 cup mushrooms, cleaned and chopped

Bring 6 cups water to boil in a casserole, and boil tongue for 20 minutes. Remove from heat, drain, let cool at room temperature, and remove the skin from the tongue.

Heat the butter in a large skillet over medium-high heat. Add the tongue, and brown on each side for about 5 minutes, turning over frequently. Season with salt, and add the onion, celery, bacon, bay leaf, and tomatoes. Simmer for another 5 minutes.

Add the wine and mushrooms, reduce heat, and cook, covered, over low heat for another 30 minutes. Do not overcook. When the tongue is tender, remove from heat and transfer to a serving platter.

OLD CLOTHES AND FRIED COW
ropa vieja y vaca frita

I think it's a given that if you are Cuban, or even half Cuban, you've got a cousin, or *primo*, somewhere, and of course about twelve of them in Miami or New Jersey. It is natural! Every time you mention a city to a Cuban, he will say, "Oh, yes, I have a *primo* there." Along that same line, there is no way you can talk about *ropa vieja* (old clothes) without inevitably bringing up its first cousin, *vaca frita* (fried cow).

My aunt and my mom say that in Cuba, if you made *vaca frita* for lunch, you could turn the leftovers into *ropa vieja* for dinner. These two recipes go together and have almost the same ingredients in two variations. One is dry (*vaca frita*) and one is wet, smothered in tomato sauce (*ropa vieja*). Maybe, like me, you have kids who prefer one or the other: My older son likes *vaca frita,* and my younger *ropa vieja.* My daughter, Alyson, who is the classic middle child, has to have a little of each on her plate. So I prepare both *vaca frita* and *ropa vieja* at the same time, to keep peace.

What makes these two recipes icons of Cuban cooking are their very funny and almost ironically unappetizing names. Who in his or her right mind would make or eat a dish called "old clothes" or "fried cow"? Before you answer, try these two homemade versions.

OLD CLOTHES CUBAN STYLE *ropa vieja*

This is a natural to throw over white rice. If you are into modern fast food, a *ropa vieja* wrap is really delicious.

4 SERVINGS

> 2 pounds flank steak
> 4 cups Vedado District basic broth (see page 52) or beef
>   consommé
> 1/3 cup olive oil
> 2 garlic cloves, chopped
> 1 onion, peeled and chopped
> 1 green bell pepper, seeded and chopped
> 1 cup tomato sauce
> 1 teaspoon salt
> 1 bay leaf
> 1/2 cup dry red wine or sherry

Place the beef in a deep saucepan, and cover with the consommé. Simmer over low heat, covered, until the meat is tender, about 1½ hours.

Allow to cool at room temperature until you can comfortably shred the meat into thin threads by cutting against the grain. Reserve the beef and the broth.

In a large skillet, heat the oil over low heat, and cook the garlic, onion, and green pepper, stirring, until the onion is tender and the mixture is fragrant.

Add tomato sauce, salt, bay leaf, and wine, and then add the shredded beef and broth.

Simmer, covered, over low heat for about 40 minutes, stirring occasionally.

FRIED COW BY CARLOS ALBERTO MONTANER *vaca frita de Carlos Alberto Montaner*

My favorite Cuban patriot is Carlos Alberto Montaner. As soft-spoken as he is soothing, he brings sanity into the passionate political-exile world. When I see him having lunch, it is usually *vaca frita*. So I decided to ask him for his recipe, and here it is.

4 SERVINGS

> 2 pounds flank steak
> 3 cups water
> 1 teaspoon salt
> 2 onions, peeled and chopped (divided)
> ½ cup olive oil
> 4 garlic cloves
> Juice of 2 sour oranges (see page 120) or 2 lemons
> ¼ teaspoon pepper
> 4 cups cooked white rice (see page 160)

In a large saucepan, cover the beef with the water, and add salt and one of the chopped onions.

Cook, covered, over low heat for about 25 minutes, or until completely tender. The meat should start breaking apart on its own.

Remove from heat, and either discard the stock or reserve it for another use. Allow the beef to cool slightly.

Shred the beef as much as possible into thin threads.

In a large skillet, heat the oil and garlic cloves over medium-high heat until fragrant, and start frying the beef shreds, stirring often, for 5 minutes. Add the remaining chopped onion to fry along with the beef threads until crisp.

Add the sour-orange juice immediately, season with pepper, and serve over white rice.

NOTE A great variation to this dish is to serve it as a *vaca frita* chop (see page 103).

THE PICADILLO FAMILY

Picadillo falls somewhere between chili, hash, and a sloppy joe. There are many variations. Some call for only ground beef, but others include lamb, pork, chorizo sausage, or ham. It is a traditional, popular, and inexpensive dish to make. *Picadillo* can be eaten by itself, with rice, or as a stuffing for *empanadas*. Kids and adults alike love it. I have included as many varieties as possible. I am sure you will experiment and find your own favorite combination, your customized *picadillo*.

CARLOS EIRE'S PICADILLO *picadillo de Carlos Eire*

Carlos Eire is a fine writer who poignantly captured the true essence of what it means to be a Cuban American in his National Book Award–winning memoir, *Waiting for Snow in Havana*. He was an Operation Peter Pan boy, one of many Cuban children who came to the United States without their parents. Eire grew up to be a successful professor at Yale University. This is his *picadillo*. I like it served with white rice (see page 160) and fried ripe plantains (see page 142).

4 SERVINGS

> 4 teaspoons olive oil
> 1 large red onion, peeled and chopped
> 1 sweet red pepper, seeded and chopped
> 4 garlic cloves, peeled and chopped
> 2 teaspoons ground cumin
> Salt and pepper to taste
> Pinch of paprika
> 1½ pounds ground sirloin
> ¼ cup raisins
> ¼ cup pitted and chopped Spanish green olives
> 1 cup tomato sauce
> 1 teaspoon balsamic or red vinegar

Heat oil in a large skillet for about 5 minutes. Add the onion, red pepper, and garlic, and sauté until the onion becomes translucent and the pepper is tender. Add the cumin, salt, pepper, and paprika.

Reduce heat, add the ground sirloin, and cook for a few minutes, until it browns. As it begins to brown, add the raisins, olives, tomato sauce, and vinegar. Simmer, stirring constantly over medium-low heat, for about 25 minutes, until meat is fully cooked and the sauce thick and creamy.

PICADILLO AL GUAPO

Guapo is an idiomatic term that Cubans use to mock the young who are full of bravado. High confidence levels have always been part of the Cuban psyche, which is a long-running joke in our culture. This *picadillo* is *guapo* because it has it all: ham, chorizo, beef, *and* pork!

Sometimes it is just wonderful to top this with a fried egg. We call that a *caballo*—literally, "on horseback." Always accompany with white rice (see page 160).

4 SERVINGS

> ¼ cup vegetable oil
> 1 onion, peeled and chopped
> 1 green bell pepper, seeded and chopped
> 2 garlic cloves, minced
> ½ pound ground beef
> ¼ pound ground pork
> ¼ pound ground ham
> ¼ pound peeled and ground chorizo sausage
> ¾ cup capers
> Salt and pepper to taste
> ¼ cup chopped pimiento-stuffed green olives
> ½ cup tomato sauce
> ¼ cup dry white wine

Heat the oil in a large skillet over medium heat for 5 minutes. Add the onion, green pepper, and garlic, and sauté for a few minutes, until the onion becomes translucent and the pepper tender.

Add the ground beef, pork, ham, and sausage, and sauté, stirring constantly, until all the ingredients mix and the meats brown. Stir in the capers, season with salt and pepper, and add the olives, stirring constantly. Add the tomato sauce and wine, lower heat, and simmer, covered, for about 25 minutes.

When the mixture is thoroughly cooked, remove from heat and serve immediately.

PICADILLO PIE *tambor de picadillo*

First you have to make mashed potatoes, and then the *picadillo*. The work is well worth it.

4 SERVINGS

FOR THE MASHED POTATOES

> 2 pounds potatoes, peeled and diced
> 1½ cups milk
> ½ cup heavy cream
> ½ stick (4 tablespoons) butter
> Salt and pepper to taste

FOR THE PICADILLO

> 2 teaspoons olive oil
> 1 onion, peeled and diced
> 1 green bell pepper, seeded and diced
> 1½ pounds ground sirloin
> ½ cup tomato sauce
> ½ cup pitted and chopped Spanish green olives
> ½ cup raisins
> 1 tablespoon dry sherry
> ½ teaspoon sugar
> Salt and pepper to taste

FOR TOPPING

> ½ cup mixture of grated Parmesan cheese and bread crumbs

In a large, heavy pot, bring 8 cups water to a boil over high heat. Add the potatoes, and when the water returns to a boil, lower heat, cover, and let the potatoes simmer for about 25 minutes.

Drain the potatoes, and mash with a potato masher, fork, or whisk. Add the milk, cream, and butter slowly, and continue whisking and mashing. Season to taste, and set aside.

Meanwhile, in a large skillet over medium heat, heat the oil. Add the onion and green pepper, and sauté for about 5 minutes, until the onion is translucent and the pepper is tender.

Add the sirloin, and cook, stirring constantly, until the meat is browned, about 5 minutes. Stir in the tomato sauce with the olives, raisins, sherry, and sugar. Simmer for about 20 minutes, to desired consistency and until fully cooked. Season with salt and pepper, and set this aside as well.

Preheat the oven to 350 degrees.

In a rectangular, square, or round greased baking pan, layer half the mashed potatoes evenly on the bottom. Cover with the sirloin mixture, and top off with the remaining half of the mashed potatoes.

Sprinkle the cheese-and-bread-crumb mixture on top, and bake for about 25 minutes, until it turns bubbly and golden.

NOTE Try mashed *malanga* (see page 134) instead of potatoes on this pie for a spectacular variation.

PORK

puerco

CUBANS AND OTHERS native to the Caribbean love pork. Cubans in particular love roasting pork, especially in the form of a whole suckling pig, and definitely on Christmas Eve. There is hardly a more festive way to enjoy a party, a holiday, a wedding, or any type of special occasion than roasting a suckling pig—it is the epitome of welcoming hospitality in many cultures around the world. It is hard to cook an entire pig in your oven, so most Cubans use La Caja China in the backyard. Literally translated, it is called "The Chinese Box"—a rectangular plywood chest lined with aluminum foil in which you can roast a whole pig weighing up to 100 pounds, not to mention a lamb, several turkeys, many chickens, or numerous fish. It follows the Chinese principle of putting the charcoal on top of the food, not underneath as in regular barbecues. The amount of heat generated in the box makes it a fast, easy way to cook just about anything, no matter how big. These Chinese Boxes are sold in Hispanic markets and hardware stores and are easily available online (see Resources, page 417). Before you invest, ask yourself how serious you are about barbecuing. You can also be a purist, like my ninety-year-old next-door neighbor, Calero, and dig a pit in your backyard to cook your pig. And, of course, there is always the oven for smaller pigs. Most butchers can order a whole pig for your special feast. Or you can settle for roasting the pork loin or pork shoulder or pork leg. I have included recipes for roasting, braising, stewing, grilling, and even frying pork that will delight your family and friends.

The most commonly used cuts of pork for preparing Cuban recipes are:

Whole suckling pig—*lechón*
Leg of pork, uncured—*pierna de puerco*
Ham—*jamón*
Spare ribs—*costillas de puerco*
Loin of pork—*lomo de puerco*
Pork chops—*chuletas de puerco*

ROAST SUCKLING PIG À LA BENNY MORÉ
lechón asado Benny Moré

Of all of Cuba's legendary singers, Benny Moré was the most revered and loved. This recipe honors his style and his great passion for Cuban life, music, and spirit. The recipe is easy and authentic! Contact your butcher well ahead of time to special-order the pig. Ask that your butcher clean, gut, and split your pig.

12 SERVINGS

> Juice of 30 sour oranges (see page 120), or juice of 20 limes and
>   10 regular oranges (reserve the orange or lime halves)
> 1 whole suckling pig (about 15 pounds), well cleaned, gutted, and
>   split
> 20 garlic cloves, 5 quartered and 15 minced
> 4 teaspoons dried oregano
> 2 tablespoons olive oil
> Salt and pepper to taste
> 1 cup coarsely chopped fresh parsley
> 4 cups mojo marinade (see page 120), plus more if needed

The day before you are to cook, rub the sour-orange halves all over the pig's body, and pour the juice all over the body and into the cavity. Cut slits all over the body of the pig, and stuff the garlic quarters into the slits.

In a bowl, mix together the minced garlic, oregano, olive oil, salt, pepper, parsley, and 2 cups of the mojo. Stuff half of this mixture inside the cavity, and rub the remaining half all over the outside. Cover the pig, and marinate for 24 hours, basting every once in a while (see page 286).

Prepare your Chinese Box, or preheat your oven to 325 degrees.

Remove the pig from the marinade, and place it facedown on a large

(continued on next page)

(continued from previous page)

baking sheet or in a large roasting pan. Cover the pig's ears, snout, and tail with aluminum foil. Cook in oven for 4 to 4½ hours; if you use a Chinese Box, it can be done in about 3 hours. The rule is about 15 to 20 minutes per pound in the oven. As you are cooking, pour in as needed the remainder of the mojo marinade, and baste as much as possible. The skin should crackle, and the meat should be completely done. The roast is done when no trace of pink or translucent meat remains and the juice runs clear when pricked by a knife. Do not allow to dry out, and add liquid or mojo as needed.

When fully cooked, remove from heat and remove the foil. Let it stand for 15 minutes, carve on a board, and transfer to a serving platter.

NOTE Here is a full sample menu:

> Slices of roast suckling pig
> White rice (see page 160)
> Black beans (see page 59)
> Cassava (*yuca*) with mojo sauce (see page 121)
> Fried ripe plantains (see page 142)
> Lettuce and tomato salad
> *Chicharrones de puerco* (see page 298)

secrets of a Cuban cook

HOW TO STORE A PIG OVERNIGHT

When your pig is marinating overnight for the big party day, store it, covered, in a cool, dry place. While it would be ideal to refrigerate it, most of us do not have the room. If you want to keep it very cold, you can store it in a large cooler with ice. Cover the whole pig with aluminum foil to retain all the juices. The important thing is to keep it covered and marinating with the citrus for a long time.

ROAST LEG OF PORK *pierna de puerco asado*

A pork leg is the same thing as a ham, except that it is fresh instead of cured. Special-order it from the butcher if you can. It is sold either boneless or bone-in, and either whole or half. The bottom half is called the shank portion, the upper half the butt portion. Both make great roasts for a larger-than-usual crowd at dinner. Serve this with *moros y cristianos* (see page 161) and a great tomato salad.

10 SERVINGS

> ½ fresh (uncured) pork leg (about 8 pounds), trimmed
> 8 garlic cloves, minced
> Salt and pepper to taste
> 2 teaspoons dried oregano
> 2 teaspoons ground cumin
> 1 tablespoon olive oil
> 2 cups juice from sour oranges (see page 120) or limes
> 1 large onion, peeled and thinly sliced

Make shallow slits all over the pork leg with the tip of a knife, and place the roast in a heavy pan. Mix the garlic, salt, pepper, oregano, cumin, and olive oil, and rub all over the roast, stuffing it into the small slits. Pour the sour-orange juice all over the roast, and refrigerate, covered, for at least 2 hours and preferably overnight.

Preheat oven to 350 degrees.

Remove the roast from the refrigerator; drain and reserve the marinade. Place roast in a baking pan, and cook for 1 hour in oven, turning it over a couple of times so it browns evenly.

Reduce the heat to 300 degrees, pour the reserved marinade over the roast, and place the sliced onion on top. Cover with aluminum foil, and continue cooking, basting occasionally, for 1 to 1½ hours, adding liquids if pork becomes dry. Now remove the foil and cook, uncovered, for another 30 minutes. Cut into it to see that it is not too pink in color. Let it stand for 15 minutes before carving. Transfer to a serving platter, and serve.

BONED PORK LOIN WITH PINEAPPLE CREAM SAUCE *lomo con salsa de piña*

6 SERVINGS

> 1 pork loin (about 3 pounds), boned, rolled, and tied
> 1 teaspoon dried thyme
> Salt and pepper to taste
> ½ stick (4 tablespoons) butter
> 1 onion, peeled and chopped
> 2 cups cubed fresh pineapple (see page 31)
> ½ cup heavy whipping cream
> 1 teaspoon Dijon mustard

Preheat oven to 375 degrees.

Untie the pork loin, and trim off the skin and fat. Lay it flat, skin side down, and sprinkle and rub thyme, salt, and pepper all over the loin. Roll up the loin again, and retie it up with string. Place on a rack in a baking pan.

Place the pan in the oven, and bake for about 2 hours, or until well cooked (check to see that it is not too pink in color).

While the loin is roasting, melt the butter in a saucepan and add the onion and pineapple. Cook over very low heat for about 25 minutes, until very soft. Remove from the heat, and allow the mixture to cool slightly. Transfer it to a food processor or blender, and add the cream and mustard. Process or blend until smooth, and season with salt and pepper to taste.

When the roast is done, remove from oven. Let it stand for 15 minutes. Just before serving, reheat the sauce if necessary. Transfer roast to a cutting board, slice evenly, and transfer to a serving platter. Serve the sauce on top of slices or on the side.

STUFFED LEG OF PORK *pierna de puerco rellena*

Your butcher may be able to prepare the pork leg for stuffing, but the home method in this recipe is more time-consuming but works equally well.

10 SERVINGS

FOR THE PORK

½ fresh (uncured) pork leg (about 8 pounds), trimmed

8 garlic cloves, minced

Salt and pepper to taste

2 teaspoons dried oregano

2 teaspoons ground cumin

1 tablespoon olive oil

2 cups juice from sour oranges (see page 120) or limes

1 large onion, peeled and thinly sliced

FOR THE STUFFING

2 teaspoons butter

½ cup chopped onion

4 cups diced ham

1 cup bread crumbs

½ cup milk

½ cup dry white wine

½ cup raisins

½ cup almonds, slivered

1 cup peeled and diced apple

⅛ teaspoon grated nutmeg

⅛ teaspoon dried thyme

⅛ teaspoon pepper

½ cup *malta*

NOTE *Malta* is a carbonated malt beverage, sold with soft drinks in the Hispanic aisle of your supermarket. You may substitute any type of glaze or syrup.

Remove the bone from the leg by cutting around the ball-and-socket joint with a sharp-pointed knife. Continue cutting down the length of the leg bone, and cut and scrape the meat away from the bone to free the bone. Lift the

(continued on next page)

(continued from previous page)

fillet end of the leg bone, and detach it from the meat. Cut out the tendons, and butterfly the meat: Laying it out flat, trim off any visible fat; then slash the thick portions of the meat and open it up in a butterfly shape so the whole leg is reasonably even in its thickness. Cover with a piece of plastic wrap, and pound with a meat mallet to flatten the meat further for easier stuffing.

In a large pan, marinate the pork with the garlic, salt, pepper, oregano, cumin, olive oil, and sour-orange juice. Place onion slices on top, cover, and refrigerate for at least 2 hours.

When your pork is marinated and you are ready to cook, make the stuffing: Heat the butter in a skillet over medium-high heat, and sauté the onion for a few minutes, until translucent. Add the ham, and cook for a few more minutes, stirring constantly. Add the bread crumbs, milk, wine, raisins, almonds, and apple, bring to a simmer, and reduce heat. Season with the nutmeg, thyme, and pepper, and continue simmering for about 10 minutes. Remove from heat and reserve.

Preheat oven to 325 degrees.

Place pork flat on a cutting board, and spread stuffing evenly (about ¾ inch thick) over pork, leaving a border. Completely enclose the stuffing by rolling up the pork neatly. Tie in several places with string, and if necessary use skewers to secure the ends. Transfer to a baking pan, fat side up, and brush with the *malta*. Bake in the oven for about 3 to 3½ hours. When fully cooked, transfer to a serving platter, garnish as you like, and slice. Serve with mashed potatoes (see page 133) or mashed *malanga* (see page 134).

GÜINES PORK CHOPS *chuletas de puerco*

Güines is a colonial municipality of Havana, and was formerly the home of many exiled Cubans. Every year in Miami these exiles throw a party that is famous and lots of fun. I got this recipe from one of those parties, which I went to with a group of friends who came from Güines.

Chuletas are always eaten by the pair, so eight chuletas are for four people. Serve with *congrí* (see page 162) or *moros y cristianos* (see page 161).

4 SERVINGS (8 CHULETAS)

> Eight ½-inch-thick center-cut pork chops
> Salt and pepper to taste
> 3 garlic cloves, minced
> ½ teaspoon dried oregano
> ½ teaspoon ground cumin
> Juice from 2 sour oranges (see page 120)
> 1 large onion, peeled and thinly sliced
> 5 tablespoons olive oil

Place the pork chops in a pan, and marinate with salt, pepper, garlic, oregano, cumin, and sour-orange juice. Arrange the slices of onions on top. Cover, and refrigerate for at least 2 hours, preferably overnight. This will make the pork chops as tender as possible.

When fully marinated, remove the chops and pat dry with paper towels. Reserve the marinade and the sliced onion.

Heat the olive oil in a large skillet over medium-high heat. When the oil is sizzling, add the chops one by one, and keep turning them over to brown evenly, about 2 minutes per side. When they have browned, set them aside on a plate. Now add the reserved onion slices to the skillet, and sauté over medium heat until translucent, about 3 minutes. Add ½ cup of the reserved marinade, return the chops to the skillet, and sauté for about 10 minutes, turning once or twice, until they are cooked through and juices penetrate. Remove to a serving platter, and spoon the onions and pan juices over them.

GARDEN-STYLE PORK

carne de puerco a la jardinera

This recipe is a mosaic of vegetables and colors. Serve with very simple white rice (see page 160) or yellow rice (rice with saffron).

4 SERVINGS

2 tablespoons vegetable shortening or butter

1½ pounds pork loin, cubed

Juice of 1 lemon

½ teaspoon dried oregano

2 garlic cloves, minced

1 large onion, peeled and chopped

1 green bell pepper, seeded and chopped

¼ cup tomato sauce

1 parsley sprig, chopped

1 carrot, peeled and very thinly sliced

1 celery stalk, chopped

½ cup thinly sliced canned beets

½ cup sweet green peas (petit pois; canned are okay)

1 cup dry white wine

1 cup water

Heat the shortening in a deep, heavy skillet over medium heat. Add the pork cubes and stir well. Cook for about 3 minutes, until the cubes brown. Then, gradually, add the lemon juice, oregano, garlic, onion, green pepper, tomato sauce, parsley, carrot, celery, beets, sweet peas, wine, and water.

Bring to a simmer, reduce heat to medium-low, and continue to simmer for about 35 minutes. When all vegetables are tender and pork cubes are fully cooked, transfer to a serving bowl.

SANTIAGO DE CUBA MEATLOAF
pulpeta santiaguera

Santiago de Cuba is a breathtakingly beautiful province. The people are rural and love to cook their pork in many different ways. This is their variation on the Cuban meatloaf (see page 272). It is stronger-tasting because there is no ground beef: Use only ground pork and deviled ham spread.

6 SERVINGS

> 1 pound ground pork
> One small can deviled ham
> $\frac{1}{2}$ cup bread crumbs or cracker meal
> 2 eggs, beaten (divided)
> Salt and pepper to taste
> $\frac{1}{2}$ teaspoon dried oregano
> 1 carrot, grated
> 4 teaspoons olive oil
> 2 garlic cloves, minced
> 1 medium onion, peeled and chopped
> 1 green bell pepper, seeded and chopped
> $\frac{1}{2}$ cup tomato sauce
> $\frac{1}{2}$ cup dry white wine

Wash your hands and roll up your sleeves. There is no better way. In a large bowl, combine the ground pork and deviled ham. To this mixture add half of the bread crumbs, one of the beaten eggs, salt, pepper, oregano, and grated carrot. Work it and knead it together until all the ingredients are thoroughly combined and the texture is moist. Shape into an oblong or rectangular loaf.

Dip the loaf in the remaining beaten egg, and sprinkle with the remaining bread crumbs to coat lightly. Refrigerate, covered, in a pan for at least 1 hour.

Heat oil in a large, heavy pot over medium-high heat. Add the loaf, and brown on all sides. Turn the loaf carefully, using two spatulas or spoons, since piercing with a fork could break up the shape. You are not cooking it at this time, just browning it, so the whole process should only take about 3 to 5 minutes.

Remove loaf from the pot, and resume heating the oil over medium-high heat. Sauté the garlic, onion, and green pepper until the onion is translucent

(continued on next page)

(continued from previous page)

and the pepper is tender. Add the tomato sauce and wine. Simmer for about 5 minutes, and then gently place the browned meatloaf back in the pot with the tomato mixture. Reduce heat to medium-low, and cook for about 45 minutes, letting the sauce simmer slowly. Spoon sauce occasionally over the loaf, and add liquid for desired consistency. When fully cooked, transfer to a serving platter and slice. Serve immediately.

FRIED PORK LOIN FILLETS *carne de cerdo frita*

Serve with a little guava marmalade or jelly on the side.

4 SERVINGS

> 1 pound pork loin, boned, cut into ¼-inch-thick fillets
> 2 garlic cloves, minced
> Salt and pepper to taste
> 2 teaspoons butter

Trim off any excess fat from the pork, rub with garlic, and season with salt and pepper.

In a skillet, heat the butter over medium-high heat and sauté the fillets, turning them over, until browned and fully cooked (about 12 minutes).

PORK MONTERÍA *montería*

The *montería* is the Cuban leftover tradition the day after a big pork feast. Whenever we roast an entire suckling pig, it is a given that we will have lots and lots of leftover pork, which must not go to waste. The day after the party (usually Christmas Day), it is traditional to prepare a one-dish fork supper with the leftovers from the night before. Just spoon this over the leftover rice and you have a great hash!

6 SERVINGS

¼ cup olive oil
2 onions, peeled and chopped
1 green bell pepper, seeded and chopped
3 garlic cloves, minced
1 cup tomato sauce
3 pounds leftover roast pork meat and skin trimmings
1 cup dry white wine
1 cup pitted Spanish green olives
½ cup capers
¼ teaspoon dried oregano
¼ teaspoon ground cumin
Salt and pepper to taste
4 cups cooked white rice (see page 160)

Heat the oil in a large skillet over medium heat. Add the onions, green pepper, and garlic and sauté for a few minutes, until the onions become translucent and the pepper is tender. Add the tomato sauce, and simmer for a few minutes.

Add the leftover pork meat and skin, wine, olives, and capers, and season with oregano, cumin, salt, and pepper. Stirring constantly, continue cooking for a few more minutes, until you have the desired saucelike consistency. Add more liquid or correct seasonings if necessary. Serve immediately over a mound of white rice.

PORK SCALOPPINI *filetes de puerco a la italiana*

You can accompany these with your favorite prepared Italian red or pink sauce. Serve over pasta.

4 SERVINGS

> 8 pork loin fillets (extra lean), thinly sliced
> 2 garlic cloves, minced
> Salt and pepper to taste
> Juice of 1 lemon
> 2 cups bread crumbs or cracker meal
> 1 cup grated cheese (Parmigiano-Reggiano, Swiss, or even cheddar)
> 3 eggs, beaten
> 1 cup vegetable oil

Make sure that your fillets are thin. If you need to, pound with meat mallet to desired thickness (¼ inch thick is ideal). Marinate with garlic, salt, pepper, and lemon juice. Cover, and refrigerate for at least 30 minutes.

Meanwhile, mix the bread crumbs in a bowl with ¾ cup grated cheese. Dip and coat the fillets in the beaten eggs and then in the bread-crumb-and-cheese mixture.

Place the oil in a skillet over medium heat. Drop in the fillets one by one, fry for about 5 minutes, turning them over often, so they brown and fry evenly. When fully cooked, remove from skillet and pat with paper towels to remove excess oil. Transfer to a serving platter. Sprinkle the remaining grated cheese on top.

BABY BACK RIBS WITH GUAVA SAUCE
costillas de puerco con guayaba

My family loves these ribs cooked in the oven. Cook as many as your oven will hold. It is slow, slow, slow roasting! If you prefer, you may use the barbecue grill, but this way is so much less messy. Serve with a Cuban creamed potato salad (see page 196).

4 SERVINGS

> **3 pounds baby back pork ribs**
> **1 onion, peeled and chopped**
> **2 garlic cloves, minced**
> **1 teaspoon ground cumin**
> **½ stick guava paste**
> NOTE Guava paste can be found in the Hispanic aisle of your supermarket. It is inexpensive and can be stored forever. You can substitute guava marmalade or guava shells puréed in the blender.
> **Juice of 1 lemon**
> **1 tablespoon soy sauce**
> **2 teaspoons ketchup**
> **1 teaspoon Worcestershire sauce**
> **Salt and pepper to taste**

In a large saucepan, combine the ribs with the onion, garlic, and cumin. Add 8 cups water or enough to cover, and bring to a quick boil over high heat. Immediately drain the ribs and place them on heavy-duty aluminum foil wide enough to tent over them.

Preheat oven to 350 degrees.

Meanwhile, process the guava paste, lemon juice, soy sauce, ketchup, and Worcestershire sauce in a blender or food processor. You may add a little water to make the sauce smoother. Add salt and pepper to taste.

Pour the sauce over ribs (reserve some for later use), and seal the aluminum foil tightly over the ribs, making a very heavy tent that will fit on an oven rack. Place the tented ribs in a baking pan, and cook this in the oven for 2 or 3 hours.

Remove the pan from oven, and let the ribs cool inside the aluminum foil tent. Carefully open the foil at the seam, check for doneness by cutting into a rib, and you will discover the most mouth-watering, fall-off-the-bone oven-baked ribs ever. Serve immediately with the reserved sauce on the side.

FOR SERIOUS PORK LOVERS
para los que de verdad les gusta de puerco

Yes, you had to know this was coming! There are certain traditional recipes in Cuban culture that may expand what is considered edible by some American standards. These recipes are 100 percent guaranteed to surprise you, but also to delight you and broaden your food horizons.

CUBAN PORK CRACKLINGS
chicharrones de puerco

It is difficult for any Cuban to find anything more appetizing to accompany a cold beer or a rum cocktail than pork cracklings, which are prepared by frying pork fat or pork skin, or actually both, sometimes alone and sometimes with a little meat. There are three types of Cuban pork cracklings: those made only with fat trimmings, those made with skin and meat and fat, and those that are made only with the skin and, once fried, are puffy and foamy. Enjoy them all!

PORK RINDS
4 SERVINGS

> ½ cup olive oil or vegetable oil
> 1 pound pork fat, cut into ½- to 1-inch cubes
> 2 cups water
> Salt to taste

Heat the olive oil in a heavy, nonstick skillet over medium-high heat. When the oil is very hot, add the cubes of fat. Fry until crispy, sprinkling with water at regular intervals while frying. Be careful not to get splattered by the oil by staying an arm's length from the skillet.

Remove one by one—cooking time will vary depending on their size. Season, and serve immediately.

PORK SKIN, FAT, AND MEAT CRACKLINGS
chicharrones de puerco

This recipe is very similar to the Cajun recipes of Deep South Louisiana. To make these cracklings, you must use a cut of pork that has the skin, the fat, and the pork meat all attached. Pork rinds (preceding recipe) use only the pork fat. The easiest source for the combination of all three, to make these fantastic cracklings, is a butt roast or rump roast.

4 SERVINGS

> **2 pounds rump roast or butt roast of pork, cut into 1-inch pieces
>   that all include meat, skin, and fat**
> **½ cup mojo marinade (see page 120)**
> **4 cups water**
> **Salt and pepper to taste**
> **1 lemon, sliced, for garnish**

Marinate the pork pieces in the mojo in a covered bowl, for about 1 hour, at room temperature.

Put the water in a saucepan large enough so the water fills only one-quarter of the depth of the pan and the pork pieces will fit. Bring water to a boil over high heat.

Place the pork pieces in the boiling water in the pan, and keep the heat high. The water will dissolve the fat and evaporate, so the pork pieces will eventually cook in their own melted grease or lard (no, it is not a dirty word!). Cook for 7 to 10 minutes; do not overcook—you want them to remain tender. Remove with a slotted spoon as they are cooked, and pat dry with paper towels to remove excess grease. Transfer to a serving platter, season with salt and pepper, and garnish with lemon slices.

PUFFED PORK CRACKLINGS *chicharrones de viento*

These are the cracklings that you see packaged as a snack. In yesterday's Cuba, street vendors would sell them in brown paper bags. The most important step in making this wonderful snack is the drying of the skin.

4 SERVINGS

> **2 pounds pork skin, cut into squares 2–3-inch squares**
> **1 cup vegetable shortening or lard**
> **Salt to taste**

(continued on next page)

(continued from previous page)

Be sure to hang the strips to dry and cure for a few days before you plan to make puffed cracklings; they must resemble a stiff and dry hide. You can keep this dry skin in a closed jar for about 20 days, so make more than you need and reserve some for later use.

Cut each dried strip into two square or rectangular pieces. Put 4 cups water in a saucepan with salt. Heat over medium heat till boiling, and add the pork pieces. Simmer slowly, so the pork pieces will become soft and pliable. Once that is accomplished, remove, drain, and reserve.

In another saucepan, heat the shortening over very high heat. Once it is hot, add the pork pieces one by one, a few at at time, because they increase in size as they puff and will need plenty of room. Fry them in the shortening for about 3 minutes, until they puff and become golden brown. Sprinkle with salt, and serve immediately.

Accompany with cold beer or mojitos (see page 14).

PIG'S FEET WITH CHICKPEAS
paticas de puerco con garbanzos

This recipe is old and traditional. It began to appear in cookbooks in Cuba around the 1920s and was very popular throughout the island, because of its Spanish roots and because it is economical and full of nutrition. What could be better or make more sense to a frugal family than using every single part of the pig, even its feet? The meat is not as fatty as you might expect and is full of protein. Bijol (annatto powder) colors rice yellow and is often used in Cuban kitchens to replace expensive saffron.

4 SERVINGS

>   1 pound dried chickpeas
>   4 pig's feet, cleaned (see page 301)
>   6 strips bacon, diced
>   ½ pound cooked Virginia ham, diced
>   2 chorizo sausages, peeled and chopped
>   ½ cup olive oil
>   4 garlic cloves, minced
>   2 onions, peeled and chopped
>   2 cups tomato sauce
>   1 green bell pepper, seeded and chopped

1 pound potatoes, peeled and diced
1 teaspoon Bijol annatto powder
1 cup pitted Spanish green olives
$\frac{1}{2}$ cup raisins
Salt and pepper to taste

In a large bowl, soak the chickpeas overnight, changing the water once during the process. Meanwhile, boil the pig's feet in 8 cups water in a large saucepan for about 40 minutes. This, too, can be done the night before.

Drain the water from the chickpeas, and rinse. Drain the water from the pig's feet, and reserve.

Place the pig's feet and chickpeas in 2 cups water in a large, heavy pot over medium-high heat. Cook slowly for about fifteen minutes as it builds to a boil. Add the bacon strips, ham, and chorizo sausages, and continue to simmer for about 1 hour, until the chickpeas become tender. If needed, add more liquid as you cook.

Heat the olive oil in a skillet over medium-high heat, and add the garlic, onions, tomato sauce, and green pepper. After the chickpeas have softened, add this mixture to the pot with the chickpeas and pig's feet, and continue cooking slowly, making sure the pot contains enough liquid. Add the diced potatoes, Bijol, olives, and raisins. Season with salt and pepper to taste, and continue cooking over low heat for about 1 hour. Remove from heat when everything is tender. Serve in bowls as a stew, or over a mound of white rice (see page 160).

secrets of a Cuban cook

HOW TO CLEAN PIG'S FEET

You must thoroughly cleanse pig's feet in order to cook them or even pickle them. There is no pretty way around this, so try not to be squeamish. The first thing to do is to scald the feet several times with boiling water. Then scrape them clean with a wire brush. Make sure they are absolutely free of dirt or hair. Submerge them in cold water with salt and let them stand for about 4 hours at room temperature. After that time, rinse them well with clean, cold water. Now they are ready to be cooked.

VEAL, SAUSAGE, AND OTHER MEATS

ternera, salchichas, y otras carnes

COLD VEAL SCALLOPS MAMÁ INÉS
ternera fría Mamá Inés

Veal is the delicate meat of young calves that are from one to six months old. It is used widely in Europe in cutlets and steaks. In Spain, veal steaks and fries are a daily meal. Mamá Inés is a character in a famous Cuban song who loved celebrations; this is named after her because it is the perfect party food—delicious served cold. Serve it with avocado and pineapple salad (see page 191).

4 SERVINGS

> 8 veal medallions from loin
> Salt to taste
> ¼ stick (2 tablespoons) butter
> 1 cup white wine

Make sure that your veal medallions are thin. If you need to, pound with meat mallet to desired thickness (¼ inch thick is ideal). Season with salt.

Heat the butter in a skillet over medium-high heat, and sauté the veal for about 1 minute on each side, or until golden brown. Add the wine, and simmer for another 5 to 7 minutes, being careful not to overcook. Remove veal from heat when cooked but still tender.

Leave at room temperature to cool. If you want, you can refrigerate it until you are ready to use it. Transfer it to a platter, and serve.

CUBAN VEAL AND VEGETABLE MOSAIC
ternera con vegetales

4 SERVINGS

> 8 veal medallions
> Salt to taste
> 2 tablespoons all-purpose flour
> 2 tablespoons red vinegar
> ¼ stick (2 tablespoons) butter
> 1 cup Vedado District basic broth (see page 52)
> 1 tablespoon olive oil
> 1 large eggplant (about 2 pounds), skin on, sliced
> 4 tomatoes, sliced

Make sure that your veal medallions are thin. If you need to, pound with meat mallet to desired thickness (¼ inch thick is ideal). Season with salt, and sprinkle all over with the flour and the vinegar.

Heat the butter in a skillet over medium-high heat, and add the medallions. Sauté for about 1 minute on each side, or until golden brown. Reduce heat, add the broth, and simmer slowly for about 15 minutes.

Heat the olive oil in another skillet over medium-high heat, and sauté the eggplant slices for about 3 minutes, turning over occasionally. Reserve and set aside.

On a serving platter, alternate a layer of eggplant with one of veal medallions, and top with the tomato slices. Serve with a potato salad.

SALPICÓN

Salpicón also comes from the French culinary influence. It is a mixture of ingredients that you might have lying around the kitchen, diced or minced with a sauce. In Cuban cuisine, a *salpicón* is used to salvage the meat leftovers. It resembles a *pisto* (see pages 215–219). We love our *salpicón* with leftover veal meat. It is very elegant and can be eaten cold as well. Just serve it with a loaf of Cuban bread (see page 78).

4 SERVINGS

> 3 tablespoons olive oil
> 4 cups shredded or diced leftover veal (fully cooked)
> 1 tablespoon red vinegar
> 4 medium tomatoes, diced
> 1 sweet red pepper seeded and chopped
> Salt and pepper to taste
> Lettuce leaves for garnish
> 3 hard-boiled eggs (see page 201), sliced

Heat the oil in a skillet over medium-high heat. Sauté the meat for 2 to 3 minutes. Add the vinegar, tomatoes, and sweet pepper and continue cooking for another 3 minutes. Season with salt and pepper.

Remove from heat, and transfer mixture to the center of a serving platter lined with lettuce leaves. Arrange the hard-boiled egg slices around the *salpicón* and serve immediately.

CHORIZO SAUSAGE WITH POTATOES
papas con chorizo

This recipe just calls out for a glass of red wine and a loaf of Cuban bread (see page 78). It can be served hot on a cold winter night, or cold as a summer lunch.

4 SERVINGS

> 2 pounds potatoes, peeled and diced
> 2 chorizo sausages, diced
> Salt and pepper to taste
> 1 parsley sprig, chopped
> 2 teaspoons olive oil

In a large saucepan, boil the potatoes in 4 cups water for about 15 minutes. Remove potatoes with a slotted spoon, drain, and set aside.

In a skillet over medium-high heat, sauté the chorizo pieces for about 3 minutes, until they start to crumble. Season with salt and pepper, and add the chopped parsley and boiled potatoes. Continue cooking for 2 to 3 minutes, and stir only once or twice, making sure that the potatoes retain their shape and texture. Transfer to a serving platter, and sprinkle with olive oil.

SIMPLE BEEF JERKY *tasajo simple*

Tasajo is made of salt-dried beef. The original *tasajo* comes from horse meat, which is a delicacy in Italy but unheard of in the United States. In any case, dried beef can now be found at many Latin bodegas, or even in the butcher shop of your local supermarket. Here's how to make your own *tasajo*. This version is basic—no sauce, just plain *tasajo a la Cubana*!

4 SERVINGS

> 1½ pounds dried beef
> ¼ cup shortening
> 2 garlic cloves, minced
> 1 onion, peeled and chopped
> Salt and pepper to taste

Soak the dried beef overnight in a casserole full of water. Discard the water.

In a large saucepan, boil 8 cups water and add the dried beef. Cook for about 1 hour over low heat, until the beef becomes soft enough to pull apart in strands. Remove the beef with a slotted spoon, and pound with a meat mallet.

Allow to cool at room temperature, and shred the meat into thin threads.

Melt the shortening in a skillet over medium-high heat, and sauté the garlic and onion until the onion is translucent. Add the shredded beef, and continue to sauté, stirring constantly, for about 15 minutes. Season with salt and pepper.

CUBAN-STYLE STEWED BEEF JERKY
aporreado de tasajo

Serve this stewed *tasajo* over a mound of fluffy white rice (see page 160). Accompany with *tostones* (see pages 148–150).

4 SERVINGS

> 1½ pounds dried beef
> ¼ cup vegetable shortening
> 1 onion, peeled and chopped
> 1 sweet red pepper, seeded and chopped
> 2 garlic cloves, minced
> 1 cup tomato sauce
> ½ cup white wine
> ½ teaspoon ground cumin
> Salt and pepper to taste

Soak the dried beef overnight in a casserole full of water. Discard the water.

In a large saucepan, boil 8 cups water and add the dried beef. Cook for about 1 hour over low heat, until the beef becomes soft enough to pull apart in strands. Remove the beef with a slotted spoon, and pound with a meat mallet to make it as thin and tender as possible.

Allow to cool at room temperature, and shred the meat into thin threads.

Melt the shortening in a skillet over medium-high heat and sauté the onion, sweet pepper, and garlic until the onion is translucent and the pepper is tender. Reduce the heat, and add the tomato sauce, wine, and cumin, and season with salt and pepper. Add the shredded beef, and simmer slowly, covered, for another 30 minutes. When meat is tender and thoroughly cooked, remove from heat and serve immediately.

ROAST RABBIT TRINIDAD *conejo asado Trinidad*

The city of Trinidad, Cuba, is an architectural gem, preserved to this day. This rabbit recipe was served in the best restaurants of that beautiful historical setting. Rabbit, a delicacy relatively unknown to most Americans, is very popular in France, and for that reason became popular in Cuba as well. Rabbit meat is fine-grained, mild-flavored, and almost all white meat. It is a good source of protein. Ask your butcher for a young, tender rabbit weighing no more than 2½ pounds. Rabbit can be prepared in any manner. This simple roast is my favorite. It goes well with saffron rice and vegetables (see page 170).

4 SERVINGS

> **One 2- to 2½-pound rabbit, cleaned, prepared, and cut into 6 pieces**
> NOTE 2 pieces from forelegs, 2 pieces from hind legs, and 2 pieces from back section.
> **5 tablespoons butter, softened**
> **3 tablespoons butter**
> **Juice of 2 sour oranges (see page 120)**
> **3 garlic cloves, minced**
> **Salt and pepper to taste**

Preheat oven to 325 degrees.

Brush the rabbit pieces with the softened butter. Place rabbit pieces in a shallow baking pan, making sure you do not crowd them. Cover pan with aluminum foil, and roast for about 45 minutes.

Meanwhile, melt 3 tablespoons butter in a skillet over medium heat. Add the sour-orange juice and garlic, and sauté for 3 to 5 minutes. Season with salt and pepper.

After about 15 minutes, remove the foil cover and baste the rabbit pieces with the sour-orange mixture, using a spoon, brush, or bulb baster. This will prevent drying out and will add flavor and color to the rabbit. Roast for another ½ hour or so. Test for doneness as you would chicken—prick with a fork; the juices should run clear. When rabbit is done and tender (do not overcook), serve immediately.

RABBIT FARMER STYLE *conejo campesino*

My grandmother Fefa, who was widowed at a very young age, had eight kids, four of them boys. Her sons, my uncles, were avid fishermen and hunters and were boisterous young men. My grandmother told me that one of the ways she kept her young men at home and at bay was cooking very "manly" meals that contained wine and liquor, such as the farmer- or *campesino*-style rabbit in this recipe. Serve this with white rice (see page 160) or mashed potatoes (see page 133).

4 SERVINGS

> One 2- to 2½-pound rabbit, cleaned, prepared, and cut into
>   6 pieces
> NOTE 2 pieces from forelegs, 2 pieces from hind legs, and 2 pieces
> from back section
> **6 garlic cloves, minced**
> **1 tablespoon olive oil**
> **2 medium onions, peeled and chopped**
> **1½ cups red wine**
> **½ cup *aguardiente***
> NOTE Literally translated "burning water"—a South American coarse
> liquor distilled from sugarcane and flavored with aniseed. If you
> cannot obtain *aguardiente,* then opt for brandy.
> **Salt and pepper to taste**
> **2 teaspoons all-purpose flour or prepared roux**
> **½ stick (4 tablespoons) butter (optional)**

Rub the rabbit pieces with the minced garlic. In a skillet, heat the oil over medium-high heat, add the rabbit pieces, and cook until they are golden brown, turning to color evenly.

Reduce heat to medium-low, and add the onions, wine, and *aguardiente.* Season with salt and pepper. Thicken the sauce with flour or a prepared roux (mixture of flour and butter slowly cooked over low heat) and butter if desired. Cover, and allow to cook over low heat for an additional 30 to 35 minutes.

CUBAN BABY FOOD
para los más pequeños

IT IS REALLY VERY SMART and frugal to make your own baby food. What could be more satisfying than knowing that your child is getting the best nutrition with few preservatives and that you are getting the best value for your money? It is also a wonderful way of introducing your baby to all kinds of different ent textures and colors in food, a great adventure in moving to solid food. Root vegetables and beans can be the perfect baby food, because they contain protein; fruits are high in vitamins and minerals; cereals are excellent low-fat carbohydrates. Mix and match, experiment, and gradually get your baby to eat cereals, beans, fruits, and vegetables daily. Most of these recipes are for babies six months and older. Remember to give your child time to get accustomed to all the flavors and combinations.

Nearly all these recipes make more than one serving, and the leftovers can be stored, refrigerated, for up to seven days in airtight containers. You can freeze them for up to 20 days.

Just for fun, I gave each recipe a traditional Cuban baby name—of course in its diminutive form, because, while growing up, a Cuban baby is called by his or her name with either an "-ita" (girl) or "-ito" (boy) at the end. I am still Raquelita to my mom, and to half the people in my life.

ALICITA'S SWEET POTATO PURÉE
puré de boniato

Literally hundreds of sweet-potato or boniato varieties are grown, ranging from long and tubular to short and circular. Some varieties are starchy and bland; others are sweet and spicy. Boniato also has enough protein to serve as a sole food for your baby, and is filling enough to satisfy the heartiest appetite. My favorite way to prepare boniato is *boniatillo,* a sweet-potato purée with cinnamon (see the variation on page 374), which is great for older kids, but this purée is a great introduction to boniato. You can make a big batch and freeze and store it.

4 SERVINGS (6 MONTHS AND OLDER)

> **2 medium boniatos (sweet potatoes), peeled and cubed**
> **2 teaspoons cream cheese (optional)**
> **½ cup Vedado District basic broth (optional; see page 52)**

In a large heavy saucepan, cover the sweet potatoes with 6 cups water and bring to a boil. Reduce heat to medium-high, and continue cooking until boniatos are very tender (about 20 minutes). Do not add salt or any seasonings.

Drain, and transfer the boniatos to a food processor. Add the cream cheese (optional), and process until very smooth. If desired, and if your child is old enough, add the broth gradually as you process.

Serve immediately, making sure it is not too hot for the baby, or freeze it for the future.

MIGUELITO'S PUMPKIN AND CHICKEN PURÉE *puré de calabaza con pollo*

4 SERVINGS (6 MONTHS AND OLDER)

> 1 pound pumpkin flesh, diced
> 1 boneless, skinless chicken breast, steamed and cubed
> 2 teaspoons butter or cream cheese
> ½ cup Vedado District basic broth (optional; see page 52)

In a large heavy saucepan, cover the pumpkin pieces with 6 cups water and bring to a boil. Reduce heat to medium-high, and continue cooking until pumpkin is very tender (about 20 minutes). Do not add salt or any seasonings. Drain, and transfer to a food processor.

Add the chicken pieces and the butter, and process until very smooth. If desired and your child is old enough, add the broth gradually as you process to get the right consistency.

Serve immediately, making sure it is not too hot for the baby, or freeze for future use.

CARMENCITA'S CARROT AND PUMPKIN PURÉE *puré de zanahoria y calabaza*

4 SERVINGS (6 MONTHS AND OLDER)

> 2 carrots, peeled and diced or cubed
> Flesh of ½ small sugar pumpkin, diced
> 2 teaspoons butter or cream cheese
> ½ cup Vedado District basic broth (optional; see page 52)

In a large heavy saucepan, cover the carrot and pumpkin pieces with 6 cups water and bring to a boil. Reduce heat to medium-high, and continue cooking until very tender (about 20 minutes). Do not add salt or any seasonings. Drain, and transfer to a food processor.

Add the butter, and process until very smooth. If desired and your child is old enough, add the broth gradually as you process to get the right consistency.

Serve immediately, making sure it is not too hot for the baby, or freeze for future use.

BARBARITA'S MALANGA PURÉE *puré de malanga*

The best thing about *malanga* is that it is probably the most hypoallergenic food in the world, so it is perfect for babies, who can digest it easily. *Malanga* is a root vegetable about the size and shape of a regular white potato; it is easily found in Hispanic as well as in Asian markets. The amount of broth or milk that you add controls the purée's consistency.

4 SERVINGS (6 MONTHS AND OLDER)

> 3 medium *malangas*, peeled and cubed
> 2 teaspoons cream cheese (optional)
> ½ cup Vedado District basic broth (optional; see page 52)
> ½ cup milk (optional)

In a large heavy saucepan, cover the *malanga* cubes with 6 cups water and bring to a boil. Reduce heat to medium-high, and continue cooking until *malanga* is very tender (about 20 minutes). Do not add salt or any seasonings.

Drain, and transfer to a food processor. Add the cream cheese (optional), and process until very smooth. If desired and if your child is old enough, add the broth and/or milk gradually as you process.

Serve immediately, making sure it is not too hot for the baby, or freeze for future use.

RAULITO'S BANANA AND ORANGE PURÉE

puré de banana y naranja

This purée *must* be served immediately and not stored, either refrigerated or frozen. The banana loses all its nutritional value once it turns dark.

1 SERVING (6 MONTHS AND OLDER)

> 1 ripe banana, peeled and diced
> ½ cup freshly squeezed orange juice

Mash the banana with a fork, and transfer to a food processor. Add the orange juice gradually, and process until very smooth. Serve immediately. If you like, you can substitute apple juice for the orange juice.

MARISOLITA'S SPLIT PEA PURÉE

puré de chícharos

When you soak and cook *chícharos* (split peas), they turn soft. Adult Cubans eat them in a thick, hearty soup with ham hock and potatoes. They are best introduced to babies in this simple purée.

4 SERVINGS (6 MONTHS AND OLDER)

> 2 cups split peas
> 1 cup Vedado District basic broth (see page 52), plus more as
>   needed
> 1 cup cubed pumpkin
> ½ cup chopped sweet ham
> 2 teaspoons butter

Wash the split peas, and soak overnight in a large casserole full of water.

Once they are soaked and softened, drain, and place in a large saucepan with 4 cups water and the cup of broth. Bring to a boil, and cook over medium heat for about 20 minutes, or until peas are very tender. Add the pumpkin cubes, and continue to simmer for another 15 minutes.

When both the split peas and pumpkin are fully cooked, remove from heat and drain well. In a food processor, process the split peas and pumpkin with the chopped ham. Add the butter and some more broth gradually until you get the desired consistency. Serve immediately, making sure it is not too hot for the baby, or freeze for future use.

ALBERTICO'S SWEET PEA PURÉE

puré de petits pois

This one is for very busy moms! It could not be simpler.

2 SERVINGS (6 MONTHS AND OLDER)

> ¾ cup sweet green peas (petits pois; canned are okay)
> 1 teaspoon cream cheese, softened
> ¼ cup Vedado District basic broth (optional; see page 52)

(continued on next page)

(continued from previous page)

Mash the sweet peas in a mixing bowl, and transfer to food processor or blender.

Add the softened cream cheese, and process until smooth. If you like, add a little water or broth for a smoother or more liquid purée. Serve at room temperature, or warm a little by adding hot broth or water.

LOLITA'S MIXED VEGETABLE PURÉE
puré de vegetales

I remember my grandmother always making this in her large kitchen, just in case any baby dropped by. Inevitably, one of my aunts or uncles would bring a baby around for this wonderful surprise vegetable baby food. The vegetables were always fresh, and the adults, too, would eat the smooth food.

4 SERVINGS (6 MONTHS AND OLDER)

> **1 pound mixed fresh vegetables, peeled and diced or cubed**
> NOTE Favorite vegetables for this purée include carrots, pumpkin, sweet potato, white potato, beets, broccoli, and green beans.
> **2 teaspoons olive oil**
> **½ cup whole milk (optional)**

In a large heavy saucepan, cover the mixed vegetable cubes with 8 cups water and bring to a boil. Reduce heat to medium-high, and continue cooking until vegetables are very tender (about 20 minutes). Do not add salt or any seasonings.

Drain, and transfer the mixture to a food processor. Add the olive oil, and process until very smooth. If desired and if your child is old enough, add a little whole milk. Serve immediately, making sure it is not too hot for the baby, or freeze for future use.

ARTURITO'S GREEN BEAN MASH
delicia de judías verdes

Green beans are rich in potassium and calcium, and are wonderful vegetables for a baby's early development. They are also full of fiber and vitamin C.

4 SERVINGS (6 MONTHS AND OLDER)

> 1 pint green beans, washed and trimmed
> 1 cup chopped carrots
> ½ onion, peeled and chopped
> 2 teaspoons butter
> 1 tablespoon instant cream of rice, prepared

In a large heavy saucepan, cover the green beans and carrots with 8 cups water and bring to a boil. Add the onion, reduce heat to medium-high, and continue cooking until very tender (about 20 minutes).

Drain, and transfer the mixture to a food processor. Add the butter, and process until very smooth. Return to the saucepan, and add the cream of rice for extra nutrition and improved consistency. Stir, and serve immediately, making sure it is not too hot for the baby, or freeze for future use.

CLARITA'S SWEET POTATO AND TOMATO PURÉE *puré de boniato y tomate*

What could be better than marrying the two flavors and all the nutrients of the sweet potato and the tomato? Tomatoes are rich in vitamin C and low in calories. The sweet potato is the perfect carbohydrate to match.

4 SERVINGS (6 MONTHS AND OLDER)

> 2 medium boniatos (sweet potatoes), peeled and cubed
> 1 tomato, peeled, seeded, and chopped
> 2 teaspoons cream cheese (optional)
> ½ cup Vedado District basic broth (optional; see page 52)

In a large saucepan, cover the sweet potatoes with 6 cups water and bring to a boil. Reduce heat to medium-high, and continue cooking until very tender (about 20 minutes). Do not add salt or any seasonings.

(continued on next page)

(continued from previous page)

Drain, and transfer to a food processor. Add the tomato and the cream cheese (optional), and process until very smooth. Add the broth for a smoother purée. Serve immediately, making sure it is not too hot for the baby, or freeze for future use.

ANGELITO'S POTATO AND APPLE PURÉE
puré de papa y manzana

The combination is both sweet and finely textured, which makes it a wonderful baby food.

4 SERVINGS (6 MONTHS AND OLDER)

>   3 potatoes, peeled and diced
>   1 apple, peeled, cored, and diced
>   1 teaspoon olive oil

In a large saucepan, cover the potatoes with 6 cups water and bring to a boil. Reduce heat to medium-high, and continue cooking until potatoes are very tender (about 20 minutes). Add the apple and simmer for another 5 minutes.

Drain, and transfer the mixture to a food processor. Add the olive oil, and process until very smooth. Serve immediately, making sure it is not too hot for the baby, or freeze for future use.

FELICITA'S DELICIOUS RICE AND PUMPKIN PURÉE *puré de arroz y calabaza*

4 SERVINGS (6 MONTHS AND OLDER)

>   1 pound pumpkin flesh, diced
>   1 cup diced carrot
>   ½ onion, peeled and chopped
>   1 tablespoon instant cream of rice, prepared
>   1 teaspoon olive oil

In a large saucepan, cover the pumpkin and carrot pieces with 6 cups water and bring to a boil. Add the onion. Reduce heat to medium-high, and continue cooking until very tender (about 25 minutes). Do not add salt or any seasonings. Drain, and transfer to a food processor. Process until very smooth.

Return the mixture to a saucepan over very low heat, and add the cream of rice. Stir in the olive oil, and remove from heat. Serve immediately, making sure it is not too hot for the baby, or freeze for future use.

ISABELITA'S FENNEL CREAM *crema de hinojo*

Fennel is a versatile vegetable that plays an important role in the dishes of France and Italy. With curative as well as nutritional value, it can be a real plus in your baby's diet. It is aromatic and has a strong flavor, so this recipe dilutes it with cream of tapioca.

4 SERVINGS (6 MONTHS AND OLDER)

> 1 fennel bulb
> 1 cup vegetable consommé (see page 53)
> ½ cup tapioca cream or pudding, prepared
> 2 teaspoons olive oil

Core the fennel bulb, cut it lengthwise, and dice.

In a large saucepan, cover the fennel with 6 cups water and bring to a boil. Reduce heat to medium-high, and continue cooking until fennel is tender (about 15 minutes).

Drain, and transfer to a food processor. Process until very smooth. Return the fennel to a saucepan over very low heat, and add the broth slowly, stirring. Mix in the cream of tapioca, remove from heat, and stir. Add the olive oil, stir again, and serve immediately, making sure that it is not too hot for the baby, or freeze for future use.

NOTE For a quick and easy homemade tapioca cream, mix ¼ cup water and ¼ cup milk with 2 teaspoons quick-cooking tapioca, 1 tablespoon butter, 1 egg (beaten), and 2 tablespoons sugar, and cook over low heat for 7 minutes, stirring constantly, until the cream has reached a smooth texture.

CARLITO'S BEET SOUP *sopa de remolacha*

It is important to get your baby used to soups and broths early on. This will help them appreciate soups in their adult diets. Soups are easily digested, often naturally low in calories, and rich in vitamins and minerals. Never underestimate the healing and comforting power of soups!

4 SERVINGS (6 MONTHS AND OLDER)

> 2 potatoes, peeled and diced
> 1 beet, peeled and diced (see sidebar below)
> 1 carrot, peeled and diced
> 1 cup milk, or more as needed

In a large saucepan, cover the diced potatoes, beet, and carrot with 6 cups water and bring to a boil. Reduce heat to medium-high, and continue cooking until tender (about 25 minutes).

Drain, and transfer to a food processor. Process until very smooth. Return the mixture to a saucepan over very low heat, and add the milk slowly, stirring. If soup is too thick, add a little more milk until soup reaches desired consistency. Serve immediately, making sure it is not too hot for the baby.

secrets of a Cuban cook

THE EASY WAY TO PEEL A BEET

To peel away the skin of beets without a fuss or a mess, first soak them in a saucepan and bring to a boil over high heat. Once the water reaches boiling point, reduce heat to medium, cover the pan, and simmer for about 8 minutes. Remove the beets and place them in cold water. Once the beets are cool enough to handle, use a small knife and peel skin from top to bottom gently. It will come off immediately.

TITO'S FIRST BATIDO *el primer batido*

A *batido*, or milkshake, is refreshing, and perfect as a between-meal snack for your baby. Introduce tropical fruits slowly, to reduce the risk of allergic reactions. Bananas are great for starters. Papaya (*fruta bomba*) can follow. Be careful with guava, tamarind, or any melons.

1 SERVING (6 MONTHS AND OLDER)

> 1 cup milk
> ½ banana, peeled and diced
> ½ cup peeled and diced apple
> ½ cup crushed ice (optional)

In a blender, process the milk, banana, and apple. Blend until very smooth. You can add a little bit of crushed ice and process thoroughly. Remember— babies do not really like foods at any extreme temperatures. Serve immediately.

RENECITO'S COLORED RICE DELIGHT
delicia de arroz de colores

This recipe is perfect for older babies who can easily eat and digest small chunks of food.

4 SERVINGS (9 MONTHS AND OLDER)

> 1 carrot, peeled and diced
> ¾ cup sweet green peas (petits pois; canned are okay)
> ½ cup green beans, washed and trimmed
> 2 cups Vedado District basic broth (see page 52)
> 1½ cups white rice

In a large heavy saucepan, cover the diced carrot, sweet peas, and green beans with the broth.

Bring to a boil, and right at the boiling point, add the rice and lower heat, cover, and cook slowly for about 25 minutes. Fluff rice, transfer to a bowl, and serve immediately, making sure it is not too hot for the baby, or freeze for future use.

TERESITA'S VEGETABLES AND CHEESE
verduras con queso

This could introduce cottage cheese to your baby. In general, cheese is not only safe but healthful for babies: packed with calcium and a source of vitamins. This recipe is perfect for families trying to raise healthy vegetarian babies. And the best part is that babies love cheese. If you start with cottage cheese, you can graduate to other types of cheese later on.

4 SERVINGS (9 MONTHS AND OLDER)

> **3 cups peeled and diced fresh vegetables**
> NOTE Favorite vegetables for this recipe include carrots, pumpkin, sweet potato, white potato, beets, and green beans.
> **¼ cup instant Nabisco Cream of Wheat or cream of rice, prepared**
> **½ cup cottage cheese**

In a large heavy saucepan, cover the diced vegetables with 5 cups water and bring to a boil. Reduce heat to medium-high, and continue cooking until tender (about 25 minutes).

Drain, and transfer to a mixing bowl. Mash with a fork until you have a chunky consistency. Add the Cream of Wheat, and put in a casserole. Stir, and add the cheese, creating a smoothly blended mixture. Serve immediately, making sure it is not too hot for the baby.

RAFAELITO'S MARINE CREAM *crema marinera*

This light recipe is a wonderful introduction to the delights of the ocean. Fresh fish—whether grouper, mahi mahi, or any other kind—is a must! To make sure that the fish is completely deboned, run your fingers over the flesh of each fillet to locate any stray bones, and pull them out with tweezers (see page 225).

4 SERVINGS (9 MONTHS AND OLDER)

> **2 small white fish fillets, skinned and deboned**
> **2 cups Lolita's mixed vegetable purée (see page 314)**
> **½ cup instant cream of rice, prepared**
> **2 teaspoons olive oil**

Gently poach or steam the fish fillets in 2 cups water until fully cooked. Drain and mash, being careful to remove any leftover bones. Reserve. If you like, process in blender for a smoother and safer consistency.

In a separate saucepan, mix the vegetable purée with the cream of rice, and simmer over very low heat for 3 to 4 minutes. Add the olive oil, and stir in the mashed fish. Remove from heat and serve immediately, making sure it is not too hot for the baby, or freeze for future use.

JUNIOR'S FRUIT BOWL *macedonia clásica*

Yes, Cuban babies are sometimes called Junior, because they are often named after their fathers. This fruit cocktail is a great way to incorporate different fruits in babies' diets as they grow older.

4 SERVINGS (9 MONTHS AND OLDER)

> 1 peach, peeled, pitted, and diced
> 1 apple, peeled, cored, and diced
> 1 cup peach or apple juice
> ½ cup natural or vanilla yogurt
> ½ cup raisins

In a saucepan, cover the peach and apple pieces with the juice, and simmer over low heat for about 12 minutes. Remove from heat, and process slowly in food processor or blender.

Add the yogurt and raisins, and transfer to a serving bowl. Serve at room temperature, and store the leftovers.

THE CUBAN PRESSURE COOKER

la olla a presión cubana

FOR YEARS, I have been terrified of but fascinated by pressure cookers. I remember that my grandmother had not one but two first-generation pressure cookers in use at the same time on her stovetop, the jiggle tops dancing to their own beat, and steam venting out with a whistle. Modern-day pressure cookers, with their spring valves, are safe and easy to use and cook extremely fast. All pressure cookers produce steam in a closed container, raising the boiling point of the liquids; since they can get hotter before boiling, foods cook more quickly. Before you cook anything in a pressure cooker there must be liquid inside the pot, at least 1 cup of water, broth, or some other liquid, which is sufficient for about 20 minutes of cooking time. Never fill a pressure cooker to the top: It needs some extra space to produce steam. Follow the manufacturer's directions for how much. Do not cook on the very high setting, and make sure you reach and maintain the necessary pressure. Do not overcook in the pressure cooker, and remove the lid only when all the pressure has been released. And, above all, enjoy making these super-quick dishes in your pressure cooker.

CUBAN POT ROAST IN THE PRESSURE COOKER *boliche en olla a presión*

4 SERVINGS

> One 2- to 3-pound rump roast, marinated in 7 cups mojo
>   marinade (see page 120) for 2–3 hours
> ¼ cup vegetable oil
> Salt and pepper to taste
> 1 large onion, peeled and chopped
> 1 green bell pepper, seeded and chopped
> 1 bay leaf
> 1 cup Vedado District basic broth (see page 52)
> ½ cup water, plus 2 tablespoons cold water
> 1 cup red wine
> 4 potatoes, peeled and diced
> 2 carrots, peeled and chopped
> 2 tablespoons all-purpose flour

Brown meat in oil in the pressure cooker. Add salt, pepper, onion, green pepper, bay leaf, broth, ½ cup water, and wine. Add potatoes and carrots. Cover, and bring to full pressure.

When steam appears, reduce heat to low and cook for 25 to 30 minutes, according to manufacturer's directions, until tender. Reduce pressure completely, remove meat and vegetables with a slotted spoon, and set aside.

Combine flour and 2 tablespoons cold water, and mix until smooth. Return broth to a simmer, stir in flour and water, and continue to cook until sauce thickens. Return the meat and potatoes to the pot, and remove from heat. Serve immediately.

RICE AND CHICKEN IN THE
PRESSURE COOKER *arroz con pollo en olla a presión*

Arroz con pollo is one of the easiest recipes for the pressure cooker.

4 SERVINGS

3 pounds bone-in chicken breasts, thighs, and drumsticks
4 teaspoons vegetable oil
½ cup sofrito (see page 119)
¼ pound ham, diced
3 bay leaves
Salt and pepper to taste
¼ teaspoon ground oregano
1 cup water
1 cup beer
1 cup chicken consommé (see page 54) or canned broth
1 pound short-grain Valencia rice
Saffron to taste
Pitted Spanish green olives for garnish

Wash the chicken parts, and blot dry with paper towels. Heat the oil in the pressure cooker. Brown the chicken pieces. Stir in the sofrito, and add the diced ham, bay leaves, salt, pepper, and oregano.

Add the water, beer, and chicken consommé. Add the rice and saffron.

Cover, and bring to full pressure.

When steam appears, reduce heat to low and cook for 25 to 30 minutes, according to manufacturer's directions, until tender.

Reduce pressure completely, and uncover as directed.

GARDEN-STYLE PORK IN THE PRESSURE COOKER

carne de puerco a la jardinera en olla a presión

This recipe is a multicolored mosaic of vegetables. Serve with very simple white rice (see page 160) or yellow rice.

4 SERVINGS

1½ pounds pork loin, cubed

2 tablespoons vegetable shortening or butter

Juice of 1 lemon

½ teaspoon dried oregano

2 garlic cloves, minced

1 large onion, peeled and chopped

1 green pepper, seeded and chopped

¼ cup tomato sauce

1 parsley sprig, chopped

1 carrot, peeled and very thinly sliced

1 celery stalk, chopped

1 cup dry white wine

1 cup water, plus 2 tablespoons cold water

2 teaspoons all-purpose flour

Brown meat in shortening in the pressure cooker. Add lemon juice, oregano, garlic, onion, green pepper, tomato sauce, parsley, carrot, celery, wine, and 1 cup water. Cover, and bring to full pressure.

When steam appears, reduce heat to low and cook for 25 to 30 minutes, according to manufacturer's directions, until tender. Reduce pressure completely, remove meat and vegetables with a slotted spoon, and set aside.

Combine flour and 2 tablespoons cold water, and mix until smooth. Return broth to a simmer, stir in flour and water, and continue to cook until sauce thickens. Remove from heat, pour over meat and vegetables, and serve immediately.

ROOT VEGETABLES STEAMED UNDER PRESSURE

viandas cocidas al vapor en olla a presión

Great-quality root vegetables are best steamed in the pressure cooker. Just add a bit of butter or olive oil and enjoy the most healthful preparation.

4 SERVINGS

2 cups water
1 small pumpkin, peeled and cut into large pieces
1 boniato (sweet potato), peeled and cut into large pieces
1 cassava (*yuca*), peeled and cut into large pieces
2 potatoes, peeled and cut into large pieces
1 ripe plantain, peeled and cut into large pieces
1 *malanga*, peeled and cut into large pieces
Olive oil for serving

First pour the water into your pressure cooker, as required by manufacturer's instructions. Set the steamer rack or basket in place.

Bring the water to a boil, and arrange the vegetables on the rack or basket in a single layer. Lock the lid in place, cover, and bring to full pressure.

When steam appears, reduce heat to low and cook for about 12 minutes, according to manufacturer's directions, until everything is still crisp but cooked. Reduce pressure completely, and remove from heat.

Serve with a drizzle of olive oil.

BACALAO AND BONIATO IN THE PRESSURE COOKER

bacalao y boniato en olla a presión

4 SERVINGS

> 1 pound salt cod (*bacalao*) strips
> 3 tablespoons olive oil
> 3 boniatos (sweet potatoes), peeled and diced
> 1 medium onion, peeled and chopped
> 2 garlic cloves, minced
> 1 medium green bell pepper, seeded and cut into julienne strips
> 1 cup tomato sauce
> Salt and pepper to taste
> 2 bay leaves
> 3 cups water
> ¼ cup dry white wine

Soak the codfish in a large bowl of water for 24 hours in the refrigerator, changing the water every few hours.

Heat the oil in the pressure cooker. Stir in the *bacalao* strips, boniatos, onion, garlic, green pepper, tomato sauce, salt, pepper, and bay leaves. Add the water and wine.

Cover, and bring to full pressure.

When steam appears, reduce heat to low and cook for 25 to 30 minutes, according to manufacturer's directions, until tender.

Reduce pressure completely, and uncover as directed.

SWEET CORNMEAL IN THE PRESSURE COOKER *harina dulce en olla a presión*

Sweet cornmeal is a great baby food—and a great dessert when we want to baby our loved ones.

4 SERVINGS

4 cups water
Salt to taste
1 cinnamon stick
1 cup finely ground cornmeal
1 cup sweetened condensed milk
¼ cup sugar
½ cup raisins
4 teaspoons butter
2 teaspoons vanilla extract
Ground cinnamon to taste

Put the water, salt, and cinnamon stick in the pressure cooker. Add the cornmeal, condensed milk, sugar, raisins, butter, and vanilla extract.

Cover, and bring to full pressure.

When steam appears, reduce heat to low and cook for 12 to 15 minutes, according to manufacturer's directions, until tender.

Reduce pressure completely, and uncover as directed. Sprinkle with ground cinnamon before serving.

CUBAN OXTAIL STEW IN THE PRESSURE COOKER *rabo encendido en olla a presión*

4 SERVINGS

2 pounds oxtails, disjointed
¼ cup olive oil
½ cup dry red wine
Salt and pepper to taste
¼ cup vegetable oil
4 garlic cloves, minced
1 large onion, peeled and chopped
1 green pepper, seeded and chopped
1 sweet red pepper, seeded and chopped
1 carrot, peeled and diced
2 cups tomato sauce
2 cups Vedado District basic broth (see page 52)
5 small potatoes, peeled and diced
1 cup chopped toasted almonds
½ cup capers
2 bay leaves

Marinate the meat in a mixture of olive oil, wine, salt, and pepper in the refrigerator for at least 8 hours or overnight. Drain marinade and discard.

Heat the vegetable oil in the pressure cooker. Add the oxtail meat and brown on all sides. Add the garlic, onion, peppers, and carrot, and sauté until the onion is translucent and vegetables are tender. Add the tomato sauce and the broth. Add the potatoes, almonds, capers, and bay leaves.

Cover, and bring to full pressure.

When steam appears, reduce heat to low and cook for about 25 to 30 minutes, according to manufacturer's directions, until tender.

Reduce pressure completely, and uncover as directed.

LIGHT CUBAN

platos ligeros cubanos

IT IS ALWAYS A GOOD IDEA to gear your recipes to a healthier lifestyle. You have the power to choose the ingredients and the method of preparation, and so you can cut out extra calories, carbohydrates, and fats. Eat in moderation, and watch those sweets. Besides following some of the recipes in this chapter, create and adapt your own. And of course exercise, don't smoke, and know the warning signs of failing health. In our family, we like to walk, and this helps us control our weight and stay healthy. In your diet:

- Eat a variety of fruits and vegetables.
- Choose whole-grain, high-fiber, fat-free, and low-fat foods.
- Eat fish and lean chicken and meats.
- Limit snacks and other high-calorie, low-nutrient foods.
- Try using cooking spray rather than butter or oil to keep food from sticking to pans.
- Cut back on trans fat and high-cholesterol-producing foods.
- Cut back on all sodas.
- Choose, cook, and prepare foods with no sodium added, and season only sparingly with salt.
- Monitor for diabetes. Diabetes is very prevalent in the Hispanic community, but most people do not even realize they have it, and not treating it can lead to devastating health problems. High blood pressure is also a

danger; blood pressure should be checked on a regular basis. Remember that this is usually reduced through proper diet. Obesity is also a major concern for Hispanics, and indeed for many Americans. Know your risks and watch your weight.

In all the recipes in this book, you can substitute low-fat and low-cal ingredients and use less salt. I have collected specific lighter Cuban recipes in this chapter over the years, to help when any of us has been on a diet. These are our favorites.

BLACK BEAN PATTIES WITH PINEAPPLE RICE

hamburguesas de frijoles negros con arroz de piña

This meal is high in protein and low in calories.

4 SERVINGS

FOR RICE

> 2 teaspoons butter or light butter substitute
> 1 cup diced pineapple (see page 31)
> 2 cups cooked brown rice

FOR BLACK BEAN PATTIES

> 2 cups black bean soup, drained (see page 59)
> 1 garlic clove, minced
> ¼ teaspoon ground cumin powder
> Salt to taste
> 1 egg white
> ½ cup shredded low-fat cheese
> 1 onion, peeled and minced
> ¼ cup cornmeal
> ¼ cup reduced-fat sour cream (optional)

To prepare the rice: Melt the butter substitute in a nonstick skillet over medium heat. Add the pineapple pieces, and sauté for about 4 minutes,

(continued on next page)

(continued from previous page)

or until pineapple begins to brown. Add to cooked rice, toss in a bowl, and keep warm.

To prepare the patties: Combine half of the beans, the garlic, cumin, and salt in a bowl. Mash with a fork. Place the other half of the beans and the egg white in a food processor or blender, and purée. Add the purée to the mashed beans, and mix in the cheese and onion. Divide and shape mixture into four patties, and coat with cornmeal. Coat skillet with cooking spray, and cook patties over medium heat for about 3 minutes on each side. Serve patties over the mound of pineapple rice. Top with reduced-fat sour cream if desired.

CHICKEN AND PLANTAIN STEW
estofado de pollo y plátano

High in potassium and low in calories and fat, this is a great one-dish diet meal.

4 SERVINGS

> 1 teaspoon olive oil
> 1 pound boneless chicken breast, diced
> 1 cup chopped onion
> 2 garlic cloves, minced
> 1 cup chopped tomatoes
> ½ cup dry white wine
> 1 teaspoon paprika
> 1 teaspoon ground cumin
> 1 teaspoon dried oregano powder
> 1 cup chicken consommé (see page 54) or low-fat, low-sodium
>   chicken broth
> 2 firm plantains, peeled and sliced

In a large saucepan, heat oil over medium-high heat. Add the chicken, onion, and garlic, and sauté for about 5 minutes, stirring occasionally, until chicken pieces brown.

Add the tomatoes, wine, paprika, cumin, oregano, and chicken consommé. Bring to a boil over high heat, reduce heat, and simmer, uncovered, for about 10 to 12 minutes. Add the plantains, and continue to simmer over low heat for another 10 minutes, or until plantains are tender and fully cooked. This dish is so rich (even if low in calories) that it can be eaten without rice, so serve it in a bowl and accompany with crackers.

CUBAN GARDEN SOUP *sopa cubana a la jardinera*

This tasty soup is low in calories and high in vegetable nutrients, with the added bonus of whole-wheat pasta.

4 SERVINGS

> 1 teaspoon olive oil
> 1 onion, peeled and chopped
> 2 cups chicken consommé (see page 54) or low-fat, low-sodium canned chicken broth
> 1 cup water
> 1 cup chopped collard greens
> 1 cup lima beans, cooked
> ½ cup whole-wheat elbow macaroni
> 1 carrot, peeled and sliced
> 2 celery stalks, chopped
> 1 garlic clove, minced

In a large saucepan, heat the oil over medium-high heat, swirling to coat the bottom. Sauté the onion for 7 to 10 minutes, or until translucent.

Reduce the heat to low, and stir in the remaining ingredients. Simmer for about 10 minutes, or until pasta is tender (longer if you like soft pasta), stirring occasionally. Serve immediately in a bowl.

MIXED SALAD GREENS WITH SHRIMP À LA VINAIGRETTE

ensalada verde de camarones con vinagreta

You can make this great entrée salad with any of my tropical vinaigrettes (see pages 107–108)

4 SERVINGS

2 teaspoons olive oil

2 cups raw shrimp, peeled, deveined, and rinsed

1 cup torn-up iceberg lettuce

1 cup chopped romaine lettuce

1 cup chopped watercress

1 cup torn-up mixed salad greens

1 cucumber, peeled and chopped

½ Bermuda onion, thinly sliced

½ cup vinaigrette dressing (see pages 107–108)

1 cup chopped tomatoes

1 lemon, cut into wedges

In a nonstick skillet, heat the oil over medium-high heat and sauté the shrimp for about 2 minutes, stirring frequently to prevent sticking. Reduce heat, and cook for 2 or 3 more minutes, or until shrimp are pink on the outside and opaque on the inside. Remove from heat and set aside.

Arrange your greens in a large salad bowl with the cucumber and Bermuda onion. Toss with the vinaigrette dressing of your choice from my homemade recipes. Top with tomatoes, and layer with the cooked shrimp. Squeeze lemon wedges over the salad, and enjoy.

DIRTY RICE WITH RED BEANS AND TURKEY CHORIZO

arroz sucio con frijoles colorados y chorizo de pavo

You will find turkey-stuffed chorizo sausage at many supermarkets.

4 SERVINGS

> 1 teaspoon olive oil
> 1 garlic clove, minced
> 1 onion, peeled and chopped
> 1 turkey chorizo sausage, sliced
> 2 celery stalks, chopped
> 1 cup cooked and drained red beans (see page 68)
> 2 cups cooked brown rice

In a large nonstick skillet, heat the oil over medium-high heat and sauté garlic and onion for about 2 minutes, or until onion becomes translucent. Add the sausage and celery, and continue to cook for about 5 minutes, stirring occasionally.

Reduce the heat to low, and add the red beans and the rice. Remove from heat and serve immediately.

GLAZED PORK CUBES *dados de puerco glaseados*

This light preparation is important, because Cubans love pork—it is the other white meat in our cooking.

4 SERVINGS

> 1 teaspoon canola oil
> 1 pound boneless pork loin, all fat discarded, cubed
> 1 onion, peeled and chopped
> 2 garlic cloves, minced
> ¼ cup fresh orange juice
> Juice of 1 lemon
> 1 tablespoon brown sugar
> 4 lettuce leaves

(continued on next page)

(continued from previous page)

In a large skillet, heat the oil over medium-high heat. Add the pork cubes and brown, stirring occasionally, for about 5 minutes. Add the onion and garlic, and sauté for an additional 2 minutes.

Reduce heat, and stir in the juices and the sugar. Simmer, covered, for about 25 minutes, until the pork is tender. Cook uncovered over high heat for another 5 minutes, until the juices have reduced to a glaze. Serve immediately over a bed of lettuce or in a lettuce wrap.

BLACK-EYED PEAS IN A POT
frijoles caritas en cazuela
4 SERVINGS

> 2 cups black-eyed peas
> 1 teaspoon olive oil
> 1 onion, peeled and chopped
> 1 garlic clove, minced
> 2 celery stalks, chopped
> ½ cup tomato paste
> ¼ cup dry white wine
> 1 bay leaf

Wash the beans with cold water, drain, and place in a large bowl. Soak the beans in 8 cups water overnight, or at least for 6 hours.

When the beans have swollen, cook in the same water they soaked in until soft, approximately 45 minutes. Drain, and set aside

In a skillet over medium-high heat, heat the oil and sauté the onion, garlic, and celery. Add the tomato paste, wine, and bay leaf. Reduce heat, add the drained black-eyed peas, and simmer, covered, for about 40 minutes, until all the ingredients are thoroughly combined.

BAKED BONIATO AND APPLES

boniato y manzanas al horno

The cinnamon helps keep blood pressure at a healthy level. This is a great food to take on a picnic. You can even sprinkle a few bacon bits on top.

4 SERVINGS

> ¼ cup brown sugar
> ½ teaspoon ground cinnamon
> 2 cups peeled and diced boniato (sweet potato)
> 1 cup peeled and diced apple
> 2 tablespoons butter or light butter substitute

In a small bowl, stir together the sugar and cinnamon.

Lightly spray a glass casserole dish with cooking spray, and preheat the oven to 350 degrees.

Arrange layers of boniato, apple, and the cinnamon-and-sugar combination in the casserole dish with the butter dotted on top. Cover with aluminum foil. Bake for about 1 hour, or until the boniato and apple are soft and tender. Serve hot or cold.

HERBED CORNMEAL   *harina de maíz con hierbas*

4 SERVINGS

> 3 cups water
> ½ cup uncooked cornmeal
> 2 teaspoons butter or light butter substitute
> 1 cup chopped fresh parsley

In a medium saucepan, bring the water to a boil over high heat. Stir in the cornmeal. Return to a boil, reduce the heat, and simmer, covered, stirring occasionally for about 20 minutes, or until thickened. Remove from heat.

Meanwhile, in a small bowl, mix the margarine, parsley, salt, and pepper.

Spoon the cornmeal into small bowls, and top each serving with the margarine-herb mixture. Serve immediately with grilled meat or chicken.

SUGARLESS TROPICAL FRUIT SORBET

sorbeta de frutas tropicales sin azúcar

This is a sugar-free, quick, delicious dessert.

4 SERVINGS

> One 3-ounce box sugar-free strawberry gelatin
> 1 cup boiling water
> 1 cup diced fresh pineapple (see page 31)
> 1 banana, peeled and sliced, plus more slices for garnish
> Juice of 1 lemon

Put the gelatin in a small bowl. Pour in the boiling water, and stir until the gelatin is dissolved.

Pour gelatin into a blender or food processor. Add the pineapple, lemon juice, and banana. Process on high speed until smooth, about 45 seconds. Pour into a glass baking pan, and freeze, uncovered, for about 2 hours, until firm. Just before serving, garnish with banana slices.

CUBAN DESSERTS
postres cubanos

IF THE BODY NEEDS NUTRITION, then the soul certainly needs desserts. Cubans love desserts, either simple or complex—popular pastries and puddings; mouth-melting marmalades and tropical fruit dishes that will delight your family and friends. Cuban cooks have enthusiastically maintained a tradition of preparing distinctive desserts, while borrowing from the French their passion for pastry, and from the Spanish the simplicity of their creams and puddings. The abundance of tropical fruit in Cuban cooking just adds a bonus. Mango marmalade, pineapple pound cake, and the ultimate tropical tiramisù that a wonderful Italian chef gave me are all included in these pages. But we must not forget the simple *timba,* or the *torrejas* (our take on French toast). And our variety of flans and custards are also prominent on our list of the most exquisite Cuban desserts. Our ice creams and sorbets are so numerous and diverse that they deserve another chapter, which follows.

LA TIMBA

The *timba* is the simplest of all traditional Cuban sweets. You can pair it with a cracker or a piece of Cuban bread or, if you are a purist, just eat it as is. You can also use guava shells in sweet syrup for this little treat.

1 SERVING

> Two ½-inch slices *queso blanco* or Swiss cheese
> Two ½-inch slices guava paste (see Resources, page 417)

Layer one slice of cheese on one slice of guava paste, and repeat.

SIMPLE SYRUP *almíbar*

Anyone who has dabbled in making desserts knows that syrup is the foundation of many confections. This is especially true of Cuban desserts. So here is a very basic recipe for that very simple syrup.

4 CUPS

> 3 cups sugar
> 3 cups water

In a saucepan, mix the sugar and water together and bring to a boil over medium-high heat.

Cook and continue stirring until sugar has completely dissolved, which should happen in about 10 minutes. To test if it is ready, drop a small amount in very cold water. It should be thick but still fluid. Remove from heat, and allow to cool. You can use it right away for your recipe, or refrigerate it in a covered container. If stored properly, syrup can last for almost 3 months.

NOTE The mixture will reach the syrup state at 212 degrees Fahrenheit. Check the temperature with a candy thermometer.

You can give flavor to your simple syrup by adding aromatics while boiling. These include cinnamon sticks, anise, ginger, citrus peels, and vanilla bean. When the syrup is ready, strain it and discard the aromatic.

CUBAN CARAMEL *caramelo*

Caramel is used for many desserts, and when it cools and hardens is the base for many brittles.

2 CUPS

3 cups sugar
3 cups water

In a saucepan, mix the sugar and water and bring to a boil over medium-high heat, stirring constantly.

Cook and continue stirring until the sugar has completely dissolved. The texture should be smooth and free of lumps, and thick enough to coat a wooden spoon. Cook a little longer, until syrup takes on a honey color for light caramel and a dark-brown color for dark caramel.

NOTE The mixture will reach the caramel state between 320 and 360 degrees Fahrenheit. Check the temperature with a candy thermometer.

SWEET MILK CARAMEL À LA BENNY MORÉ
dulce de leche Benny Moré

Benny Moré was the greatest Cuban singer of all time. His expression, his beat, and his great tenor voice were masterful. His personal life, on the other hand, was a mess. Our Elvis! Elvis may have had his signature peanut-butter-and-banana sandwiches, but Benny had his *dulce de leche*. The extra ingredients, besides the simmering milk and sugar, give it special properties and flavor. Serve this with cookies, or as a filling in pies or cakes. My family loves it between two sugar cookies.

4 SERVINGS

One 12-ounce can evaporated milk
½ cup water
1 teaspoon white vinegar
Peel of 1 lemon
1 cup sugar
1 cinnamon stick

(continued on next page)

(continued from previous page)

Put the evaporated milk, water, vinegar, and lemon rind in a medium heavy saucepan, and cook over medium heat until the milk curdles. Add the sugar and cinnamon stick.

Reduce heat to the lowest possible setting, and continue to cook without stirring, for about 1 hour. The *dulce de leche* will become thick and spreadable. Remove from heat, and discard cinnamon stick.

DOMINIQUE'S BANANAS WITH RUM AND RAISINS *bananas con pasas al ron a la Dominique*

My friend Dominique, who is a Haitian hotelier, gave me this wonderful recipe back when we were in college. Haitian rum, though not as famous as the Cuban brands, is mellow and works perfectly in any dessert recipe.

4 SERVINGS

> 1 cup raisins
> ½ cup white rum
> ½ stick (4 tablespoons) butter
> ½ cup sugar
> 4 bananas, peeled and cut in half lengthwise
> Juice of 1 lemon
> ½ cup ground peanuts
> 1 cup maraschino cherries, without stems

Soak the raisins in a cup with the rum for about 30 minutes. Drain, and reserve both rum and raisins.

In a mixing bowl, beat the butter and the sugar by hand or electric mixer until you form a cream. Add a tablespoon of the reserved rum to add flavor.

Preheat oven to 350 degrees.

Transfer your banana halves to a baking pan, and sprinkle them with lemon juice. Pour the butter-and-sugar mixture on top of the bananas, and then the rum-soaked raisins. Top with the peanuts and maraschino cherries, and heat in oven for about 3 minutes. Serve immediately.

GYPSY ROLL *brazo gitano*

I just could not translate the name of this dessert literally. It really should be called "Gypsy arm," but who wants to eat that? When finished, this dessert will look like a log; when cut, the portions have a pinwheel design. This roll can be made with any of your favorite fillings. Cubans love guava marmalade and the very special *dulce de leche,* but you can experiment with your own favorite flavors, whether simple or fancy, to fit the occasion. I am including the basic recipe and a few filling recipes for you to enjoy.

6 SERVINGS

> ½ stick (4 tablespoons) butter, for greasing pan and
>   parchment paper
> 6 eggs, separated
> 1 cup granulated sugar
> 1 cup all-purpose flour
> 1 teaspoon baking powder
> Salt to taste
> 1 teaspoon vanilla extract
> Confectioner's sugar, for dusting

Butter a jelly-roll pan (a rectangular baking pan with shallow sides, designed for very thin cakes that are coated with a layer of jelly), and line with buttered parchment paper.

With an electric mixer, beat the egg whites at medium speed until soft peaks form. Add the granulated sugar little by little, and increase the speed in the mixer. Beat until you get stiff peaks. Set aside.

Preheat oven to 375 degrees.

In a separate mixing bowl, beat the egg yolks until you get a pale-yellow color and the mixture becomes fluffy. In yet another mixing bowl, sift together the flour, baking powder, and salt.

Fold the egg yolks into the egg whites, and then fold in the flour and add the vanilla. Pour this batter into the jelly-roll pan, and spread it evenly to the edges of the pan. Bake in oven for about 15 minutes. Test for doneness by inserting a toothpick in the center; if it comes out clean, the cake is ready. Trim off the edges.

Invert the cake into a damp, very clean kitchen towel dusted with confectioners' sugar. Peel off the parchment paper and roll up the cake in the towel. Allow to cool for 10 minutes. Prepare filling (recipe suggestions follow).

(continued on next page)

(continued from previous page)

When cake is cool and filling is ready, unroll the cake. Evenly spread the filling over the cake, making sure you leave borders all around. Roll up the cake once again, and place it seam down on a serving plate. Dust the cake with confectioners' sugar, or frost with simple whipped cream or store-bought frosting, or drizzle with chocolate syrup. Slice the cake and serve.

secrets of a Cuban cook

SEPARATING AND FOLDING TECHNIQUES

Separating eggs is super-easy if you take a homemade approach. To separate whites from yolks, you can simply use the cracked shells. Transfer the yolk to the other shell half over a small bowl, letting the whites fall into the bowl and concentrating on keeping the yolk in the shell.

Folding is a technique used to mix or combine very gently a light, airy mixture such as egg whites with a heavier mixture, such as flour. Place the light mixture on top of the heavier mixture in a bowl, and, starting at the back of the bowl, mix in a sequence of down, across, up, and over motions—sort of like a figure eight. This combines ingredients in the gentlest way. It's a very careful, tender, and gradual procedure.

GUAVA FILLING *relleno de guayaba*

> Half 18-ounce bar guava paste, cut in slices
> Juice of ½ lemon
> 1 teaspoon rum
> 1 teaspoon grated lemon zest (see page 345)
> 2 teaspoons confectioners' sugar
> ½ cup whipped cream

Mix in food processor the guava paste, lemon juice, rum, and zest, and pulse until it becomes a spread.

DULCE DE LECHE FILLING *relleno de dulce de leche*

One 14-ounce can sweetened condensed milk

To prepare in the can: Submerge the unopened can completely in water in a saucepan. Bring the water to a boil. Reduce heat, and keep the water at a very low boil for about 2 hours. Make sure the water does not evaporate and the can is always submerged. Let the can cool before you open it. You can then pour contents into a small bowl, ready to spread on the cake.

To prepare in a heavy saucepan: Pour the condensed milk into a small heavy saucepan, and simmer over very low heat, stirring constantly, until it becomes dark amber in color and thick in texture. Let cool slightly before spreading on cake.

CHOCOLATE RUM FILLING *relleno de chocolate y ron*

$\frac{1}{4}$ **cup water**
$\frac{1}{4}$ **cup plus 1 tablespoon sugar**
2 tablespoons white rum
1$\frac{1}{4}$ cups heavy cream
1 tablespoon cocoa powder

(continued on next page)

secrets of a Cuban cook

LEMON ZEST

What is lemon zest? If you are asking the question, you probably only remember the bath soap with the catchy name and TV commercials. Actual lemon zest can be gotten easily by peeling or grating the yellow part of a lemon's skin. To remove the zest from the fruit, use a sharp paring knife or vegetable peeler. Peel off only the colored portion of the rind (the white is quite bitter). Mince the zest or leave it in strips, as your recipe dictates. If a recipe calls for grated zest, then simply grate the lemon as you would any vegetable—again, making sure you are grating only the colored part of the rind. The process is the same for limes or oranges. You can also purchase dried zest in the spice section of your supermarket, but it is never as good as fresh.

(continued from previous page)

In a small saucepan, combine water and ¼ cup sugar. Bring to a boil, reduce the heat, and simmer for about 3 minutes, until the sugar has dissolved. Remove from heat, add rum, and allow to cool. In another bowl, beat the cream, the cocoa powder, and the tablespoon of sugar, and whip until soft peaks form.

When you unroll the cake, spread the chocolate whipped cream over the cake, then spread the rum mixture over that, and carefully roll back up.

PINEAPPLE FILLING *relleno de piña*

> ½ stick (4 tablespoons) butter
> 1 cup evaporated milk
> 1 cup pineapple chunks (see page 31), puréed in the blender
> 1 cup sugar
> 1 teaspoon vanilla extract

Melt the butter in a heavy saucepan over medium heat. Stir in the evaporated milk and the pineapple purée, and continue to simmer for about 10 minutes. Reduce the heat, and sift in the sugar, whisking continuously. Simmer for an additional 3 to 5 minutes, until the mixture is thick and syrupy. Add the vanilla. Remove from heat, and allow to cool at room temperature.

TANGERINE CHOCOLATE FILLING
relleno de mandarina y chocolate

> ⅓ cup heavy cream
> 4 ounces semisweet chocolate, finely chopped
> ⅓ cup (about 2½ ounces) cream cheese, softened
> ½ stick (4 tablespoons) butter, softened
> 1 tablespoon tangerine liqueur

Heat the cream in a small, heavy saucepan over medium heat. Add the chocolate, and continue to cook over very low heat for 2 to 3 minutes, until melted. Whisk in the cream cheese, butter, and tangerine liqueur, and continue to simmer slowly for an additional 3 minutes, until all ingredients are thoroughly mixed and texture is thick. Allow to cool at room temperature.

NOTE You can substitute any tropical fruit liqueur for the tangerine to make delicious variations of this filling.

WIND PUFFS *buñuelos*

Buñuelos—"wind puffs"—originated in Spain and are a traditional Christmas dessert. They are fritters made of a very simple dough, usually flavored with anisette liqueur. There are many different types of *buñuelos*. I decided to opt for the most traditional version, which uses the Cuban root vegetables of cassava (*yuca*) and *malanga*. In Cuba, *buñuelos* are also traditionally twisted into a figure eight. Serve with *café con leche* (see page 406).

20 BUÑUELOS

> $\frac{1}{2}$ **pound cassava (*yuca*), peeled and diced**
> $\frac{1}{2}$ **pound *malanga*, peeled and diced**
> **2 eggs, beaten**
> **4 teaspoons anisette liqueur**
> **1$\frac{1}{2}$ cups all-purpose flour, plus more for work surface**
> **1 cup vegetable oil**
> **Simple syrup (see page 340) to taste**
> **Sugar for dusting**

In a large saucepan, boil 8 cups water and add the cassava and *malanga*. Cook for about 25 minutes, or until both vegetables are done and tender.

Remove from heat, drain, and purée the root vegetables in a food processor or blender. Add the eggs and anisette liqueur. Sift the flour into a mixing bowl, and combine with the cassava-and-*malanga* purée. Continue mixing until well combined for a soft dough.

Turn the dough onto a lightly floured board, and knead for about 1 minute. Roll out the dough to $\frac{1}{2}$-inch thickness. Use your lightly greased fingers to roll out about a tablespoon of dough into a long strand, making a rope about 8 inches long. With a twist of the wrist, turn the dough rope into a figure eight.

Make as many as you can with the dough that you have.

(continued on next page)

(continued from previous page)

In a large, heavy skillet, heat the oil over medium-high heat for about 3 minutes, and fry the dough pieces in the oil until golden brown, light, and fluffy. Serve immediately with a simple syrup, and sprinkle with sugar.

IRMA'S PINEAPPLE POUND CAKE
panetela de piña

Irma created my idea of the perfect Friday happy hour. Every Friday, at about four in the afternoon, she stops by my bookstore in downtown Miami and drops off the most delicious pound cakes that you could possibly imagine. We finish one off at the bookstore before we close, and I take the other home for the family. Obviously, it doesn't last through the weekend. This is her recipe for my very favorite pineapple pound cake. Thank you, Irma López, for your pound cakes, your generosity, and your recipe!

6 SERVINGS

> 2 sticks (8 ounces) butter, plus more for greasing tin
> 1½ cups granulated sugar
> 5 eggs
> 1¼ cups all-purpose flour
> 1 teaspoon salt
> ½ teaspoon baking powder
> 1 cup pineapple juice
> 1 cup diced pineapple (see page 31)
> ½ teaspoon vanilla extract
> Confectioners' sugar for dusting

Put the butter in a large, deep bowl, and beat with an electric mixer at medium speed, or beat with a wooden spoon, until the texture is soft and pliable. Add the granulated sugar, and continue mixing at medium-high speed until the mixture turns pale and fluffy and the sugar is completely incorporated. This should take from 4 to 5 minutes with an electric mixer.

To this mixture add the eggs, one at a time, beating well for about 45 seconds after each egg is added. Scrape the bowl once in a while, so all ingredients are evenly combined.

Preheat oven to 350 degrees.

Sift the flour with the salt and the baking powder. Beat the flour into the egg mixture at low speed a little at a time. Alternate adding pineapple juice and diced pineapple with the flour. Add the vanilla extract toward the end, and continue to beat at low speed until ingredients are combined. The resulting batter should have a smooth texture.

Pour the mixture into a greased loaf tin, and bake in oven for about 1 hour. To test for doneness, insert a toothpick into the center; it should come out clean. Remove from the oven, let cool, sprinkle with confectioners' sugar, and serve with sauce, ice cream, or by itself.

NOTE A great variation of this recipe is to dress it up with a glaze to make a festive and elegant pineapple rum cake. Once you remove the pound cake from the oven, let it sit in the pan for about 20 minutes. While you are waiting, melt ½ cup butter in a small pan over medium heat. Stir in ½ cup brown sugar and ½ cup white sugar, bring to a gentle simmer for about 5 minutes, and stir in 1 cup rum. Cook for another 5 minutes, until the sugars have dissolved, then remove from heat. Gently poke holes in the cake with a fork and pour glaze evenly over entire cake.

CAFÉ CON LECHE POUND CAKE
ponetela de café con leche

What could be more Cuban than a pound cake with coffee and *dulce de leche*? The fantastic taste and texture make this cake a perennial favorite.

6 SERVINGS

2 sticks (8 ounces) butter, plus more for greasing tin
1½ cups granulated sugar
4 eggs
1¼ cups all-purpose flour
1 teaspoon salt
½ teaspoon baking powder
4 teaspoons *dulce de leche* (see below)
¼ cup prepared Cuban coffee (see page 404)
½ teaspoon vanilla extract
Confectioners' sugar for dusting

(continued on next page)

(continued from previous page)

Put the butter in a large, deep bowl, and beat with an electric mixer at medium speed, or beat with a wooden spoon, until the texture is soft and pliable. Add the granulated sugar, and continue mixing at medium-high speed until the mixture turns pale and fluffy and the sugar is completely incorporated. This should take from 4 to 5 minutes with an electric mixer.

To this mixture add the eggs, one at a time, beating well for about 45 seconds after each egg is added. Scrape the bowl once in a while so all ingredients are evenly combined.

Preheat oven to 350 degrees.

Sift the flour with the salt and the baking powder. Beat the flour at low speed into the egg mixture, a little at a time. Alternate adding *dulce de leche* and the Cuban coffee with the flour, beating constantly. Add the vanilla extract toward the end, and continue to beat at low speed until all ingredients are combined. The resulting batter should have a smooth texture.

Pour the mixture into a greased loaf tin, and bake in oven for about 1 hour. To test for doneness, insert a toothpick into the center; it should come out clean. Remove from the oven, let cool, sprinkle with confectioners' sugar, and serve with sauce, ice cream, or by itself.

NOTE For this recipe, make the *dulce de leche* with the saucepan method: Pour the sweetened condensed milk into a small heavy saucepan, and simmer over very low heat, stirring constantly, until it becomes dark amber in color and thick in texture. Let cool slightly.

COCONUT POUND CAKE *panetela de coco*

This cake is creamy and delicious. Cream of coconut is readily available, but you can also use homemade coconut milk (see page 30), prepared without the ice.

This cake is excellent with ice cream or sauce, or just by itself.

6 SERVINGS

> 2 sticks (8 ounces) butter, plus more for greasing tin
> 1½ cups granulated sugar
> 5 eggs
> 1¼ cups all-purpose flour

1 teaspoon salt
1/2 teaspoon baking powder
1 cup Coco López cream of coconut
1/2 cup toasted coconut flakes
1/2 teaspoon vanilla extract
Confectioners' sugar for dusting

Put the butter in a large, deep bowl, and beat with an electric mixer at medium speed, or beat with a wooden spoon, until the texture is soft and pliable. Add the granulated sugar, and continue mixing at medium-high speed until the mixture turns pale and fluffy and the sugar is completely incorporated. This should take from 4 to 5 minutes with an electric mixer.

To this mixture add the eggs, one at a time, beating well for about 45 seconds after each egg is added. Scrape the bowl once in a while, so all ingredients are evenly combined.

Preheat oven to 350 degrees.

Sift the flour with the salt and the baking powder. Beat the flour at low speed into the egg mixture, a little at a time. Alternate adding cream of coconut and coconut flakes with flour. Add the vanilla extract toward the end, and continue to beat at low speed until all ingredients are combined. The resulting batter should have a smooth texture.

Pour the mixture into a greased loaf tin, and bake in oven for about 1 hour. To test for doneness, insert a toothpick into the center; it should come out clean. Remove from the oven, let cool, sprinkle with confectioners' sugar, and serve.

secrets of a Cuban cook

HOW TO TOAST COCONUT

Preheat oven to 350 degrees. Arrange shredded or flaked coconut in a single layer on a cookie sheet, and bake for 10 to 15 minutes, or until golden brown. Stir and check frequently to prevent burning. Remove from oven, and of course allow to cool before using in recipe.

TROPICAL TIRAMISÙ BY FRATELLI MILANO

tiramisù tropical

A Cuban twist on the traditional Italian dessert. This is one of my favorite recipes, because it comes from one of my favorite places, a restaurant just down the street from our family bookstore in Miami. Operated by twin Milanese chef brothers, Roberto and Emanuele, and gently managed by Roberto's wife, Fiorella, Fratelli Milano is a dreamy, cozy little restaurant where great cooking and great friendships take place. When you try this tiramisù, you cannot help but think that life is beautiful.

8 SERVINGS

> 2 cups water
> 3 cups sugar
> ¾ cup light rum
> 5 eggs
> 2 cups mascarpone cheese
> NOTE Mascarpone is a buttery, rich, delicate-tasting double-cream to triple-cream cow's-milk cheese from Italy's Lombardy region. It is available in most markets.
> 2 cups heavy cream
> 20 ladyfingers
> 3 cups diced mixed fresh fruit (papaya, mango, pineapple, and strawberries)
> 1 cup shredded coconut, toasted (see page 351)

In a large saucepan, combine water, 2 cups of the sugar, and rum, and boil over medium-high heat for about 3 minutes. Remove from heat, cool to room temperature, and set aside. (You will use this later for dipping ladyfingers.)

In a bowl, mix the eggs, the remaining 1 cup sugar, mascarpone cheese, and heavy cream, and beat with electric mixer at medium-high speed until mixture thickens. Be careful not to overbeat it.

Dip each ladyfinger in the rum and sugar, and reserve.

In a 9-inch square glass baking pan, spread a layer of the cream mixture, then a layer of dipped ladyfingers, and follow with a layer of the diced mixed fruit. Repeat the process twice so you have three layers of each, then top off with an extra layer of the cream mixture. Refrigerate, covered, overnight. Before serving, sprinkle with toasted shredded coconut.

CUBAN FRIED CREAM *crema frita*

It is not just the Italians who enjoy this wonderful dessert. This is how we make it Cuban style.

4 SERVINGS

> 8 eggs
> 2 cups all-purpose flour
> 3 cups milk
> Zest of 1 lemon, grated (see page 345)
> ¾ cup granulated sugar
> Salt to taste
> 2 teaspoons butter
> 1 cup ground sweet butter cookies
> 1 cup vegetable oil
> 1 tablespoon confectioners' sugar
> Slices of fruit (pineapple, pear, or apple) for serving

Combine two of the eggs and the flour in a mixing bowl, and whisk together with an electric mixer until pale and thick. Beat five of the remaining eggs in a separate bowl, then add to the flour mixture.

In the meantime, boil the milk for a couple of minutes in a saucepan, and add the lemon zest. Remove from heat and allow to cool. Add this also to the original flour mixture.

In a heavy saucepan, cook the mixture over low heat for 5 minutes, stirring constantly so it won't stick to bottom of pan. Add the granulated sugar, salt, and butter, and stir again. Remove from heat just as you see the first bubbles but before it begins to foam. Pour into an ample, fairly deep dish, spreading it to a thickness of about ¾ inch, and let it cool completely.

When completely cool, cut the cream into diamonds, squares, or your favorite shape. Beat the last egg, dip each piece of cream in the beaten egg, and coat lightly with the ground sweet butter cookies.

Heat the oil in a skillet over medium-high heat, and fry the cream squares or diamonds until golden. Drain on paper towels to absorb excess oil, dust with confectioners' sugar, and serve immediately. Accompany with slices of pineapple, pear, or apple.

CUBAN CAPUCHINOS *capuchinos*

These *capuchinos* are not named after coffee, but after Capuchin monks, who wore peaked hoods as part of their habits. These custard-like pastries are fun; served really drenched in syrup, they have a lovely golden color.

20 CAPUCHINOS

> **10 egg yolks**
> **1 egg white**
> **¼ cup sugar**
> **4 teaspoons cornstarch**
> **4 cups simple syrup (see page 340), infused with 1 cinnamon stick**

Prepare the cones by rolling sheets of parchment paper into 1-inch cones; stand them up vertically in a muffin tin.

In a mixing bowl, beat the egg yolks, egg white, and sugar with an electric mixer for about 10 minutes, until mixture becomes very thick. Add the cornstarch slowly while mixing vigorously.

Preheat oven to 350 degrees.

Place the batter in a pastry bag with a medium tip, and fill the cones with the batter. Do not fill to the top of the cones, because the *capuchinos* will grow in size while baking.

Place the rack of *capuchinos* in oven, and also place a shallow pan of water in the center of the oven beneath them to keep them moist. Bake for 25 to 30 minutes, until the tops turn golden brown. Remove from oven, and remove the parchment-paper cones.

Transfer *capuchinos* to a shallow container, and pour at least 3 of the 4 cups of the simple syrup on top, until the *capuchinos* are drenched and have absorbed a lot of the syrup. Refrigerate overnight, and serve the next day with the reserved syrup.

PRUNES IN SIMPLE SYRUP
ciruelas pasas en almíbar

This sweet dessert simply must be accompanied by cream cheese and some Cuban crackers. It's also great with muffins.

4 SERVINGS

> ½ **pound prunes, pitted**
> **2 cups simple syrup (see page 340), infused with 1 cinnamon stick**

Wash prunes, and soak in water for 30–50 minutes, until tender, soft, and plump.

Place prunes in a large saucepan with 3 cups water, and bring to a boil over medium-high heat. Reduce heat, and simmer for about 20 minutes, stirring occasionally.

Transfer the prunes to the syrup, and continue to cook over very low heat for about 10 minutes, or until the consistency is thick.

CRISPY COCONUT *coco quemado*

This is a super treat, perfect for an evening party. Fresh coconut makes all the difference.

4 SERVINGS

> **1 coconut**
> **1 cup brown sugar**
> **2 egg yolks, beaten**
> **Butter for greasing tins**
> **Dollop of whipped cream for serving**

Crack the coconut (see page 356). Scoop out the coconut meat, grate, and set aside in a mixing bowl. Reserve the coconut juice.

Prepare a simple syrup using the coconut juice and the brown sugar: In a saucepan, mix the sugar and coconut juice together and bring to a boil over medium-high heat. Cook and continue stirring until sugar has completely dissolved, which should happen in about 10 minutes. Reduce heat, add grated coconut, and stir to mix thoroughly. Continue to simmer for another 5 to 7 minutes, until syrup is thick.

(continued on next page)

(continued from previous page)

Preheat oven to 375 degrees.

Remove mixture from heat, add the egg yolks, and stir well. Pour into four individual greased muffin tins, and bake in oven for about 25 minutes, until browned and crispy on top. Allow to cool, remove from muffin molds, and serve with whipped cream.

NOTE You can also pour the coconut mixture into a square glass baking dish and, when baked and cooled, cut it into squares.

secrets of a Cuban cook

HOW TO CRACK A COCONUT

Hold the coconut over a bowl in one hand so the middle section rests in the middle of your palm with the tip on one end and the eyes of the coconut on the other. Whack the coconut with the blunt side of a cleaver a few times in the center, until it cracks open cleanly into two halves. Catch the coconut juice in the bowl as it drains. You can, if necessary, substitute a 16-ounce can of coconut in heavy syrup for one fresh coconut, but, again, fresh coconut is best.

CUBAN APPLESAUCE *compota de manzana*

Choose apples that are naturally sweet; it is best to use a mixture, not just one type. Some types of apples you will find in the market are Red Delicious, Empire, Gala, Fuji, and Rome. Your applesauce or compote can be a dessert, but is also delicious as a side dish to pork or even rabbit.

4 SERVINGS

8 apples, peeled, cored, and cut into ½- to 1-inch wedges
6 cups water
2 cups sugar
1 cinnamon stick
1 cup raisins
Ground cinnamon to taste

Place apple wedges in a large, heavy saucepan with water, and boil over medium-high heat for about 15 minutes. When tender, add the sugar and the cinnamon stick. Lower heat, and simmer for an additional 20 minutes, stirring occasionally. Add the raisins in the last 10 minutes of cooking.

Apple chunks should be tender but retain their shape. When they are ready, remove from heat, transfer to a bowl, and add ground cinnamon to taste. Remove cinnamon stick, cover, and refrigerate. Serve in glass cups—or even wineglasses, for a festive effect.

PEAR AND PRUNE COMPOTE
compota de peras y ciruelas pasas

Add a few more teaspoons of sugar to this recipe for a really sweet treat. This compote also makes an excellent pie filling.

4 TO 6 SERVINGS

> **8 pears, peeled, cored, and diced**
> NOTE You can use a melon baller to scoop out the core, and cut out the stem and base with a small knife.
> **2 cups pitted prunes, diced**
> **8 cups water**
> **2 cups sugar**
> **1 cinnamon stick**
> **Zest of 1 lemon, grated (see page 345)**

In a large saucepan, place the pears and prunes with the water and boil for about 10 minutes over medium-high heat.

Reduce heat to low, and add the sugar, cinnamon stick, and grated lemon zest. Continue to cook for approximately 10 more minutes. Be sure the fruits are tender but still retain their shape and do not become mushy. Remove from heat, remove cinnamon stick, and bring to room temperature. Cover and refrigerate. Serve in cups.

GUANÁBANA DESSERT *dulce de guanábana*

In Cuba we call it *guanábana*. The soursop sprouts on the trunk and branches of a tree in Ecuador, Peru, Mexico, and the Caribbean. It is very much like a custard apple. The flesh has a grainy texture but when ripe is soft and creamy, and fragrant of pineapple, banana, and vanilla. It is delicious as juice and in milkshakes, ice cream, and this *dulce* (dessert with simple syrup). This dessert is perfect with a big chunk of cheddar or American cheese or some whipped cream. Double up on this recipe and store some for a midnight snack.

2 SERVINGS

> 1 *guanábana* (soursop), peeled and seeded
> 2 cups simple syrup (see page 340)
> 1 cinnamon stick
> 1 piece of lemon peel

Once the *guanábana* is peeled and seeded, cut into big chunks.

In a medium saucepan, heat the simple syrup, stir in the *guanábana* chunks, and cook, stirring continuously, for about 15 minutes. Add the cinnamon stick and the lemon peel. If the syrup gets too thick during this cooking, add ½ cup water and continue to simmer, stirring all the ingredients together.

Remove from heat, discard the cinnamon stick and lemon peel, let cool to room temperature or warm, and serve in small dessert bowls.

PINEAPPLE DESSERT *dulce de piña*

It is hard to get enough of pineapple—it is such a refreshing fruit and can be served in so many different ways. This dessert is one of the simplest. Serve it with sugar cookies.

4 SERVINGS

> 1 very ripe pineapple, peeled and cubed (see page 31)
> Salt to taste
> 2 cups simple syrup (see page 340)

Place pineapple in a bowl with 3 cups water, and leave to soak for about 30 minutes.

In a large saucepan, heat the simple syrup over medium heat, and when the syrup begins to bubble, add the pineapple chunks. Return to a simmer, reduce heat, and continue to simmer for about 10 minutes, stirring continuously. The dessert is ready when the pineapple chunks appear to be translucent in color. Remove from heat, let cool to room temperature, and serve in dessert bowls.

GRAPEFRUIT DESSERT *dulce de toronja*

Cubans are not great fans of grapefruit. But this sweet-and-sour dessert is a favorite on most Cuban tables. Serve it with toasted Cuban bread (see page 78) or brioche, and cream cheese.

4 SERVINGS

> 4 grapefruits, peeled, seeded, and cut into wedges
> 2 cups simple syrup (see page 340)

In a large saucepan, bring 4 cups water to a boil and drop in the grapefruit wedges. Reduce heat slightly and continue to simmer for about 30 minutes, until the grapefruit is tender.

Remove from heat and drain the grapefruit. Purée the grapefruit in a food processor or blender. Strain for a smoother blend.

In a separate saucepan, heat the simple syrup, stirring frequently. Add the grapefruit purée. Cook and stir for about 5 minutes over low heat. Remove from heat, cool to room temperature, and serve immediately.

secrets of a Cuban cook

HOW TO PEEL AND PREPARE GRAPEFRUIT

To peel all citrus fruits completely, cut a slice from the top and from the base. Set the fruit base down on a surface and, using a small sharp knife, cut following the curve of the fruit lengthwise in thick strips. Be sure to take the soft white spongy layer out, since it is bitter. To cut into segments or wedges, hold the peeled fruit in your cupped hand, over a bowl to catch the juice. Work from the side of the fruit to the center, slide the knife down one side of a separating membrane to free flesh, and then slide the knife down the other side of the membrane to free it from there as well. Drop the wedge into the bowl and continue until the grapefruit is completely cut. Squeeze all the juice out of the membrane into the bowl. You are ready to use in recipe.

CUBAN FRENCH TOAST *torrejas*

This is not for breakfast but is served as a filling dessert—or a sweet snack anytime.

4 SERVINGS

> ¼ cup dry white wine
> 1 cup whole milk
> 1 cup evaporated milk
> 1 teaspoon ground cinnamon
> 2 teaspoons vanilla extract
> 3 eggs, beaten
> 8 slices white bread
> 1 cup vegetable or corn oil
> 2 cups simple syrup (see page 340)

In one mixing bowl, combine the wine, whole milk, evaporated milk, cinnamon, and vanilla extract. Place the beaten eggs in another bowl, and set aside.

Dip the bread slices in the milk mixture, making sure they are completely soaked but not letting them break apart. Then dip in the beaten egg. Work in batches!

In a large, deep frying pan, heat the oil over medium heat. When oil is hot enough to sizzle, carefully place the bread slices in it one by one, and fry for 2 or 3 minutes on each side, until golden brown. Drain on paper towels, and repeat with all the slices. Transfer to a large serving platter, and refrigerate or cool to room temperature for about 1 hour. Pour the simple syrup over the *torrejas* and serve.

MARMALADES
mermeladas

Cuban desserts include very simple marmalades, usually smooth purées (not chunky), often served with a piece of fresh unripened cheese (cream cheese or cottage cheese) or hard cheese (Swiss or cheddar). We love the Cuban *queso blanco*, white cheese, which is just farmer's cheese—pressed cottage cheese. The simplicity is the key.

Of course, you do not always have to go the homemade route. There are great marmalades in the Hispanic aisle of your supermarket, your local Latin bodega, and online.

These homemade marmalades also make excellent pie fillings (see page 363).

GUAVA MARMALADE COLÓN
mermelada de guayaba Colón

Serve this with lots of crackers, lots of cheese, and lots of appetite.

4 SERVINGS

> **1 pound guavas (about 4 or 5 guavas), peeled, seeded, and diced**
> NOTE You do not have to peel guavas, though I prefer to for this recipe. You need only cut them in half, scoop out the seeds, and dice.
> **4 cups water**
> **2–3 cups sugar**
> **1 cinnamon stick**

Place guava pieces in a large, heavy saucepan with water and boil over medium-high heat for about 15 minutes. When tender, add the sugar and the cinnamon stick. Lower heat, and simmer for an additional 20 minutes, stirring occasionally and making sure it does not stick to bottom of pan.

When the mixture has become thick, remove from heat, discard the cinnamon stick, and transfer to a food processor. Process the guava mixture until very smooth. If it is too thick, add some water.

MANGO MARMALADE *mermelada de mango*

This is great alone or with a piece of cheese, and can also be used as a filling for pies and other pastries.

4 SERVINGS

> **6 mangoes (not too ripe), peeled and diced**
> **3 cups water**
> **1 cup sugar**

(continued on next page)

(continued from previous page)

Place mango pieces in a large, heavy saucepan with water, and boil over medium-high heat for about 15 minutes. When tender, add the sugar. Lower heat, and simmer for an additional 20 minutes, stirring occasionally and making sure it does not stick to bottom of pan.

When the mixture has become thick, remove from heat and transfer to a food processor. Process until very smooth. If it is too thick, add some water.

NOTE If you *are* using overripe mangoes, there is no need to boil. Just process the fresh fruit in a food processor, place in a saucepan with 2 cups of simple syrup (see page 340), and heat for 10 minutes, stirring constantly.

ORANGE MARMALADE *mermelada de naranja*
4 SERVINGS

> **8 oranges, peeled and cut into crosswise slices**
> **3 cups water**
> **2 cups sugar**
> **Zest of 1 lemon (see page 345)**

Place orange slices in a large, heavy saucepan with water, and boil over medium-high heat for about 15 minutes. When tender, add the sugar and lemon zest. Lower heat, and simmer for an additional 20 minutes, stirring occasionally and making sure it does not stick to bottom of pan.

Strain mixture, and transfer to a food processor. Process until very smooth. If it is too thick, add some water.

PINEAPPLE MARMALADE *mermelada de piña*
This is also wonderful as a sauce.
4 SERVINGS

> **1 fresh pineapple, peeled and diced (see page 31)**
> **3 cups water**
> **Salt to taste**
> **1 cup sugar**

Leave the pineapple pieces to soak in a bowl of water for about 3 hours. Drain, and discard the water.

Place pineapple chunks in a large heavy saucepan with the 3 cups fresh water, and boil over medium-high heat for about 25 minutes. When tender, add the salt and sugar. Lower heat, and simmer for an additional 15 minutes, stirring occasionally and making sure it does not stick to bottom of pan.

Strain mixture, and transfer to a food processor. Process until very smooth. If it is too thick, add some water. If you are going to use it as a pie filling, on the other hand, make sure consistency is thick.

CUBAN DOUBLE-CRUST PIE *pastel camagüeyano*

This double-crusted pie is a perfect, foolproof recipe. The list of possible fillings for this pie is endless, but the authentic, traditional fillings are:

> Guava marmalade colón (see page 361)
> Mango marmalade (see page 361)
> Orange marmalade (see page 362)
> Pineapple marmalade (see page 362)
> Cuban applesauce (see page 356)

6 SERVINGS

> **2 cups unbleached all-purpose flour, plus more for dusting**
> **¼ cup sugar**
> **Pinch of salt**
> **2 teaspoons baking powder**
> **1 stick (8 tablespoons) unsalted butter**
> **¼ cup ice water**
> **1 large egg**
> **2 teaspoons white vinegar or dry white wine**
> **2 cups any filling you desire**

Sift the flour, sugar, salt, and baking powder into a mixing bowl. Add and combine the butter (chilled if possible): Working with your fingertips, cut the butter into the flour mixture and rub it until the mixture is coarse and crumblike.

(continued on next page)

(continued from previous page)

In a separate bowl, beat together water, egg, and vinegar. Add to flour mixture, and with a fork toss gently, mixing and moistening it to form a soft dough.

Press the dough or scrape it up into a ball. If it is too dry, add a little more ice water. Wrap the dough ball with plastic wrap or wax paper, and refrigerate for at least 2 hours.

Remove dough ball from the refrigerator, and divide it in half. Roll one half out to ¼-inch thickness on a floured surface. If you are new to pie crusts, remember to use even pressure with your rolling pin and work from the center of the dough to the edge, easing pressure as you reach the edge. From time to time as you are rolling, lift up the dough and give it a small turn, to prevent it from sticking to the work surface. If the dough tears, patch it up with a piece of moistened dough. Work quickly, because the dough becomes sticky quickly.

Roll dough around rolling pin, then unroll it and drape it over a 9-inch pie plate, pressing gently to fit into the pan.

Put the filling of your choice inside the pie shell, and spread it evenly.

Roll out a second piece of dough to ¼-inch thickness on a floured surface. This time, roll it out to a circle that is about 1 inch larger than the first one. Roll it up around the rolling pin, and unroll and drape over the pie filling. Press edges together to seal and trim overhang on both edges. With fingertips or with floured fork prongs, press evenly and firmly all around the edge.

Make several 2-inch slits on the top crust to vent steam during baking. Refrigerate entire pie for 15 to 20 minutes before baking.

Preheat oven to 400 degrees.

Place pie in oven, lining the rack below with foil to catch any juices. Bake 10 minutes, reduce heat to 375 degrees, and continue to bake for 60 to 75 minutes more, until both bottom and top crusts are golden and juices are bubbling. Tent with foil if top crust starts to brown too quickly.

Remove from oven, and transfer to a wire rack to let cool completely, for at least 3 hours. Tent with aluminum foil if saving for the next day, but do not refrigerate.

THE FAMOUS FLANS
los flanes

The Cuban flan is elegant, upscale, and classy. Most of all, it is delicious, and brings out the purity of its ingredients. It can be enhanced with the addition of coconut, cream cheese, tropical fruits, honey, and even almonds. You can use ramekin molds or flan molds, or you can make one big flan, round or square. It is your preference because it is your flan! The following recipes are for one big round flan.

TRADITIONAL MILK FLAN WITH CUBAN CARAMEL *flan de leche con caramelo cubano*

6 SERVINGS

1 recipe Cuban caramel (see page 341), freshly made or reheated

FOR FLAN

1 cup whole milk
1 cup evaporated milk
1 cup sweetened condensed milk
6 egg yolks
3 eggs
1 cup sugar
Pinch of salt
1 teaspoon vanilla extract

Carefully pour hot caramel syrup into a 9-inch round glass cake pan with high sides, turning the pan to coat the bottom and sides evenly. Set aside.

Now make the flan: In a small saucepan, heat the whole, evaporated, and sweetened condensed milk over low heat for about 4 to 5 minutes, making sure that the mixture does not start to boil. Remove from heat.

Preheat oven to 325 or 350 degrees.

Meanwhile, using an electric mixer at low speed, mix the egg yolks and eggs in a mixing bowl. Add the sugar, salt, and vanilla extract. Now gently mix

(continued on next page)

(continued from previous page)

in the milk mixture, slowly and gradually, until thoroughly blended. Strain if you want at this point to achieve a really smooth texture.

Pour your flan mixture into the round caramelized and prepared pan. Set the pan in a hot-water bath.

Bake in oven for 1 hour to 1 hour, 15 minutes, or until the center of the flan is firm to the touch. Remove from heat, and allow to cool to room temperature. Refrigerate, covered, overnight.

To unmold and serve, run a sharp knife very carefully around the edge of the pan. Place a rimmed serving plate upside down over the top of the flan, flip it over, and invert onto the serving plate. Serve immediately.

COCONUT FLAN *flan de coco*

For a coconut flan, add in 1 cup shredded fresh coconut when you add the sugar, salt, and vanilla to the beaten eggs. Gently mix in the milks, slowly and gradually, until thoroughly combined. Pour into a blender, and process at low speed to get a really smooth mixture. Proceed with the recipe as above.

PINEAPPLE FLAN *flan de piña*

For this refreshing variation, add in 1 cup fresh pineapple chunks (see page 31) when you add the sugar, salt, and vanilla to the beaten eggs, and then add 1 cup fresh pineapple juice. Gently mix in the milks, slowly and gradually, until thoroughly combined. Pour into a blender and process at low speed to get a really smooth texture. Proceed with the recipe as above.

secrets of a Cuban cook

THE BAÑO MARÍA

The French call the hot-water bath a *bain-marie* and Cubans call it a *baño María*. Place a container of food in a large shallow pan of warm water, to surround the food with gentle heat whether in the oven or on the stovetop.

PUMPKIN FLAN *flan de calabaza*

6 SERVINGS

>1 recipe Cuban caramel (see page 341), freshly made or reheated

FOR FLAN

>3 cups peeled and diced pumpkin
>2 cups milk (or 1 cup whole and 1 cup evaporated)
>5 eggs
>1 cup sugar
>Pinch of salt
>1 teaspoon ground cinnamon
>½ teaspoon grated lemon zest (see page 345)
>1 tablespoon butter
>2 teaspoons cornstarch

Carefully pour hot caramel syrup into a 9-by-5-inch rectangular glass loaf pan with high sides, turning the pan to coat the bottom and sides evenly. Set aside.

Now make the flan: Boil the pumpkin pieces in 5 cups water in a saucepan over high heat for about 15 minutes, or until tender. Remove from heat, drain, and purée the pumpkin in a food processor or blender to make a smooth mixture. Reserve.

In a small saucepan, heat the milk over low heat for 4 to 5 minutes, making sure that it does not start to boil. Remove from heat.

Preheat oven to 325 degrees.

Meanwhile, using an electric mixer at low speed, beat the eggs in a mixing bowl. Add the sugar, salt, ground cinnamon, and lemon zest. Add the pumpkin purée, butter, and cornstarch. Now gently mix in the milks, slowly and gradually, until thoroughly combined. Strain if you want at this point to achieve a really smooth texture.

Pour your flan mixture into the caramelized and prepared loaf pan. Set the pan in a hot-water bath (see page 366).

Bake in oven for 1 hour to 1 hour, 15 minutes, or until the center of the flan is firm to the touch. Remove from heat, and allow to cool to room temperature. Refrigerate, covered, overnight.

To unmold and serve, run a sharp knife very carefully around the edge of the pan. Place a rimmed serving plate upside down over the top of the flan, flip it over, and invert onto the serving plate. Serve immediately.

CREAM CHEESE FLAN *flan de queso*

This is an easy flan variation—a blender does most of the work.

6 SERVINGS

1 recipe Cuban caramel (see page 341), freshly made or reheated

FOR FLAN

1 cup whole milk

1 cup evaporated milk

1 cup sweetened condensed milk

6 egg yolks

2 eggs

1 cup sugar

8 ounces cream cheese, softened

1 teaspoon vanilla extract

Salt to taste

Carefully pour hot caramel syrup into a 9-inch round glass cake pan with high sides, turning the pan to coat the bottom and sides evenly. Set aside.

Now make the flan: In a small saucepan, heat the whole, evaporated, and sweetened condensed milk over low heat for 4 to 5 minutes, making sure that the mixture does not start to boil. Remove from heat.

Preheat oven to 325 or 350 degrees.

Combine the egg yolks, eggs, sugar, cream cheese, vanilla extract, and salt in a blender, and process at low speed. Now gently pour in the milk mixture, and blend again at low speed until thoroughly smooth.

Pour your flan mixture into the round caramelized and prepared pan. Set the pan in a hot-water bath (see page 366).

Bake in oven for 1 hour to 1 hour, 15 minutes, or until the center of the flan is firm to the touch. Remove from heat, and allow to cool to room temperature. Refrigerate, covered, overnight.

To unmold and serve, run a sharp knife very carefully around the edge of the pan. Place a rimmed serving plate upside down over the top of the flan, flip it over, and invert onto the serving plate. Serve immediately.

HEAVEN'S DELIGHT FLAN *tocino del cielo*

I really love making this flan, because you get to mix most of the caramel into the flan itself. Use individual ramekins for this recipe. The finished *tocino* will be small, pretty, and deep golden in color, since you use only egg yolks.

6 SERVINGS

1 recipe Cuban caramel (see page 341), freshly made or reheated

FOR TOCINO

12 egg yolks

¼ cup sugar

1 teaspoon pure vanilla extract

Reserve in a bowl all but ½ cup of the caramel. Divide the ½ cup caramel equally among six small individual ramekins (4- to 6-ounce size).

Preheat oven to 325 or 350 degrees.

Now make the *tocino*: Using an electric mixer at low speed, beat the egg yolks and mix in the sugar and vanilla. Add the reserved cooled syrup little by little, until fully mixed and incorporated. Divide this equally among the ramekins, on top of the caramel.

Set ramekins in a hot-water bath (see page 366).

Bake in oven for 45 minutes, or until the center of each *tocino* is firm to the touch. Remove from heat, and allow to cool to room temperature. Refrigerate, covered, overnight.

To unmold and serve, run a sharp knife very carefully around the side of the ramekins. Invert each ramekin onto a small dessert plate, and serve immediately.

CUBAN PUDDINGS
pudines cubanos

Every culture seems to have its own versions of pudding. Many have a traditional bread pudding, which is an excellent way to use up stale (in our case Cuban) bread. I have included our classic rice puddings as well as the very famous diplomatic pudding, which is usually served during the Christmas season.

SIMPLE CUBAN BREAD PUDDING *pudín de pan*
6 SERVINGS

> 1 recipe Cuban caramel (see page 341), freshly made or reheated

FOR PUDDING

> 1 loaf day-old Cuban bread (see page 78), torn into 2-inch pieces
> 1 cup sweetened condensed milk
> 2 ounces anisette liqueur
> 5 eggs, beaten
> 4 teaspoons butter
> 1 teaspoon vanilla extract
> $\frac{1}{2}$ cup raisins
> $\frac{1}{2}$ cup toasted almonds

Carefully pour hot caramel syrup into a 9-by-12-inch rectangular baking dish with high sides, turning the dish to coat the bottom and sides evenly. Set aside.

Now make the pudding: In a mixing bowl, soak the bread pieces in the condensed milk and the anisette liqueur. Leave the bread soaking for about 30 minutes.

Preheat oven to 350 degrees.

Meanwhile, beat eggs lightly, by hand for 2 or 3 minutes or with electric mixer for 1 minute. Add butter and vanilla, and pour into the bread-and-milk mixture. Stir in raisins and almonds, and let it sit for a few minutes.

Pour this pudding mixture into the caramelized and prepared baking dish. Bake in oven for about 1 hour. To test for doneness, insert a toothpick into the center; it should come out clean. Serve warm, or set aside to cool to room temperature and refrigerate, covered.

CUBAN RICE PUDDING *arroz con leche cubano*

A very elegant dessert that is quite common at a Cuban family dinner.

6 SERVINGS

> ½ **cup white rice**
> 1½ **cups water**
> **Zest of 1 lemon, grated (see page 345)**
> **1 cinnamon stick**
> **4 cups milk**
> **Salt to taste**
> **1 cup sugar**
> **1 teaspoon vanilla extract**
> **Ground cinnamon to taste**

Rinse rice, and boil in a large saucepan with water, lemon zest, and cinnamon stick for approximately 20 minutes, until rice is soft and fully cooked.

Reduce the heat, and add the milk, salt, sugar, and vanilla. Continue to cook over medium-low heat for approximately 1 hour, until mixture thickens. Stir frequently, so the rice does not stick to the bottom of the pan or burn. When it reaches your desired consistency, remove from heat.

Take out the cinnamon stick, and transfer pudding to individual dessert bowls. Let cool to room temperature, or refrigerate. Sprinkle with cinnamon at time of serving.

NOTE You can achieve a wonderful flavor and texture if you use more than one type of milk. Instead of just whole milk, try using equal parts evaporated, sweetened condensed, and whole milk.

MATANZAS RICE PUDDING
arroz con leche de Matanzas

Matanzas is the central province of Cuba, with lots of beaches and historical homes. The people are laid-back and are famous for their siestas. This rice-pudding recipe comes from that region.

6 SERVINGS

> ½ **cup rice**
> 1½ **cups water**
> **Zest of 1 lemon, grated (see page 345)**
> **1 cinnamon stick**
> **4 cups milk, preferably mixture of whole, evaporated, and**
> **sweetened condensed milk**
> **1 cup sugar**
> **2 teaspoons anisette liqueur**
> **Salt to taste**
> **Ground cinnamon to taste**

Rinse rice, and boil in a large saucepan with water, lemon zest, and cinnamon stick for approximately 20 minutes, until rice is soft and fully cooked.

Reduce the heat, and add the milk, sugar, anisette liqueur, and salt. Continue to cook over medium-low heat for approximately 1 hour, until it thickens. Be sure to stir frequently, so the rice does not stick to the bottom of the pan or burn. When it reaches desired consistency, remove from heat.

Take out the cinnamon stick, and transfer pudding to individual dessert bowls. Let cool to room temperature, or refrigerate. Sprinkle with cinnamon at time of serving.

DIPLOMATIC PUDDING *pudín diplomático*

This is called "diplomatic pudding" because it was originally served at diplomatic functions. It is based on a Hungarian dessert. For Cubans, the diplomatic pudding is part of a holiday feast. Ideal as a Christmas dessert, it is also wonderful on New Year's Day, when my family likes to have it in the early afternoon with a cleansing cup of jasmine tea. This is our little tradition.

6 SERVINGS

1 recipe **Cuban caramel (see page 341), freshly made or reheated**

FOR PUDDING

½ **cup evaporated milk**

1 cup sweetened condensed milk

1 cup whole milk

1 cinnamon stick

1 teaspoon grated lemon zest (see page 345)

6 eggs

1 cup sugar

1 teaspoon pure vanilla extract

Salt to taste

1 tablespoon brandy or amaretto liqueur

2 cups fruit cocktail (homemade or canned)

1 loaf bread (Cuban, French, Italian, or your favorite), torn into 2-inch pieces

Carefully pour hot caramel syrup into a 9-by-12-inch rectangular glass baking pan with high sides, turning the pan to coat the bottom and sides evenly. Set aside.

Now make the pudding: In a large saucepan over medium heat, heat the evaporated, condensed, and whole milks with the cinnamon stick and lemon zest until boiling point. Remove from heat, discard the cinnamon stick, and allow to cool to room temperature.

Preheat oven to 325 or 350 degrees.

Meanwhile, beat eggs lightly, by hand for 2 or 3 minutes or with electric mixer for 1 minute. Add sugar, vanilla, salt, and brandy. Now gently pour in the milk mixture, and blend again, at low speed, until thoroughly smooth. Gently

(continued on next page)

(continued from previous page)

mix in the fruit cocktail, and toss in the bread pieces. Transfer this mixture into the caramelized and prepared baking pan.

Set the pan in a hot-water bath (see page 366). Bake in oven for 1 hour to 1 hour, 15 minutes, or until the center of the pudding is firm to the touch. Remove from heat, and allow to cool to room temperature. Refrigerate, covered, overnight.

To unmold and serve, run a sharp knife very carefully around the edge of the pan. Place a rimmed serving plate upside down over the top of the pudding, and invert the pudding onto the serving plate.

SWEET POTATO PUDDING *boniatillo*

This is wonderful to introduce to your children as a first dessert. It is nutritious yet light.

6 SERVINGS

> **1 pound white boniatos (sweet potatoes), peeled and diced**
> **1½ cups milk**
> **2 cups sugar**
> **2 egg yolks, beaten**
> **½ cup whipped cream, lightly sweetened, plus more for serving**
> **Ground cinnamon to taste**

Bring 8 cups water to a boil in a large saucepan, and boil the sweet-potato pieces over medium-high heat for approximately 25 minutes, until they are soft and tender. Remove with a slotted spoon, and purée in a food processor or blender, adding milk as needed until it reaches a smooth, creamy consistency.

Preheat oven to 325 degrees.

Add remaining milk and sugar to the purée, and strain the entire mixture. Heat over low heat in a saucepan for about 5 minutes to blend thoroughly. Beat the egg yolks with the whipped cream, and slowly add to the sweet-potato purée. Remove from heat, and pour equal amounts of the mixture into each cup of a nonstick muffin tin.

Bake in oven for about 20 minutes. Remove from oven. To unmold, run a thin knife around the inside of each tin to loosen. Gently ease out, then transfer to dessert plates. Top with a dollop of whipped cream, and sprinkle with cinnamon.

NOTE A delicious variation of this pudding is to substitute cream of coconut for the whipped cream.

COLONIAL VANILLA CUSTARD *natilla*

Just your old-fashioned, comforting, rich French-vanilla pudding. This homade custard is also the basis for a very rich ice cream. If you make it plain, just top with cinnamon, cinnamon sugar, whipped cream, or a little bit of *dulce de leche*. This *natilla* is super-rich because it uses whole, sweetened condensed, and evaporated milks.

6 SERVINGS

> **2 cups whole milk**
> **1 cup sweetened condensed milk**
> **1 cup evaporated milk**
> **1 cinnamon stick**
> **Peel of 1 lemon**
> **Salt to taste**
> **8 egg yolks**
> **1 cup sugar**
> **4 teaspoons cornstarch**
> **2 teaspoons vanilla extract**
> **Ground cinnamon or cinnamon sugar to taste**

Place the three types of milk, the cinnamon stick, lemon peel, and salt in a heavy saucepan, and bring to a boil over medium-low heat, watching very closely and stirring as much as possible to avoid scorching or curdling. When the milk starts to boil, remove from heat and allow to cool a couple of minutes. Remove and discard the cinnamon stick and lemon rind.

In a mixing bowl, lightly beat the egg yolks by hand (or with an electric mixer at extra-low speed) until smoothly blended and creamy. Then add the sugar and cornstarch, and continue to beat until completely smooth. Gradually add the warm milk mixture to the egg-yolk mixture, stirring constantly (with a wooden spoon if possible).

(continued on next page)

(continued from previous page)

Transfer to a saucepan, and heat the custard over medium heat until you bring it to a boil, stirring constantly. Reduce heat to low, add the vanilla extract, and cook for another 5 to 6 minutes, still stirring constantly, until the custard thickens to a creamy consistency that coats the spoon. Remove from heat.

Pour the custard into individual bowls or cups, cover, and refrigerate. Sprinkle with ground cinnamon or cinnamon sugar. You may also serve at room temperature, or even warm, with whipped cream.

NOTE You can play around and mix in grated chocolate for chocolate custard, brandy for an elegant custard, and orange zest for an orange-flavored custard. Add any of these ingredients when you beat the egg yolks.

SWEET CORNMEAL *harina dulce*

Here is a version of this delicious dessert that is made without a pressure cooker (see page 328).

4 SERVINGS

4 cups water
Salt to taste
1 cinnamon stick
1 cup finely ground cornmeal
1 cup sweetened condensed milk
¼ cup sugar
½ cup raisins
4 teaspoons butter
2 teaspoons vanilla extract
Ground cinnamon to taste

Pour the water, salt, and cinnamon stick into a large heavy saucepan, and bring to a boil over medium-high heat. Once it begins boiling, add the cornmeal, lower the heat to medium, and cover.

Simmer the mixture for about 45 minutes, making sure you stir occasionally to prevent sticking. If heat is too high, lower to medium-low. Once the cornmeal is fully cooked, remove from heat and allow to cool to room temperature.

Once cooled, add the condensed milk, sugar, raisins, and butter. Cook over low heat, stirring constantly, for about 5 minutes, until all the ingredients are thoroughly mixed. Add the vanilla extract, and be sure to remove the cinnamon stick. Serve immediately in dessert bowls, sprinkled with ground cinnamon.

NOTE This dessert can also be refrigerated and served the next day.

CARIBBEAN CORN PUDDING *majarete*

Majarete is a type of corn pudding. There is great dispute as to whether it is Dominican, Cuban, or Puerto Rican in origin. Some cooks include coconut milk or cream of coconut, but the purists leave that out. Be sure to use fresh sweet white corn if possible, for the most authentic recipe. It is also a custom to reserve some for the next morning for breakfast—a Cuban take on oatmeal.

4 TO 6 SERVINGS

> **4 cups freshly cut corn kernels (from 6–8 ears of corn), coarsely ground**
> **6 cups milk, whole or skim**
> **1 cup sugar**
> **2 teaspoons vanilla extract**
> **1 cinnamon stick**
> **Ground cinnamon to taste**

Strain the corn kernels through a colander or sieve with ½ cup of the milk. The result should have a milky texture.

Transfer to a large saucepan and add all the ingredients except for the ground cinnamon. Simmer over low heat for about 15 minutes, stirring constantly to prevent sticking. When you achieve the desired consistency (according to taste, but rather thick), remove from heat and pour into bowls or cups. Sprinkle with ground cinnamon and let cool to room temperature before serving.

FLOATING ISLAND *isla flotante*

This dessert will impress guests and delight your family. So sweet!

4 TO 6 SERVINGS

> 1 recipe Cuban caramel (see page 341), freshly made or reheated
> 6 eggs, separated
> 1 cup sugar
> 6 cups milk
> Salt to taste
> Zest of 1 lemon, grated (see page 345)
> 1 teaspoon vanilla extract
> 1 teaspoon all-purpose flour

Carefully pour hot caramel syrup into a 9-inch round glass cake pan with high sides, turning the pan to coat the bottom and sides evenly. Set aside.

In a mixing bowl, beat the egg whites with ¼ cup of the sugar until peaks are formed.

Meanwhile, in a large saucepan, boil over medium heat the milk, salt, and lemon zest. When the milk comes to a boil, add the egg white mixture slowly, one spoonful at a time, to avoid burning and to make sure the milk continues at a slow boil. Continue to simmer over medium-low heat for about 5 minutes, stirring constantly. Remove from heat.

Preheat oven to 250 degrees.

In another mixing bowl, beat the egg yolks with the remaining sugar and the vanilla extract to form a cream. Add the flour, and beat again. Add this mixture slowly and carefully to the milk mixture, and stir until mixture is smooth. Pour into caramelized and prepared pan.

Set the pan in a hot-water bath (see page 366).

Bake for about 15 minutes. Turn off the oven, but do not remove the dessert until it has cooled inside the oven so it does not lose shape with the sudden change of temperature. Serve directly from oven.

CUBAN COOKIES AND CHURROS
galleticas y churros

Almost every culinary tradition has a basic cookie recipe. Our Cuban cookies have a wonderful variety of additions to the dough, including but not restricted to guava, cinnamon, lemon, chocolate, almonds, coconut, raisins, sweet caramel, strawberry, and orange.

Churros, on the other hand, are unique to Spanish and Latin American cultures. They are tubular in shape and are sprinkled with sugar.

BASIC CUBAN COOKIES *galletas cubanas típicas*
40 COOKIES

> 3 cups all-purpose flour
> 1½ teaspoons salt
> 1½ teaspoons baking soda
> 2 sticks (1 cup) butter
> 1½ cups sugar
> 2 eggs
> 1 teaspoon vanilla extract
> 1 to 2 cups flavoring additions, in chunks or chopped

Preheat oven to 350 degrees, placing one rack in center and one rack in bottom third of the oven. Line two cookie sheets or baking trays with parchment paper.

In a mixing bowl, whisk together the flour, salt, and baking soda. In another mixing bowl, place the butter and sugar and stir with a wooden spoon, or use an electric mixer for 2 or 3 minutes, until the mixture is light and fluffy. Add the eggs to the butter and sugar, one at a time, and the vanilla extract, and continue mixing. Make sure the mixture is smooth, and all the ingredients are thoroughly mixed.

Add the flour mixture to the butter mixture, and beat well with the mixer on low speed. This is the time to add flavorings, such as guava chunks, cinnamon, lemon, chocolate chips, slivered almonds, grated coconut, raisins,

(continued on next page)

(continued from previous page)

sweet caramel, strawberry pieces, or grated orange. Add at least 1 cup, and up to 2 cups.

Using a scoop or spoon, drop dough mixture onto the prepared cookie sheets to form 1½-inch mounds, spaced about 2 inches apart. Bake for 13 to 15 minutes, until golden brown at the edges and set in the center. For evenly browned cookies, rotate sheets halfway through baking, from top to bottom racks and from back to front. Remove from oven when done, and cool on sheets for about 5 minutes. Transfer cookies to a wire rack to cool completely, and serve, or store in an airtight container.

CUBAN SHORTBREAD COOKIES
torticas de Morón

These cookies, also called *mantecados,* come from the town of Morón, located in central Cuba. The original *mantecado* was a rich confection traditionally served at Christmas, made with almonds, lard, and not much else. The recipe dates to the fifteenth century, when the Spaniards sought to put surplus lard to good use. But if you make these cookies with vegetable shortening, they will have an equally delicate, light, and crumbly texture. We sometimes call these by the same name as our *mantecado* ice cream, because they too will melt in your mouth.

40 COOKIES

> 1 cup lard or vegetable shortening
> 1½ cups sugar, plus more (optional) for filling
> 3 cups all-purpose flour
> 1 teaspoon baking powder
> ½ teaspoon salt
> 1 teaspoon grated lemon zest (see page 345)
> White sugar for dusting (optional)
> 1 cup guava marmalade (see page 361) or jelly of your choice
> (optional)

In a large mixing bowl, use an electric mixer to beat the lard until fluffy. Add the sugar, and continue beating until the mixture is creamy and light. Set aside.

Sift together the flour, baking powder, and salt, and add lemon zest. Stir, making sure the dry ingredients are well combined. Add this to the lard mixture, 1 cup at a time, and beat until the dough is stiff and forms a smooth ball.

Turn the dough onto a piece of plastic wrap, and form into a cylinder. Wrap, and chill in refrigerator for about 1 hour.

Preheat oven to 350 degrees, placing one rack in center and one rack in bottom third of the oven. Line two cookie sheets or baking trays with parchment paper.

When dough is chilled, remove from refrigerator and roll out to a thickness of ½ inch. Using a round cutter, cut the dough into 2-inch circles and arrange them a couple of inches apart on the prepared cookie sheets. With your finger, make a small depression in the center of each cookie. Bake in oven for about 12 minutes, until light golden brown at edges and firm in center. For evenly browned cookies, rotate sheets halfway through baking, from top to bottom racks and from back to front. Remove from oven when done, and cool on sheets for about 5 minutes. Transfer cookies to a wire rack to cool completely. Sprinkle the cooled *torticas* lightly with sugar, or fill the depressions in the center with guava marmalade or jelly. Serve, storing leftovers in an airtight container.

CUBAN POWDERED COOKIES *polvorones*

Have a batch of these ready for your weekend *cortadito* (see page 405) routine. *Polvorones* comes from the word *pólvora*, which means "powder." They are probably called this because they are "pulverized," or broken up easily, in your mouth. The resulting powder is just delicious!

20 COOKIES

> **4 cups all-purpose flour**
> **1 cup sugar**
> **2 sticks (1 cup) butter, softened**
> **1 teaspoon vanilla extract**
> **½ teaspoon almond extract**
> **Confectioners' sugar or ground cinnamon to taste**

(continued on next page)

(continued from previous page)

In a large mixing bowl, use an electric mixer to beat the flour, sugar, and butter together until fluffy. Add the vanilla and almond extract, and continue beating to mix thoroughly.

Turn the dough onto a piece of plastic wrap, and form into a cylinder. Wrap, and chill in refrigerator for about 1 hour.

Preheat oven to 350 degrees, placing one rack in center and one rack in bottom third of the oven. Line two cookie sheets or baking trays with parchment paper.

When dough is chilled, remove from refrigerator and roll out to a thickness of ½ inch. Shape into 1-inch balls or cylinders. Arrange them a couple of inches apart on the prepared cookie sheets. Bake in oven for 20 to 25 minutes, until golden brown. For evenly browned cookies, rotate sheets halfway through baking, from top to bottom racks and from back to front. Remove from oven when done, and cool on sheets for about 5 minutes. Transfer cookies to a wire rack to cool completely. Sprinkle or roll the cooled *polvorones* lightly with confectioners' sugar or powdered cinnamon before serving.

ENGLISH SPONGE RUSKS *bizcochos ingleses*

Why has this traditional Anglo dessert become a Cuban dessert? It seems that teatime was a custom honored in some private schools and clubs in Havana, and sponge rusks were served at this *merienda* (snack). At home, I remember having homemade *bizcochos* with my afternoon *café con leche* (see page 406). My children enjoyed them with hot chocolate.

24 BIZCOCHOS

3 eggs, separated (see page 344)
1 cup sugar
¾ cup flour
1 tablespoon baking powder
½ teaspoon salt
1 teaspoon vanilla

In a large mixing bowl, use an electric mixer to beat the egg yolks with the sugar until very thick. Set aside.

Sift flour with baking powder and salt, and set aside. In another mixing bowl, beat the egg whites with an electric mixer until stiff. Now fold in the egg-yolk mixture and the dry ingredients, add the vanilla, and continue beating until all the ingredients are thoroughly mixed.

Preheat oven to 350 degrees, placing one rack in center and one rack in bottom third of the oven. Line two cookie sheets or baking trays with parchment paper.

Turn the dough onto a piece of plastic wrap, and form into a cylinder. Wrap, and chill in refrigerator for about 1 hour.

When dough is chilled, remove from refrigerator and roll out the dough to a thickness of ½ inch. Shape or cut into 1-inch-long strips. Arrange them a couple of inches apart on the prepared cookie sheets.

Bake in oven for 20 to 25 minutes, until golden brown. For evenly browned *bizcochos,* rotate sheets halfway through baking from top to bottom racks and from back to front. Remove from oven when done, and cool on sheets for about 5 minutes. Transfer *bizcochos* to a wire rack to cool completely.

ALFAJORES

The *alfajor,* a favorite South American pastry, made its way into the hearts of Cubans way back in the 1940s in Havana, where everything from movie stars to food trends was imported from Argentina. In Miami's culinary melting pot, Cuban Americans have claimed *alfajores* as their own. *Alfajores* are like shortbread cookies filled with delicious *dulce de leche* and rolled in coconut flakes—perfect for any occasion.

12 ALFAJORES

> 1½ sticks (¾ cup) butter, plus more for greasing cookie sheet
> 1 cup sugar
> 1 egg
> 2 egg yolks
> 2 tablespoons Cognac
> 2½ cups corn flour or cornstarch
> 1 teaspoon vanilla extract
> ½ teaspoon baking powder
> Zest of ½ lemon, grated (see page 345)
> 1½ cups *dulce de leche* (see page 341)
> 1 cup grated coconut

(continued on next page)

(continued from previous page)

With an electric mixer, cream the butter and sugar together. Add the egg and egg yolks, Cognac, corn flour, vanilla extract, baking powder, and lemon zest. Beat to mix well and combine ingredients thoroughly. Wrap the dough in plastic wrap and refrigerate for about 30 minutes.

Preheat oven to 300 degrees.

When the dough is chilled, remove from the refrigerator. Roll out on a lightly floured surface to about ¼-inch thickness. Cut into 2-inch rounds. You should have about twenty-four.

Transfer the cookies to a lightly greased cookie sheet, and bake in oven for about 20 minutes. Remove from oven with a slotted spatula, transfer to a wire rack, and allow to cool.

When the cookies are cool, spread *dulce de leche* gently on half of them. Press the remaining cookies on top, to make sandwiches, allowing some of the *dulce de leche* filling to escape from the sides. Roll the sides in the coconut flakes until completely covered. Serve right away, or store covered.

SPANISH FRITTERS *churros*

As a teenager, I took the traditional trip to Spain with a bunch of my Cuban American girlfriends, chaperoned by one very strict but sleepy tour guide. One night we left her resting and took off to a disco. We danced the night away and went for churros and hot chocolate (see page 407) early the next morning. To our surprise, we found that churros and hot chocolate, a treat for us, was a hearty and affordable breakfast for the working men and women of Madrid. What a great time, and what great churros. This is the recipe. There are *churreras*, or churro makers, on the market, but they are not really necessary. Use a cookie press instead, or just a simple pastry bag with a large star tip.

12 CHURROS

> 1 cup water
> ½ stick (4 tablespoons) butter
> 1 cup all-purpose flour
> ¼ teaspoon baking powder
> ⅛ teaspoon salt
> 1 teaspoon sugar
> 3 cups vegetable oil, or more if needed
> Sugar, cinnamon, or honey for topping

Pour the water into a medium saucepan, and heat over medium-high heat. Add the butter, and bring to a boil.

Meanwhile, sift together the flour, baking powder, salt, and sugar in a mixing bowl. Stir, making sure the dry ingredients are well combined. Slowly pour the boiling water from the saucepan into the flour mixture. Stir constantly with a fork until you have a smooth dough without lumps—stir, do not beat, for a firm and sticky dough.

Heat the vegetable oil in a large, heavy skillet over medium-high heat, making sure you have enough oil so the churros will be able to float freely and be covered completely. Test the temperature of your oil by placing a small amount of dough in it; the dough should bubble right up.

Spoon dough into a large cookie press or a pastry bag with a star tip. Carefully squeeze dough into the hot oil forming a large ring, and fry for 3 or 4 minutes on each side, or until golden brown. Make sure that you do not put too many pieces in at one time, and monitor that the churros float freely while frying. It is best to fry in batches.

As each is done, remove it with tongs and transfer to drain on a paper towel. Once all the churros are done and drained, cut them into approximately 4-inch lengths. Sprinkle with sugar, cinnamon, or honey, and serve. (The pros just dump the sugar on the pile of churros, or shake the churros up with the sugar in a paper bag—feel free to try that if you like!)

EGG CHURROS *churros de huevo*

This is a much heavier churro mixture. If you wish, you can even substitute a half-milk, half-water mixture for the water.

20 CHURROS

> **1 cup water**
> **⅔ stick (⅓ cup) butter**
> **1 cup all-purpose flour**
> **¼ teaspoon baking powder**
> **½ teaspoon salt**
> **2 tablespoons sugar, plus more for topping**
> **2 eggs**
> **½ teaspoon vanilla extract**
> **3 cups vegetable oil, or more if needed**

(continued on next page)

(continued from previous page)

Pour the water into a medium-sized saucepan, and heat over medium-high heat. Add the butter, and bring to a boil.

Meanwhile, sift together the flour, baking powder, salt, and sugar in a mixing bowl. Stir, making sure the dry ingredients are well combined. Slowly pour the boiling water from the saucepan into the flour mixture. Stir constantly with a fork until you have a smooth dough without lumps—stir, do not beat, for a firm and sticky dough.

In a separate bowl, beat the eggs and vanilla extract together with an electric mixer, and add this mixture to the flour. Stir until well blended and the dough has a firm, sticky consistency.

Heat the vegetable oil in a large, heavy skillet over medium-high heat, making sure you have enough oil so the churros will be able to float freely and be covered completely. Test the temperature of your oil by placing a small amount of dough in it; the dough should bubble right up.

Spoon dough into a large cookie press or a pastry bag with a star tip. Carefully squeeze dough into the hot oil, forming a ring, and fry for 3 or 4 minutes on each side, or until golden brown. Make sure that you do not put too many pieces in at one time, and monitor that the churros float freely while frying. It is best to fry in batches.

As each is done, remove it with tongs and transfer to drain on a paper towel. Once all the churros are done and drained, cut them into 4-inch lengths. Sprinkle with sugar and serve. (The pros just dump the sugar on the pile of churros, or shake the churros up with the sugar in a paper bag—feel free to try that if you like!)

FLAKY CUBAN PASTRIES *pastelitos cubanos*

These are found everywhere, including virtually every Latin coffee shop. Think of *pastelitos* and old men making sure they don't spill any guava filling on their crisply tailored *guayaberas*. Also think of *pastelitos* and small children spilling most of the filling on their uniforms during an after-school snack. Parents will often cater mini-*pastelitos* for their kids' birthday parties, which is actually very funny, because *pastelitos* is already a diminutive word. *Pastelitos* are usually made with flaky puff pastry, even though other doughs can be used. The fillings need not be sweet. There are ground-beef *pastelitos*, cheese *pastelitos*, ham *pastelitos* (called *cangrejitos*), and pizza *pastelitos*. But the sweet ones are the favorites. Guava, coconut, and guava-cheese *pastelitos* are among the most popular. This is the recipe for the dough. Use your imagination and whatever is in your cupboard for your filling.

12 PASTELITOS

> **3 cups all-purpose flour, plus more for the work surface**
> **1 teaspoon salt**
> **½ cup ice water**
> **½ stick (4 tablespoons) butter, chilled**
> **1 egg, beaten with 2 teaspoons water**
> **¼ cup simple syrup (see page 340)**

Place about 2¾ cups flour in a mixing bowl. Refrigerate the remaining ¼ cup flour.

Dissolve the salt in the ice water, and stir the water mixture into the flour. When the flour is moistened, turn the dough onto a work surface and gather it into a ball. Wrap in plastic wrap and refrigerate for at least 45 minutes.

Once the dough has chilled, remove from the refrigerator and roll out on a floured work surface into an even square, approximately 12 inches on a side.

Mash the butter, and sprinkle with the chilled ¼ cup flour. Knead this mixture with your hands and the rolling pin until it is smooth and the flour is completely mixed in. On a floured board, roll and shape it into a rectangle about 6 by 12 inches. (It should roll out like pie crust; if too soft, chill longer.)

Place the butter on one half of the dough. Turn other half of dough over butter to encase it. Pinch edges together to seal. Dust with some flour and roll it out gently into a rectangle, about 8 by 12 inches. Fold one end a third

(continued on next page)

(continued from previous page)

of the way over and then fold the other end over that (like folding a letter).

Let dough rest for 15 minutes in the refrigerator, and roll out again into a rectangle. Fold one end a third of the way, and then fold the other end over that. Let dough rest again for about 15 minutes in the refrigerator, and repeat the process of rolling out and folding in. Repeat this process three more times, so you will eventually have "folded" the dough six times, making sure you let the dough rest for about 15 minutes in the refrigerator each time.

Preheat the oven to 350 degrees.

Roll out the dough to a rectangle about ⅛ inch thick. With a knife, cut the flattened dough into 4-inch-wide strips the length of your baking pan. Lay one strip on a sheet pan lined with parchment paper, and put about 1 tablespoon of filling lengthwise in the middle, in a continuous stripe about ¾ inch wide. Brush edges of strip with water, and cover with another 4-inch strip of dough the same size as the bottom strip. Press the edges together all the way around. Brush the top with the egg wash. Bake for about 35 minutes.

Remove from oven, brush with simple syrup, and return to bake for another 5 to 7 minutes.

Remove from oven, and cut crosswise into 12 pieces.

NOTE For traditional guava filling, all you need is a 16-ounce can of guava shells in heavy syrup! Just purée guava shells and syrup in a food processor or blender, processing until it reaches a smooth consistency. Pour purée into a medium saucepan, and cook over low heat until reduced to a very thick consistency. Remove from heat, let cool to room temperature, and use as filling.

CUBAN ICE CREAMS AND FROZEN TREATS

helados y granizados cubanos

ICE CREAMS AND FROZEN DESSERTS are of course the perfect ending to a dinner in a tropical climate. The variety of fruits and flavors can entice even a novice into trying some of these wonderful frozen desserts.

To help you with this crowded field, here is a scorecard:

- Ice creams have a high milk-fat content and include a sweetening agent.
- Sherbets are fruit-flavored but also contain a milk product, though with a low milk-fat content.
- Sorbets are nondairy, based on fruit juice or fruit.
- Snow cones, or water ices, are desserts usually made of crushed or shaved ice with a fruit-flavored syrup. In Cuba and in most Cuban American neighborhoods, snow cones are known as *granizados*.
- *Durofríos* are Cuban ice pops.

Ice cream is divided into two types: custard style, which includes eggs and requires cooking, and American style, which contains no egg yolks, is based purely on cream and sugar, and does not require cooking.

There are an infinite variety of ice-cream makers, ranging from the manual to the electric; from simple, inexpensive, old-fashioned wooden buckets with a metal inner container, to expensive electric ice-cream machines that have the freezing units built in. If you are serious about preparing frozen desserts, invest your money in a small electric unit, even if it relies on a prefrozen canister—which you place in the freezer 24 hours in advance.

Good fresh ingredients make great ice cream. Add perfectly ripe fruits and berries to your ice-cream base; sprinkle fruit with sugar, and crush it with a potato masher before mixing it in, for the full flavor.

When you add nuts, chocolate, or crumbled cookies, let the ice cream reach a soft-serve consistency before stirring in these ingredients; then pack in airtight containers and freeze until firm.

Do the same when you add extracts to custard-type ice cream.

In the unlikely event that you have leftover homemade ice cream, store it airtight with a layer of plastic wrap pressed onto the surface, to prevent it from absorbing odors. You can store custard-type ice creams for up to three days.

CUSTARD-STYLE ICE CREAM
helado de natillas

MANTECADO ICE CREAM *helado de mantecado*

Why is it so hard to describe and actually to find *mantecado* ice cream? Many will say that it is just French-vanilla-flavored ice cream, but Hispanics who remember the ice-cream trucks and carts of their childhood know that *mantecado* is even creamier than French vanilla and has flavor almost like butter pecan. It will hook you for life. I found a homemade recipe and tried it with my kids and my mom. This *mantecado* ice cream received the seal of approval from three generations of one Cuban family.

8 SERVINGS

> 1 cup evaporated milk
> 1 cup whole milk
> 2 teaspoons all-purpose flour
> 1/4 teaspoon ground cinnamon
> 1/4 teaspoon salt
> 1 1/2 cups sugar
> 3 tablespoons vanilla extract
> 6 egg yolks
> 3 egg whites
> 2 teaspoons light corn syrup

Combine evaporated milk, whole milk, flour, cinnamon, salt, and 1/2 cup of the sugar in a medium saucepan over medium-high heat. Add the vanilla extract, and reduce heat at once. Cook the mixture, stirring occasionally, for 3 to 5 minutes, until it begins to show small bubbles, making sure not to allow it to actually boil. Remove from heat, cover, and let cool for about 30 minutes to room temperature.

In a medium bowl, whisk the egg yolks with another ½ cup of the sugar until smooth and all the sugar is dissolved. Add 1 cup of the milk mixture to the egg yolks in a slow stream, whisking continuously to combine and to avoid curdling. Then whisk the egg mixture back into the milk mixture in the saucepan.

Return the saucepan to the stovetop and cook over low heat, stirring and whisking constantly, for 5 to 7 minutes, until the custard thickens and can coat the back of a spoon. Again, don't let it boil. Remove from heat.

In another bowl, beat the egg whites with the remaining ½ cup sugar, a little at a time, until the whites hold stiff peaks. Add this to your custard.

Strain the custard through a fine sieve into a bowl set in an ice-water bath (put the bowl in a shallow pan of iced water), and stir in the corn syrup.

Allow custard to stand until cold, stirring occasionally. Cover with plastic wrap and refrigerate until very cold, ideally overnight.

When the custard is cold, transfer to an ice-cream maker and freeze according to the manufacturer's directions. The ice cream will be soft, creamy, and so delicious. If you want firmer ice cream, put it in the freezer for a couple of hours before serving. You may also choose to store in the freezer for up to 3 days.

MANGO ICE CREAM *helado de mango*

Be sure that your mangoes are really ripe!

6 SERVINGS

2½ cups peeled, pitted, and diced mango
2 cups sugar
2 tablespoons lime juice
1 cup whole milk
1 cup evaporated milk
5 egg yolks
1 cup whipping cream

(continued on next page)

(continued from previous page)

In a stainless steel mixing bowl, combine the mango pieces, ½ cup of the sugar, and the lime juice. Cover and refrigerate for 1 or 2 hours until pieces are completely chilled.

Combine whole milk, evaporated milk, and another ½ cup of the sugar in a medium saucepan over medium-high heat. Reduce heat at once and cook the mixture, stirring occasionally, for 3 to 5 minutes, making sure not to allow it to boil. Remove from heat, cover, and let cool for about 30 minutes, to room temperature.

In a medium bowl, whisk the egg yolks with another ½ cup of the sugar until smooth and all the sugar is dissolved. Add 1 cup of the milk mixture to the egg yolks in a slow stream, whisking continuously to combine and to avoid curdling. Then whisk the egg mixture back into the milk mixture in the saucepan.

Return the saucepan to the stovetop and cook over low heat, stirring and whisking constantly, for 5 to 7 minutes, until the custard thickens and can coat the back of a spoon. Again, don't let it boil. Remove from heat.

Strain the custard through a fine sieve into a bowl set in an ice-water bath (put the bowl in a shallow pan of iced water).

When the custard is cold, sprinkle the fruit with the remaining sugar and crush it with a potato masher to give the fullest flavor. Stir the mango pieces into the custard mixture. Now stir in the whipping cream. Taste the mixture for sweetness, adding even more sugar if necessary.

Transfer to an ice-cream maker and freeze according to the manufacturer's directions. The ice cream will be soft and creamy. If you want firmer ice cream, put it in the freezer for a couple of hours before serving. You may also choose to store in the freezer for up to 3 days.

COCO LOCO COCONUT ICE CREAM
helado de coco

Coconut is a favorite ingredient in Cuban desserts—you can never have too much. Top this dessert with toasted coconut flakes (see page 351) and small pineapple chunks.

6 SERVINGS

> **1 cup evaporated milk**
> **1 cup whole milk**
> **1 cup sugar**
> **Flesh of 1 fresh coconut, diced (see page 356)**
> **6 egg yolks**
> **Salt to taste**
> **1 cup heavy cream**
> **½ teaspoon vanilla extract**

NOTE You can also substitute ½ cup evaporated and ½ cup sweetened condensed milk for the 1 cup evaporated milk.

Combine evaporated milk, whole milk, and ½ cup of the sugar in a medium saucepan over medium-high heat. Reduce heat at once and cook the mixture, stirring occasionally, for 3 to 5 minutes, until small bubbles appear, making sure not to allow it to actually boil. Remove from heat.

Place the diced coconut flesh in a blender or food processor with half the hot milk mixture. Process for about 2 minutes, until the coconut is completely processed and mixture is smooth. Add the rest of the hot milk and process for an additional 30 seconds. You will now have coconut milk.

In a medium bowl, whisk the egg yolks with the remaining ½ cup sugar until smooth and all the sugar is dissolved. Add the cream, salt, and vanilla. Add 1 cup of the coconut milk to the egg yolks in a slow stream, whisking continuously to combine and to avoid curdling. Then whisk the egg mixture back into the coconut milk in the saucepan.

Return the saucepan to the stovetop and cook over low heat, stirring and whisking constantly, for 5 to 7 minutes, until the custard thickens and can coat the back of a spoon. Don't let it boil. Remove from heat.

Strain the custard through a fine sieve into a bowl set in an ice-water bath (a shallow pan of iced water surrounding the bowl).

(continued on next page)

(continued from previous page)

When the custard is cold, transfer to an ice-cream maker and freeze according to the manufacturer's directions. The ice cream will be soft and creamy. If you want firmer ice cream, put it in the freezer for a couple of hours before serving. You may also choose to store in the freezer for up to 3 days.

AMERICAN-STYLE ICE CREAM
helado americano

GUAVA AND CREAM CHEESE ICE CREAM
helado de guayaba y queso

What a fun take this is on the most traditional of Cuban fruit desserts, guava shells with cream cheese. There's no egg custard in this, and no cooking is required.

6 SERVINGS

> One 16-ounce can guava shells in heavy syrup (found in Hispanic aisle at supermarket), chilled, drained, and diced
> 1 cup sugar
> 2 tablespoons lime juice
> Two 8-ounce packages cream cheese
> Salt to taste
> 1 teaspoon pure vanilla extract
> 2 cups heavy cream
> 1 cup whole milk

In a stainless steel mixing bowl, combine the guava pieces, $\frac{1}{2}$ cup of the sugar, and lime juice. Cover, and refrigerate for 1 or 2 hours.

In another bowl, beat the cream cheese with the remaining $\frac{1}{2}$ cup sugar, the salt, and the vanilla extract with an electric mixer. As the mixer is running, gradually add the heavy cream and milk in a slow, steady stream, and continue to beat for about 1 minute, or until completely smooth.

Stir in the guava pieces, and whisk for an additional 20 seconds. Transfer to an ice-cream maker and freeze following the manufacturer's directions.

DULCE DE LECHE ICE CREAM
helado de dulce de leche

This is the best loved of all Latin American desserts, gone frozen.

6 SERVINGS

> **1 cup whole milk**
> **1 recipe *dulce de leche* filling (see page 345)**
> **1½ cups heavy cream**
> **Salt to taste**
> **1 teaspoon vanilla extract**

In a heavy saucepan, heat the milk and *dulce de leche* over medium heat just to the boiling point, stirring constantly until the *dulce de leche* is completely mixed in.

Remove from the heat, and beat in the heavy cream with an electric mixer. As the mixer is running, gradually add the heavy cream in a slow, steady stream, and add the salt and vanilla extract. Continue to beat for about 1 minute, or until completely smooth.

Transfer to an ice-cream maker and freeze following the manufacturer's directions.

SHERBETS
sorbetes

Some sherbets are served during the course of a meal to cleanse your palate for the next course. Try it for a nice twist during a tropical dinner.

ORANGE SHERBET *sorbete de naranja*
6 SERVINGS

> 2 cups fresh orange juice
> 1½ cups water
> 1 cup heavy cream
> 4 tablespoons honey
> ¼ cup sugar
> 1 tablespoon pure vanilla extract

In a stainless steel mixing bowl, combine all the ingredients.

Transfer to an ice-cream maker and freeze following the manufacturer's directions.

LIME SHERBET *sorbete de lima*
6 SERVINGS

> Zest of 2 limes, grated (see page 345)
> 1 cup sugar
> 3 cups heavy cream
> Juice of 4 limes
> ½ cup water
> Pinch of salt
> Lime slices or mint sprigs for garnish

In a large mixing bowl, stir together all the ingredients until well blended.

Pour into an ice-cream maker and freeze following the manufacturer's directions.

Garnish each serving with a slice of lime or sprig of mint.

PINEAPPLE SHERBET *sorbete de piña*

6 SERVINGS

2 cups diced fresh pineapple (see page 31)
¼ cup simple syrup (see page 340)
1 cup whole milk
1 cup heavy cream
2 teaspoons lemon juice

In a food processor or blender, process the pineapple chunks until you have a smooth purée.

In a mixing bowl, combine the pineapple mixture, simple syrup, milk, and cream. Add the lemon juice.

Transfer to an ice-cream maker and freeze following the manufacturer's directions.

SORBETS

These are even lighter than sherbets because they are made with no dairy at all.

GUANÁBANA SORBET *sorbete de guanábana*

Guanábana is also known as soursop, very like cherimoya, or custard apple. It is from a tree native to Central and South America. This sherbet is creamy-tasting without any cream.

6 SERVINGS

2 cups peeled and diced fresh *guanábana* (soursop)
1 cup sugar
2 cups water
Juice of 1 lemon
Lemon slices for garnish

In a large mixing bowl, stir together all the ingredients until well blended.

Pour into an ice-cream maker and freeze following the manufacturer's directions.

Garnish each serving with a lemon slice.

WATERMELON SORBET *sorbete de sandía*

This recipe requires no extra water.

6 SERVINGS

> 3 cups peeled, seeded, and diced watermelon
> 1½ cups simple syrup (see page 340)

Place watermelon in a food processor, and process until very smooth. Pass through a fine sieve, strain, and reserve.

In a mixing bowl, add simple syrup to the watermelon, and stir until it is well combined. Cover the bowl, and refrigerate for at least 1 hour, until well chilled.

Transfer to an ice-cream maker and freeze following the manufacturer's directions.

STRAWBERRY AND GUAVA SORBET
sorbete de fresa y guayaba

6 SERVINGS

> 2 cups chopped strawberries
> 1 cup peeled, seeded, and chopped guava shells
> 2 tablespoons water
> 1½ cups simple syrup (see page 340)

Place strawberries, guava pieces, and water in a food processor, and process until very smooth. Pass through a fine sieve, strain, and reserve.

In a mixing bowl, add simple syrup to the fruit mixture, and stir until well combined. Cover the bowl, and refrigerate for at least 1 hour, until well chilled.

Transfer to an ice-cream maker and freeze following the manufacturer's directions.

LEMON SORBET *sorbete de limón*

6 SERVINGS

> Juice of 8 lemons (approximately 1½ cups), strained
> 1¼ cups simple syrup (see page 340)

Beat the lemon juice in a blender or food processor.

In a mixing bowl, add simple syrup to the lemon juice, and stir until smooth and well combined. Cover the bowl, and refrigerate for at least 1 hour, until well chilled.

Transfer to an ice-cream maker and freeze following the manufacturer's directions.

SNOW CONES AND POPSICLES
granizados and durofríos

MANGO POPSICLES *paletas de mango*

6 SERVINGS

> 2 cups peeled, pitted, and diced mango
> 1 cup sugar
> ½ cup water
> 1 cup crushed ice

Place mango pieces, sugar, water, and ice in a food processor or blender, and process until very smooth and frosty.

Pour the mixture into Popsicle molds or ice cube trays, and freeze until solid, about 2 hours.

TROPICAL POPSICLES *durofríos tropicales*

A variety of tropical fruits are used for this all-around pleaser.

6 SERVINGS

> 1 cup pineapple juice
> ¾ cup fresh orange juice
> ¼ cup fresh lemon juice
> ⅔ cup sugar
> ½ cup finely chopped pineapple

Beat the juices together in a blender or food processor. Add the sugar, and beat to blend completely.

Stir in the finely chopped pineapple, pour into Popsicle molds or ice cube trays, and freeze until solid, about 2 hours.

FIZZ AND FRUIT POPSICLES *durofríos de fruta*

This recipe is great to try when you are expecting to have lots of kids around.

6 SERVINGS

> One 12-ounce can peach or other fruit nectar, chilled
> One 12-ounce can Sprite, chilled
> 1 cup crushed ice

Mix the fruit nectar, Sprite, and ice. Chill again for at least 10 minutes.

Pour into Popsicle molds or ice cube trays, and freeze until solid, about 2 hours.

GUAVA CREAM POPSICLES
durofríos de guayaba y crema

6 SERVINGS

> One 16-ounce can guava shells in their own syrup
> 1 cup heavy cream
> 1 teaspoon honey

Place guava shells, cream, and honey in a food processor or blender, and process until very smooth and frosty.

Pour into Popsicle molds or ice cube trays, and freeze until solid, about 2 hours.

HONEYDEW AND BASIL POPSICLES
durofrío de melón y albahaca

This is an icy treat for the adult palate.

6 SERVINGS

> **2 cups peeled and cubed honeydew melon**
> **½ cup fresh lemonade, chilled**
> **½ cup sugar**
> **½ cup chopped fresh basil**

Beat the fruit and lemonade together in a blender or food processor. Add the sugar and basil, and beat to blend completely.

Pour into Popsicle molds or ice cube trays, and freeze until solid, about 2 hours.

GRAPEFRUIT SNOW CONE *granizado de toronja*

6 SERVINGS

> **4 cups fresh grapefruit juice, strained**
> **2 cups simple syrup (see page 340)**

Combine the grapefruit juice and the simple syrup in a mixing bowl, and pour into a 10-inch-deep metal roasting pan.

Freeze, uncovered, for about 4 hours, whisking occasionally. Remove from freezer, let stand at room temperature for about 5 minutes, and scrape surface with a fork until it has the texture of shaved ice.

CUBAN COFFEE SNOW CONE
café cubano granizado
6 SERVINGS

> 6 cups Cuban coffee (see page 404)
> ½ cup water
> 1½ cups sugar
> 1 teaspoon vanilla extract

Mix all the ingredients in a medium saucepan over low heat, and simmer for 3 to 5 minutes, or until the sugar is completely dissolved. Pour into a 10-inch-deep metal roasting pan.

Freeze, uncovered, for about 4 hours, whisking occasionally. Remove from freezer, let stand at room temperature for about 5 minutes, and scrape surface with a fork until it has the texture of shaved ice.

TANGERINE SNOW CONE *granizado de mandarina*
6 SERVINGS

> 4 cups fresh tangerine juice, strained
> 2 cups simple syrup (see page 340)

Combine the tangerine juice and the simple syrup in a mixing bowl, and pour into a 10-inch-deep metal roasting pan.

Freeze, uncovered, for about 4 hours, whisking occasionally. Remove from freezer, let stand at room temperature for about 5 minutes, and scrape surface with a fork until it has the texture of shaved ice.

ANISE SNOW CONE *granizado de anís*

6 SERVINGS

> **4 cups water**
> **4 teaspoons anise extract**
> **2 cups simple syrup (see page 340)**

Combine all the ingredients in a mixing bowl, and pour into a 10-inch-deep metal roasting pan.

Freeze, uncovered, for about 4 hours, whisking occasionally. Remove from freezer, let stand at room temperature for about 5 minutes, and scrape surface with a fork until it has the texture of shaved ice.

CUBAN COFFEE, CORTADITO, AND MORE

café cubano, cortadito, y más

WHEN CUBANS and Miamians leave the city, the first thing they miss is their Cuban coffee. Regular espresso just will not do! The most important thing about Cuban coffee is that it is actually sweetened as it is being brewed. It is sweet and thick, and served in very small cups. The truly brave drink it in one shot. It is common to drink a *cafecito* first thing in the morning at home. Then it is also common to drink one after meals, and always during social, cultural, and business activities. A shot of Cuban coffee and a handshake will always seal a deal. Most Cuban restaurants all over the United States and Cuba have walk-up windows where friends meet during the day and perfect strangers strike up conversations while waiting for their *cafecito*. Many journalists have attributed the energy of Miami to the Cuban coffee. The coffee itself is dark-roasted and is more finely ground than the espresso you might be used to. You can find many brands of Cuban coffee in the Hispanic aisle of your supermarket. I will give you my own personal recipe for Cuban coffee with foam or *espumita* (see below), not to mention the most popular and delicious variations to enjoy with family and friends.

CUBAN COFFEE *cafecito*

There are really two ways to brew Cuban coffee. I prefer the espresso-pot method on top of the stove. It is traditional and quick and makes great foamy coffee. But you can also use your own espresso machine by following the directions provided with it. Just add sugar to the pitcher that the coffee drips into, and stir this into the first two or three drops of brewed coffee. That will also give you the foamy *espumita*. This recipe makes an entire brew that we normally call a *colada*, which is enough for four or five people.

4 SERVINGS

> **3 cups cold water**
> **5 tablespoons dark-roasted finely ground coffee**
> **8 teaspoons sugar**

Pour cold water into the bottom half of a two-part espresso coffeepot (an Italian *moka*), to the maximum line. Fill the top half loosely with the ground coffee. Screw the halves together.

Place over medium-high to high heat, and wait for it to start brewing.

Meanwhile, pour the sugar into a cup, preferably a metal one. As the coffee begins to percolate, pour the first two or three drops into the cup with the sugar—just enough to moisten it, so that when you mix it, it becomes a paste.

Once the coffee is fully brewed, pour it slowly into the metal cup, gently mixing it with the sugar paste. This leisurely ritual will ensure the famous *espumita*, or foam. Serve your perfect *cafecito* immediately, in small cups.

MINI-COFFEE AND MILK *cortadito*

For breakfast or after a heavy dinner, there is nothing better than a *cortadito*, which is 75 percent Cuban coffee and 25 percent milk. You can use whole, skim, or, even better, evaporated milk.

1 SERVING

> **½ cup brewed and sweetened Cuban coffee (see preceding recipe)**
> **⅛ cup whole, skim, or evaporated milk, heated**
> **Sugar to taste**

Pour Cuban coffee into your serving cup.

Add the heated milk and, if needed, add extra sugar. Serve immediately.

COFFEE AND MILK *café con leche*

This is two-thirds milk and one-third Cuban coffee. It's definitely the breakfast of choice for Cuban Americans and has become a staple item at many restaurants throughout South Florida. Similar to a French *café au lait,* it is enjoyed with Cuban toast, or maybe a croquette or two. My aunts in Cuba would have a *café con leche* right after dinner, and another one right before going to bed. This is the way children are initiated into Cuban coffee: You might be too young for a straight shot of Cuban coffee, but you're never too young to enjoy *café con leche.* I will testify that I have seen babies with *café con leche* in their bottles!

4 SERVINGS

> **4 cups whole or skim milk**
> **2 cups brewed and sweetened Cuban coffee (see page 404)**
> **Sugar to taste**

Heat milk in a small saucepan over low heat. Watch closely, and bring it nearly to a boil. When it reaches the boiling point, remove from heat.

Pour the milk into serving cups, and top off with a shot of the Cuban coffee. You can control the lightness or darkness of your *café con leche* by adding less or more coffee.

Stir gently, and if needed add sugar to taste. Serve immediately.

NOTE Even though it is not traditional, there's no reason not to enjoy *café con leche* cold or iced or in a frappé.

CAFÉ BON BON

This is a great version of a *cortadito*. Just don't count the calories! This is the way the Vietnamese drink their coffee, since it comes from a French tradition. This is also excellent iced, in a frappé.

1 SERVING

⅓ cup brewed and sweetened Cuban coffee (see page 404)
4 tablespoons sweetened condensed milk

Pour Cuban coffee into your serving cup.

Add the milk, and if needed heat for a couple of seconds in microwave. Serve immediately.

CUBAN HOT CHOCOLATE *chocolate caliente*

Cuban hot chocolate is thick and almost puddinglike. Don't miss the chance to dip your churros in it (see pages 384–386) on a cold night.

4 PORTIONS

Two 1-ounce squares pure unsweetened dark chocolate or baker's
    chocolate
Grated nutmeg to taste
Ground cinnamon to taste
4 cups milk
1 teaspoon cornstarch, dissolved in a little water
Vanilla extract to taste
Sugar to taste

Break up the chocolate into small pieces. Place in a small saucepan, and melt over low heat with the nutmeg, cinnamon, and milk.

Whisk in the cornstarch solution and vanilla, and continue cooking while stirring. Be careful not to let it boil over. Cook over low heat, whisking constantly, until the hot chocolate reaches your desired thickness. Pour into cups, and add sugar to taste. Serve immediately.

NOTE You can also make hot chocolate with half sweetened condensed milk and half water. Do not add sugar to this variation—it will be sweet enough!

CUBAN CANDIES:
Old- and
new-fashioned

caramelos cubanos

THE BASIS of all candy making is simple syrup (see page 340). It goes through many stages at different temperatures, and we'll need virtually all of the varieties for these candy recipes. The stages are measured by one simple test, dropping a small amount of sugar syrup in very cold water. You can also use a candy thermometer to measure exact temperatures.

- Simple syrup (212 degrees Fahrenheit)—stays thick but still fluid.
- Thread (223–234 degrees Fahrenheit)—forms a soft thread.
- Soft ball (234–240 degrees Fahrenheit)—forms a soft ball that flattens on its own when removed from the cold water.
- Firm ball (241–248 degrees Fahrenheit)—forms a firm but pliable ball, does not lose shape.
- Crack (300–310 degrees Fahrenheit)—separates into hard and brittle threads.
- Light caramel (320–338 degrees Fahrenheit)—turns pale golden and transparent.
- Dark caramel (350–360 degrees Fahrenheit)—turns dark amber to brown.

MINI MERINGUES *merenguitos*

Many bakeries add food coloring when they beat the egg whites, to create a beautiful effect.

20 MERENGUITOS

1 tablespoon butter for greasing pan
6 egg whites
½ teaspoon salt
1½ cups sugar

Preheat oven to 350 degrees.

In a bowl, with an electric mixer, beat the egg whites on high speed until very thick. Gradually beat in the salt and sugar, and keep testing until it holds peaks. Add more sugar to taste, then continue beating for about 3 more minutes, until stiff.

Spoon the mixture onto a lightly greased 9-by-12-inch baking pan. Arrange the heaping spoonfuls of icing a couple of inches apart, and bake in oven for about 10 minutes, until just hard and crisp but not browned.

NOUGAT *turrón*

1 TURRÓN BAR OR APPROXIMATELY 10 PIECES

5 egg whites
1 cup finely chopped toasted almonds
1 cup finely chopped hazelnuts
1 cup honey
1 cup sugar

In a bowl, beat the egg whites with an electric mixer until very stiff. Add the egg whites to the nuts, and stir to form a paste.

In a medium saucepan over low heat, cook the honey and sugar until completely mixed and melted. Add the nut-paste mixture, and continue to cook, stirring constantly, for about 10 minutes, until thoroughly heated and combined.

Transfer to a shallow rectangular tray lined with parchment paper, and allow to cool at room temperature. Cut into 2-inch pieces when set, and serve.

SESAME BARS *barritas de sésamo*

This is such a great candy. It is still sold by street vendors in—and out—of Cuba. Cheap, easy, and quick to make, it's a perfect family project.

16 BARS

> ³⁄₄ **cup honey**
> ¹⁄₄ **cup sugar**
> **2 cups hulled sesame seeds**

In a medium saucepan, bring the honey and sugar to a boil over medium heat. Reduce the heat slightly, and add the sesame seeds slowly. Continue cooking and stirring for 7 to 10 minutes over low heat, until the sugar has completely dissolved and the mixture takes on a light-brown color and reaches the dark caramel stage (see page 408).

Pour the mixture into a 20-by-15-inch inch baking tray lined with parchment paper, and smooth the top with a spatula. While still warm, cut evenly into 1-inch bars with a sharp knife. Let the mixture cool, and refrigerate for about 1 hour, till bars are firm. Remove from refrigerator, wrap individually, and serve. You can store in an airtight container in the refrigerator for a week.

NOTE You can also add slivered almonds or crushed peanuts to the mixture for a different, richer flavor and texture.

SUGARED PEANUTS *garrapiñadas*

2 CUPS PEANUTS

> **1 cup raw shelled, unpeeled peanuts**
> **1 cup sugar**
> **2¹⁄₂ cups water**

Put the peanuts, sugar, and water in a medium skillet, and bring to a boil over medium heat, stirring constantly. Reduce the heat, and continue to simmer for about 10 minutes. Stir occasionally, until water evaporates.

Reduce to low heat, and continue to cook and stir until the mixture is completely dry. Make sure that the peanuts are completely coated with the sugar mixture.

Remove from heat, and cool on a marble or stone surface, if possible. Allow to cool to room temperature, place in small plastic bags, and tie these with colorful string. Store for up to 2 weeks.

NOTE You can also dry the peanuts well by heating them on a baking sheet in a very low oven for about 5 minutes. This will ensure that the peanuts come out crunchy, with minimum effort.

CARAMEL AND CHOCOLATE DUO
dobles de chocolate y caramelo
Why not make both caramel and chocolate candy? Cut in squares and enjoy.
12 SQUARES, 6 OF EACH KIND

> 2 cups heavy cream
> 1 stick (8 tablespoons) butter
> 1 cup sugar
> 2 tablespoons glucose syrup or corn syrup
> 1 teaspoon vanilla extract for the caramels
> ½ cup chopped semisweet chocolate

For the caramel candy: In a nonstick saucepan over low heat, combine 1 cup of the cream, 4 tablespoons of the butter, ½ cup of the sugar, 1 tablespoon of the corn syrup, and the vanilla extract, and mix well, stirring, until you get a firm-ball consistency (see page 408). Stir constantly.

For the chocolate candy: In a nonstick saucepan over low heat, combine 1 cup of the cream, 4 tablespoons of the butter, ½ cup of the sugar, 1 tablespoon of the corn syrup, and the chopped chocolate, stirring well, until you get a firm-ball consistency (see page 408). Stir constantly.

Pour into two separate cooking-sprayed aluminum-foil-lined 6-inch square baking pans with deep sides. Allow to cool. When cool, cut into squares, and wrap individually.

HONEY DROPS *caramelos de miel*

These are great for kids' sore throats!

18 CANDIES

¼ cup sugar
¼ cup honey
5 tablespoons water
Granulated sugar to roll candies in

In a nonstick saucepan, over low heat, combine sugar, honey, and water, and cook over low heat until you reach the crack stage (see page 408).

Spoon mixture into 8-inch candy-mold trays. Allow to cool. When cool, remove from trays, coat candy in sugar, and wrap individually.

CUBAN LOLLIPOPS *pirulíes*

20 LOLLIPOPS

1 cup sugar
½ cup white corn syrup
2½ cups water
⅓ teaspoon each of fruit extracts (strawberry, lime, orange)
1 teaspoon each of food coloring (pink, green, orange)
20 lollipop sticks

In a nonstick saucepan, combine sugar, syrup, and water, and cook over low heat until you reach the crack stage (see page 408). Do not stir until you reach that stage. Remove from heat, divide the syrup into three portions, and add extracts and matching coloring quickly.

Pour mixtures into cylinder-shaped candy molds, and insert a stick in the middle of each candy.

Allow to cool. Remove from molds, and wrap individually.

AFRICANA COOKIES *africanas*

These popular cookie-candies are wrapped in colored aluminum foil and sold on street corners and in popular candy stores all over South Florida.

17 AFRICANAS

> 1 cup flour
> Pinch of salt
> ½ teaspoon baking soda
> 1 stick (8 tablespoons) butter
> ¾ cup sugar
> 1 egg, beaten
> 1 teaspoon vanilla extract
> 8 ounces dark or semisweet chocolate

Prepare cookies: Preheat oven to 350 degrees, placing one rack in center and one rack in bottom third of the oven. Line two cookie sheets or baking trays with parchment paper.

In a mixing bowl, whisk together the flour, salt, and baking soda. In another mixing bowl, place the butter and sugar and stir with a wooden spoon, or use an electric mixer, to mix for about 2 or 3 minutes, until light and fluffy. Add the egg and vanilla extract, and continue mixing. Make sure the mixture is smooth and all the ingredients are thoroughly blended.

Add the flour mixture to the butter mixture, and beat well with the mixer on low speed.

Using a scoop or spoon, drop dough mixture onto the prepared cookie sheets to form 1½-inch mounds spaced about 2 inches apart. Bake for about 13 to 15 minutes, until golden brown at the edges and set in the center. For evenly browned cookies, rotate sheets halfway through baking from top to bottom racks and from back to front. Remove from heat when done, and cool on baking sheets for about 5 minutes. Transfer cookies to a wire rack to cool completely.

Prepare chocolate coating: This is the time to take shortcuts. Chop chocolate into pieces.

Melt chocolate chunks in a microwavable bowl in the microwave, using the "defrost" setting or no more than 20 percent power. Heat for 90 seconds, stir,

(continued on next page)

(continued from previous page)

and repeat, until the chocolate is mostly melted. Continue stirring until the chocolate is smooth and remaining chunks are completely melted.

Dip cooled cookies in the chocolate, transfer to a wire rack, and allow to cool.

COCONUT BALLS *bolitas de coco*

Candy or dessert? You choose.

16 COCONUT BALLS

1 egg white
¼ cup honey
16 marshmallows
1 cup grated coconut flakes

In a mixing bowl, beat the egg white and honey lightly.

Roll the marshmallows in this mixture, and coat with the coconut flakes. Place on a cookie sheet covered with wax paper, and allow to dry for at least 15 minutes.

ACKNOWLEDGMENTS

I must give a tender special thanks to my agent, Diane Stockwell, who motivates and disciplines me at the same time! It was also my great luck to work under Sheila O'Shea, an editor with lots of patience and great humor. I am grateful, too, to my team of friends, especially Edith Velasquez who wrote with me way into the night—and she is not even Cuban! And of course I am forever grateful to the best bookseller in the world, Mitchell Kaplan, my mentor and my buddy who gave me the confidence to see this and introduced me to Paul Bogaards at Alfred A. Knopf, who saw the vision for this book in Spanish and now in English.

And thanks to everyone at Knopf who made this book come to market: Kathleen Fridella for your input, instruction, sharp eye, and patience; Carol Carson for the gorgeous cover; Maggie Hinders for the book's beautiful design; production manager Lisa Montebello; my copy editor, Terry Zaroff-Evans, and proofreaders, Louise Collazo and Judy Eda; and to Kathy Hourigan for overseeing this book through to publication.

RESOURCES

THESE SUGGESTED sites and stores will help you stock your Cuban pantry and enhance your cooking repertoire as a whole, because the international and Latin items in my recipes can be used in non-Latin recipes as well. The Internet is a playground for cooks, with dozens of specialty-item websites to order from. Many of my favorites are listed below. If you live in an urban area or an area with diverse cultures, you very well may find many of these Latin items in your local grocery store aisles. Most canned items mentioned can be found from Miami to Milwaukee at your local supermarket chain.

Enjoy building your Cuban pantry!

PANTRY ITEMS, SPICES, AND UTENSILS
Amazon.com Gourmet Food
www.amazon.com

Amigo Foods
Latino grocery store offering a variety of choices organized by country. Includes soups, beverages, meats, and condiments.
www.amigofoods.com

Bi-Rite Market
San Francisco's neighborhood grocery store, selling delicious locally and responsibly produced meat, fish, and produce.

3639 Eighteenth Street
San Francisco, CA 94110
(415) 241–9760
www.biritemarket.com

Broadway Panhandler
The cook's best resource for kitchen items, pans, and utensils.
65 East Eighth Street
New York, NY 10003
(212) 966–3434

Central Market
There are eight store locations in Texas.
www.centralmarket.com

Chef Shop
(877) 337–2491
www.chefshop.com

Cuban Food Market
A terrific online and mail-order resource.
Whatever Cuban item or food you're looking
for, you can get it here . . . Cuban Food
Market has more than 2,700 products in
its Cuban store: Cuban foods, coffee, and
guayabera, and more.
(877) 999–9945
www.cubanfoodmarket.com

CyberCucina
An online supermarket that has a variety of
imported Mediterranean gourmet foods and
beverages.
www.cybercucina.com

Dean & Deluca
Gourmet foods and cookware; there are
store locations in New York, California,
Kansas, North Carolina, and the District of
Columbia.
560 Broadway
New York, NY 10012
(800) 221–7714
www.deandeluca.com

Fairway
There are seven locations in the New York
Tri-State area.
(212) 595–1888
www.fairwaymarket.com

Formaggio Kitchen
Has multiple locations in the Northeast.
244 Huron Ave
Cambridge, MA 02138
(888) 212–3224

268 Shawmut Ave
Boston, MA 02118
(617) 350–6996

120 Essex Street
Essex Street Market
New York, NY 10002
(212) 982–8200

www.formaggiokitchen.com

Fox & Obel
401 East Illinois Street
Chicago, IL 60611
(312) 410–7301
www.foxandobel.com

igourmet
(877) 446–8763
www.igourmet.com

Kalustyan's
Spice resource.
(212) 685–3451
123 Lexington Avenue
New York, NY 10016
www.kalustyans.com

My Latin Food
This site delivers authentic Latin American
groceries nationwide from every corner of
Latin and South America.
www.mylatinfood.com

Specialty Grocery.net
www.specialtygrocery.net

Sur La Table
www.surlatable.com

Whole Foods Market
www.wholefoodsmarket.com/stores

Williams–Sonoma
www.williams-sonoma.com

Zingerman's
(888) 636–8162
www.zingermans.com

BUTCHERS/FISHMONGERS
Lobster and shellfish:

www.floridalobster.com

www.stonecrabandlobster.com

Butcher:

Lobel's of New York
Since 1840, Lobel's of New York has provided the most tender, flavorful prime beef and gourmet meats—straight from the butcher shop to your door.
www.lobels.com

INDEX

A NOTE ON THE TYPE

This book was set in Verlag, a font created for Abbott Miller by Hoefler & Frere-Jones in 1996 for the Solomon R. Guggenheim Museum. It was inspired by Frank Lloyd Wright's lettering on the facade of the museum in New York and was originally called Guggenheim. When Hoefler & Frere-Jones released the font publicly in 2006 it was renamed Verlag and the six original styles were expanded to thirty.

Composed by North Market Street Graphics, Lancaster, Pennsylvania

Printed and bound by RR Donnelley, Harrisonburg, Virginia

Designed by Maggie Hinders